Lost Champions

LOST CHAMPIONS

*Four Men, Two Teams,
and the Breaking of
Pro Football's
Color Line*

GRETCHEN ATWOOD

B L O O M S B U R Y

NEW YORK • LONDON • OXFORD • NEW DELHI • SYDNEY

Bloomsbury USA
An imprint of Bloomsbury Publishing Plc

1385 Broadway   50 Bedford Square
New York   London
NY 10018   WC1B 3DP
USA   UK

www.bloomsbury.com

BLOOMSBURY and the Diana logo are trademarks of Bloomsbury Publishing Plc

First published 2016

© Gretchen Atwood, 2016

ISBN: HB: 978-1-62040-600-7
        ePub: 978-1-62040-602-1

Library of Congress Cataloging-in-Publication Data is available.

2 4 6 8 10 9 7 5 3 1

Typeset by RefineCatch Ltd, Bungay, Suffolk
Printed and bound in the U.S.A. by Berryville Graphics, Berryville, Virginia

To find out more about our authors and books visit www.bloomsbury.com. Here you will find extracts, author interviews, details of forthcoming events and the option to sign up for our newsletters.

Bloomsbury books may be purchased for business or promotional use. For information on bulk purchases please contact Macmillan Corporate and Premium Sales Department at specialmarkets@macmillan.com.

In honor of
the many pioneering athletes and activists in this book;
those who came before and
those who will follow

Contents

Introduction

THE MOST COMMON QUESTION PEOPLE ASKED ME when I was working on this book was, "What made you decide to write about this?" My answers were almost always based on what they meant by *this*.

If it's regarding the integration of pro football, the answer is easy. Years ago I helped my then girlfriend move to Atlanta, Georgia. I was sitting in her living room, surrounded by boxes, thumbing through *America's Game* by Michael MacCambridge. I stumbled upon the brief mention of the signing of Kenny Washington and Woody Strode by the Los Angeles Rams in the spring of 1946.

"Wait, what?!" was my first thought. Nineteen forty-six? I had always assumed that I knew little about the men who integrated modern pro football because they must have come after Jackie Robinson broke the color barrier in Major League Baseball in 1947. Everyone knows about Robinson—the books, movies, his retired jersey number, etc. He was the first, therefore he gets the lion's share of public attention and accolades.

But this was telling me he wasn't the first to integrate professional team sports. Sure, baseball was more popular than football then, but that would explain why we know more about Robinson, not why we know very little about the others. It also revealed that I, a former sportswriter with a deep interest in sports, social justice, and twentieth-century American history, was woefully uninformed about this important facet of American sports history. Thus began my journey to answer the question "If these guys came before Jackie, why do we know so little about them?" This book is my answer.

The second meaning of the query, "What made you decide to write about this?" is why would I, a white person, write about black history? It's generally not asked with the intent to say that I shouldn't even try, but with the timeworn weariness that it often ends badly, with the stories told through an unexamined cultural and historical lens that centers whiteness. Kenny Washington, Woody Strode, and many others are not acknowledged as trailblazers precisely because of this lens. As journalist Elliot Jaspin noted, "History is what we choose to remember," and choosing to remember the people in this book—and others like them—is an attempt to reject the lens that determines who is considered a part of capital-*H* History.

In my efforts to center the people in the book, their stories, and the stories of the black communities they were a part of, I prioritized black sources. This includes family and friends of the football players, periodical sources such as black newspapers and magazines, oral histories, and additional scholarly works. In many cases the white/mainstream press didn't cover these events or comment on their significance, probably because it was assumed they didn't have any. The black media (newspapers, magazines, newsletters) were the only ones thoroughly covering the civil rights battles of the 1940s. But when multiple sources covered topics or events I was writing about, I prioritized the oral histories of black individuals who were involved or alive at that time, or the coverage of the black press, over other sources.

I cannot say there will be nothing problematic in this book or in how I approached its writing. I examined my choices constantly and reviewed them with others to see where I might be bringing my own subconscious biases. I imagine some are still there, despite my efforts, and I take full responsibility for everything on these pages. I am open to feedback from readers who feel I've committed the same mistakes that I seek to criticize. I can be reached at gretchenatwood@gmail.com. I can't promise I'll reply to all e-mails, but I will give them my full consideration.

A note on language and word choices: If people preferred specific labels, those are what I used for them. When talking more generally about *white people* or *black people*, those are usually the terms I use, along with *African American*. Several individuals expressed a strong preference for *black* over *African American*, and I made sure to use that label when referring to them individually or as part of a larger group.

I don't write out the *N* word in my book. I do use the term *Negro* when quoting a source from the time I'm writing about. I don't use the mascot names for the Washington, D.C., pro football team or the Cleveland pro baseball team. The only time I use *Indian* is when quoting someone who is Native American or First Nations or they themselves are quoting someone who is and is using the term. All of the conversations and interactions I describe in the book happened, or sources reported they did. I took some liberties to imagine the exact wording of conversations that were not caught verbatim, but that is the extent of my creative license.

Writing this book has led me to a better understanding of so much more than I ever imagined and led me to meeting some of the most amazing people. For that, and them, I will always be grateful.

—San Francisco, 2016

Prologue

Downey Avenue Playground
Los Angeles, California

1925

KENNY WASHINGTON WATCHED THE WHITE MEN CHUCK a frayed baseball back and forth. Bats clattered out of a burlap sack while one man motioned players to fan out across the diamond. Even at six years old, Kenny knew the sport. Blue Washington, his father, had barnstormed with some of the best Negro league teams in the country, pitching for the Chicago American Giants and playing first base for the Kansas City Monarchs. Kenny had previously seen this local, white semipro team play at the Downey Avenue Playground, just two blocks from his house.

The Los Angeles River gurgled immediately west of the park, and the chaparral-studded foothills bobbed along the eastern horizon. The playground formed the western edge of Lincoln Heights, a neighborhood northeast of downtown. Originally the area was home to wealthy families, but as the neighborhood industrialized, those with money moved farther west and left Lincoln Heights to the immigrants who drove the trains and maintained the railroads.

The baseball players Kenny Washington watched were sons and grandsons of these railroad men. As was Kenny, whose grandfather was a cook on the trains and who later ran a mess tent for miners working in the nearby San Gabriel Mountains. The Washingtons were likely the only black family in the neighborhood at the time, and Kenny the only African American kid the ballplayers had seen at the park.

"Hey, boy," the team's coach called to Kenny. "We're about to start practice. Do you want to chase down the balls and throw them back?"

Washington said yes.

He ran to where the coach had pointed, an unhooked strap of his overalls dancing against his back. As Kenny skipped sideways into position, the batter connected with the pitch. Kenny ran after it. He was knock-kneed, and from head-on or behind, his legs formed a skinny X when he ran. But he was so fast that his gait looked fluid despite the odd angles. Kenny swooped onto the ball, hurled it toward the infield, and immediately set himself for the next one.

Batter after batter took his turn. Washington tracked down each ball and flung it back. The coach watched the kid's throws, which were reaching the infield on the fly. How far could this youngster throw? He waved for Kenny to stand deeper in the outfield. If anyone had thought about it, they might have suspected Washington was older than he looked. But they didn't. The players continued to swing, the gray balls sliced into the outfield, and the coach motioned Kenny back even farther.

CHAPTER 1

First Quarter

Cleveland Municipal Stadium
Cleveland, Ohio

1950

As the Cleveland Browns took the field for the 1950 National Football League Championship Game, the temperature had dipped below thirty degrees, and the previously thawing field was frozen hard. Nineteen fifty was the Browns' first season in the NFL after four years in the upstart All-America Football Conference. Cleveland, with its tactical-minded coach, Paul Brown, and a high-powered offense, had dominated the AAFC every year of the league's short existence. At first the success of the Browns was celebrated, but as the AAFC faltered, critics dismissed the Browns as merely the best among far-inferior teams. Prevailing opinion held that any good NFL squad would crush the AAFC's finest. Now Cleveland had its shot to prove the naysayers wrong. To do so, they would have to stop the most dangerous passing attack pro football had ever seen in the 1950 Los Angeles Rams.

The Rams and their two star quarterbacks, veteran Bob Waterfield and newcomer Norm Van Brocklin, had broken nearly every NFL passing record during the 1950 regular season. They rolled up almost 40 points and nearly 300 yards passing per game, roughly double league averages. It would be thirty years before another NFL team averaged more passing yards per game.

The Browns could also claim to be the best in the league, given their strengths in all phases of the game. Marion Motley's punishing running complemented Otto Graham's passing magic on offense, and a relentless defense held opponents to 12 points per game, fewer than the Rams defense had held any opponent all year.

But the numbers only tell part of the story. This championship game would separate pro football's future from its past in two ways. Nineteen fifty was the birth of the modern NFL offense, predicated on defeating opponents through the air rather than on the ground. A few passers had put up eye-popping numbers in years prior, notably Washington's Sammy Baugh, but the Rams and the Browns were the first teams to prioritize passing as the way to beat defenses.

In 1950 most NFL teams ran a version of the modern T formation offense, where two ends lined up hip to hip with the linemen and either blocked on rushing plays or ran routes as primary receivers.

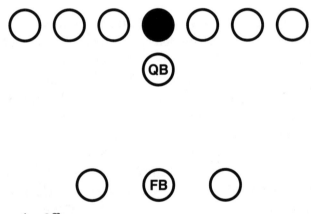

1940s T Formation Offense
Ends tight to offensive line, halfbacks and fullback even in backfield.

Several squads, including Cleveland and Los Angeles, lined up their ends out wide, apart from the down linemen, and sent halfbacks in motion to run routes out of the backfield. In 1949, the Rams had moved halfback Elroy "Crazy Legs" Hirsch to a spot a little outside of the end, creating the flanker position. The Rams were the first team to regularly line up three receivers, and their two-ends-plus-flanker alignment would become the base NFL offense in future decades.

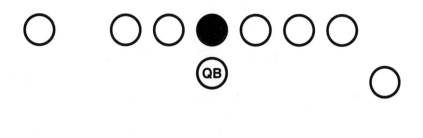

Rams T Formation with Two Ends and Flanker
Flanker is off the line, outside of a "tight" end. Opposite end is split wide.

Paul Brown's Cleveland teams revolutionized the sport in other ways. The Browns were the first offense to use the entire width of the field in the passing game. Not only did their halfbacks flare wide for passes, but their ends mastered routes such as the out and the comeback that stretched defenses to the sidelines. The Browns also had a quarterback in Otto Graham with the arm strength, timing, and touch to make these difficult throws. And if opponents shaded their linebackers to the outside to cover potential receivers, the Browns ran Motley up the middle. A total of ten players who were on the field for the 1950 NFL title game, including three quarterbacks and three receivers, would end up in the Pro Football Hall of Fame.

The teams stood out in another manner, too—a distinction overlooked even by many who follow football closely. In 1950, the majority of NFL franchises were still all white. This championship game featured the two teams with the most black players in the league, by far. The Browns and the Rams each had five, and their total of ten was more than the rest of the teams in the league combined.

When the NFL was founded in the early 1920s, it periodically fielded a handful of black players. Back then white fans didn't care as much about the racial line in pro football because many didn't think highly of the pro version of the sport. For all the images of sportsmanship and school spirit the college game elicited, the pro game raised concerns about violence, gambling, and cheating. Nonfans likened it to pro wrestling in its legitimacy as a "real" sport.

Class played a role, too. In the years before the 1944 GI Bill made a college education attainable for more middle-class and working-class families, the young men who enrolled in universities—and thus played college football—skewed white, Protestant, and well-off. After graduation many chose management-track jobs in business. Playing professional football at that time meant risking catastrophic injury on chewed-up fields studded with rocks. Teams emerged and folded in weeks, and paychecks were often late or didn't come at all. Playing pro ball was considered a better option, perhaps, than working in a coal mine or a steel mill, but it wasn't a common choice for many of the college football stars in the early part of the twentieth century.

By the 1930s the white public may still not have thought much about the color line in pro football, but NFL owners had. The driving force behind the hardening of the color line was the Boston franchise's new owner, George Preston Marshall. He opposed black players on his team and in the league. And no one was better than Marshall at the parliamentarian maneuvering and gamesmanship that often prevailed in dictating league policy at the annual owners' meeting.

Marshall and other owners justified not hiring black players because of the Great Depression, saying they couldn't give a roster spot to a black player when so many white men needed jobs. If any owner opposed that thinking, he didn't say so publicly. Marshall joined the league as an owner in 1932, and by 1934 the few black players in the league were gone. Several years later, Marshall renamed the team and moved it to the nation's capital. It was the only NFL franchise below the Mason-Dixon Line, and Marshall marketed it as the "team of the South," including setting their fight song to the tune of "Dixie."

The most sustained opposition to the color line in sports came from black sportswriters. Writers at black newspapers long fought for integration and pushed owners to try out black stars in both football and baseball, which had barred black athletes since the late 1800s. The journalists upped their efforts during and after World War II. In the fall of 1945 this pressure and additional factors helped convince Brooklyn Dodgers general manager Branch Rickey to sign Jackie Robinson to a contract with the Montreal Royals, the Dodgers' minor-league affiliate in Canada.

In the spring of 1946 the NFL's Los Angeles Rams signed Kenny Washington and Woody Strode. The Rams became the first modern NFL team to integrate and did so a year before Robinson was promoted to the major leagues in baseball. Several months after the Rams signed Washington and Strode, the Cleveland Browns inked Bill Willis and Marion Motley to contracts. These four men broke the color line in modern pro football.

Integration moved slowly at first. Many squads signed a token black player only to cut him the following year, often after limiting the player's chances to prove himself. The teams that did retain a black player usually had just the one, or maybe two, to give the first one a roommate on road trips. A black player was expected to be quiet and accept the conditions his team imposed on him if he wanted to stay on the roster. Detroit Lion Bob Mann led the NFL in receiving yards in 1949 yet was asked to take a 20 percent reduction in pay after the season. He refused and the team cut him. Only late the following year did Mann sign on with another team, despite his evident talent.

Early in 1950, the *Chicago Defender*, one of the largest African American newspapers in the country, reported that former San Francisco 49er standout Bob Mike had been fired from a scouting job with the team because he had brought a light-skinned female companion with him to an off-season practice. San Francisco owner Tony Morabito mistook Mike's presumed date for white, and he and Mike were later seen arguing in Morabito's office before it was revealed that Morabito had axed him.

The black men who did play in the NFL in the years immediately after World War II faced long odds and active resistance from players on other teams, fans, the media, and even their own coaches and teammates. Years before what many consider the beginning of the modern civil right movement—the Montgomery Bus Boycott in 1955—the black men who made it onto the field not only changed the sport but also helped reshape society.

A lasting place in history was not a major concern for the players preparing for the 1950 title game, however. In the week leading up to the game, both the Browns and the Rams angled for an advantage. Rams first-year head coach Joe Stydahar worried his Los Angeles squad would slip on the frozen field, so he had his equipment manager shave the players' cleats shorter and sharper. But as the team finished warm-ups, the referee did a boot check and ruled the Rams' shoes illegal. The visitors trudged back to their bench to change into regulation cleats. Paul Brown's team wore mostly rubber-soled basketball shoes, with some opting for cleats. Quarterback Otto Graham chose Chuck Taylors. Fullback Marion Motley wore cleats. Middle guard Bill Willis donned cleats at first, then changed to sneakers during the game. Placekicker Lou Groza wore both: a basketball shoe on his left foot and a football boot without cleats on his kicking foot.

Strategizing about what shoes his team should wear wasn't the only way Paul Brown tried to outsmart the Rams. In the previous week's playoff game, Cleveland barely beat a New York Giants team that had used an unusual "umbrella" defense against them. Instead of rushing the quarterback or trying to contain running plays to the outside, the Giants defensive ends backed off the line of scrimmage to cover the halfbacks running routes out of the backfield.

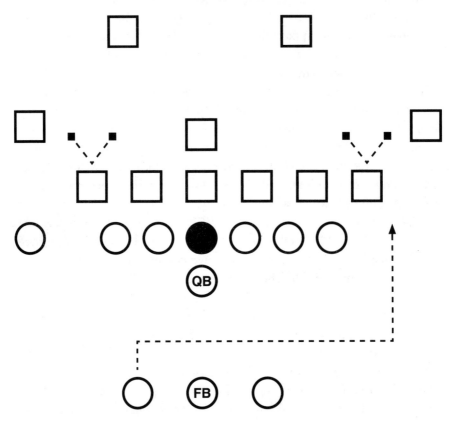

Brown's T Split End with Man-in-Motion vs. 6-1-4 "Umbrella" Defense
One end split wide; before snap, halfback goes in motion. Defensive ends can rush the passer, stay to stop the run, drop back to cover backs or ends coming out for passes.

During practices before the title game, Coach Brown talked freely with reporters about utilizing the same defensive approach against the Rams' high-flying offense. He wanted Los Angeles to waste time preparing for the new look, but only intended to show it for a few plays before reverting to the Browns' base defense.

As kickoff approached, each team finished its preparations. Nearly 30,000 fans wrapped in wool coats and scarves huddled in their seats in Municipal Stadium, a concrete C squatting on the edge of Lake Erie. Twenty-eight-mile-per-hour winds lashed the field, howling and swirling inside the stadium. The fans and players knew the unpredictable winds could wreak havoc on field goal attempts at the stadium's open end. Browns placekicker Lou Groza swore that in a past game the wind had knocked one of his field goal attempts *backward* past him.

At one thirty P.M. the Browns fanned out across their 30-yard line, facing the Rams. The home team ran forward in unison. Groza chopped his stride and swung his right foot into the leather, rocketing the ball toward the Los Angeles end zone. Rams halfback Vitamin Smith caught the ball at the five, swept left, and slid out of bounds at the 18-yard line, narrowly missing a packed snowdrift just off the field. The 1950 NFL Championship Game was under way.

Bob Waterfield led the Rams out for their first series. He had swapped starts with Norm Van Brocklin during the season, but Coach Stydahar went with the veteran for the title game. On the first play from scrimmage the Rams sent halfback Glenn Davis upfield as a receiver. Backup defensive end Jim Martin turned to track Davis and slipped. As Waterfield dropped back, he saw Davis break open and hit him near midfield. The Cleveland defensive back on that side also stumbled, and Davis darted down the sideline for an 82-yard touchdown. Twenty-seven seconds in, and the prolific Rams offense had already scored.

On Cleveland's sideline, Paul Brown crossed his arms across his chest. If the Browns had been in their base defense and not the decoy umbrella scheme, Martin wouldn't have been called on to cover Davis. And if starter Len Ford hadn't been injured halfway through the season, the Browns wouldn't have had to rely on Martin to blunt the Los Angeles attack. Paul Brown scrapped the umbrella defense even sooner than planned and told Len Ford to get ready. He would go in, injury or no injury.

Ford, another of Cleveland's black players, had suffered a fractured jaw 10 weeks earlier when the Chicago Cardinals' Pat Harder elbowed him in the face, knocking out several of his teeth. Doctors wired Ford's mouth shut following surgery, and he dropped 15 pounds during his recovery. Before the title game, team doctors were unsure if he could play. The equipment manager fashioned him an ad hoc facemask from padded plastic and attached it to his helmet.

Meanwhile the Rams lined up and Waterfield kicked off—many quarterbacks handled kicking duties in the NFL of 1950. The Browns returned the ball to their 28-yard line. Now Cleveland quarterback Otto Graham had a chance to show what he could do. Graham and the Browns had reigned over the AAFC, but in the NFL season leading up to the title game, Graham had thrown for only 1,943 yards and 14 touchdowns, a down year by his standards. This further fueled suspicions that his AAFC numbers had been inflated by facing weak opponents.

Part of the reason for Graham's modest numbers may have been Marion Motley's success running the ball. The 238-pound fullback led the league in 1950 with a 5.8 yard rushing average. Against Pittsburgh earlier in the season, Motley had piled up 188 yards on only 11 carries. But rushing wasn't Motley's only contribution to the offense. According to Cleveland assistant coach Blanton Collier, Motley was the best all-around football player he'd ever seen. Paul Brown's son, Mike, said, "My dad always felt Marion was the greatest back he ever had," and that included another Cleveland great, Jim Brown. Motley excelled in both rushing and pass blocking, earning him the nickname Otto Graham's Bodyguard.

Defensive linemen battled to get past their offensive counterparts only to get stonewalled by Motley, who often outweighed them. Motley had also mastered Cleveland's unusual pass-protection scheme, which had linemen and backs create a "cup" in front of their quarterback, something all teams would eventually copy, now known as the pocket. Since the Los Angeles run defense hadn't been tested all year—most opponents had to throw the ball to keep up with the Rams offense—and because of unpredictable weather, many expected Cleveland to start out on the ground. As did the Rams.

The Los Angeles defense stopped Motley on his first attempts. Seeing the Rams were stacking the line to thwart Motley, Graham took to the air. He hit Dub Jones and Dante Lavelli for completions. The quarterback then took off on a 22-yard gallop to the Rams 31-yard line.

Graham's gain was partly set up by how his team lined up. The Browns split their ends wide on both sides and did similarly with two halfbacks, leaving Motley the only back behind Graham, an unusual formation when the standard modern T had three backs in the backfield. Rams defenders had to account for the extra receivers out wide and thus didn't have as many defenders close in on the line of scrimmage. Graham went back to pass but didn't see anyone open. Motley blocked a defensive end past Graham, creating an escape route for the quarterback, who bolted down the left side. Graham's speed allowed him to elude linemen chasing him from behind, and downfield blocking from the end helped him extend the run.

On the next play, the Browns kept their ends lined up tight with Motley in the backfield and sent halfback Dub Jones wide. Graham took the snap and backpedaled. Los Angeles defensive end Larry Brink shot around the right side of the offensive line, heading straight for Cleveland's quarterback. Motley crab-stepped sideways and slammed his right forearm into Brink's chest, knocking him beyond Graham. Graham stepped up into the space created by the block and arced a pass toward the right corner of the end zone. Dub Jones raced to the spot and the ball dropped over his shoulder into his hands for a touchdown, just before the receiver galloped into a two-foot hedge of snow beyond the end line. The crowd roared. Lou Groza popped through the extra point, and the title game was tied, 7–7.

How would the Rams offense respond? A common misconception about the 1950 Rams was that they racked up so many passing yards with long throws. While Van Brocklin had a strong arm, Waterfield did not. Waterfield made his yards with accurate short-to-medium passes, hitting his receivers in stride so they could keep running after the catch. The Rams' bread and butter was to throw to Tom Fears over the middle.

Fears owned the middle because the Rams' speed guys cleared out defenders by going deep or out wide. Since Los Angeles had converted Crazy Legs Hirsch from a halfback to a flanker, then to an end, they mostly lined him up outside. Halfback Glenn Davis split time between flanker and a backfield spot, either running the ball or going in motion wide before turning upfield as he had on the Rams' first touchdown. Few squads had more than one or two players who excelled at pass defense, and they locked in on Hirsch and sometimes Davis, leaving Fears room between the hash marks.

That's where Waterfield looked on the Rams' second drive. As Browns defensive linemen Bill Willis, George Young, and others charged, Waterfield backpedaled, then lofted the ball over their heads to a halfback or end who had slipped into the space behind them. Los Angeles mixed in passes to halfbacks out to the flats with throws over the middle to Fears, including a 44-yard completion. Once deep inside Browns territory, Bob Waterfield turned to their "Bull Elephant" backfield to pummel their way to a score.

The Rams had come up with the heavy backfield—all three backs weighing around 220 pounds—during a previous game on a wet, slow field. The coaches had realized that having two big backs blocking for a third was nearly impossible to stop, especially when opponents struggled to keep their footing. Veteran fullback Dick Hoerner led the group. Second-year man Paul "Tank" Younger and rookie "Deacon" Dan Towler joined Hoerner in the Bull Elephant backfield. The Rams had signed Younger out of Grambling State, making him the first NFL player signed from a historically black college or university. In 1950 Los Angeles drafted Towler, also black, in the twenty-fifth round.

The Rams lined up at the Cleveland three-yard line. Waterfield took the snap, spun around, and held the ball out for Hoerner, who grabbed it and plowed over for a touchdown. Waterfield kicked the extra point, and the Rams led 14–7 at the end of the first quarter.

CHAPTER 2

The Last Word

The Last Word Café
Los Angeles, California

1946

MEETINGS OF THE RECENTLY CREATED LOS ANGELES Coliseum Commission tended to be dry administrative affairs, highlighted . by political skirmishes between the local representatives who sat on the commission and the businesses who wanted use of the stadium. But when the commissioners took their seats for their January 15, 1946, meeting, constituents from across the city packed the wood-paneled conference room. Just three days earlier the NFL champion Cleveland Rams had announced they were moving to Los Angeles.

The news shocked most football fans. Why would the league's defending champion suddenly leave their home for the unchartered territory of the West Coast, which had no pro franchises in the top leagues of any major sport? Few people realized that Rams owner Dan Reeves had wanted to move his team west for years. The population of Los Angeles had boomed during World War II, and Reeves felt the region offered a larger potential fan base and more lucrative financial opportunities than did Cleveland.

But to move, Reeves needed a majority of the other NFL owners to support his proposal, and until 1946, not enough of them did. Having a team located so far away from the geographical base of the league, the Northeast to upper Midwest, would require longer trips, which cost more, especially since air travel had yet to become routine for most pro franchises. But in 1945 the newly formed AAFC announced plans for two California teams: the San Francisco 49ers and an as-yet-unnamed team in Los Angeles. That goosed the NFL into action. It didn't want to cede the entire region to a rival league, so the NFL owners approved the Rams' move at the league's annual meeting on January 12.

Getting league approval to move wasn't the only hurdle Reeves and the Rams faced. The day after announcing their relocation, Rams general manager Charles "Chile" Walsh and other team executives flew to Southern California to negotiate with the Coliseum Commission about leasing the 100,000-seat arena.

The football teams of the University of Southern California and the University of California, Los Angeles, were the Coliseum's only regular tenants, and sports reporters expected both schools to oppose the Rams' bid at the Coliseum Commission meeting. The new All-America Football Conference franchise also wanted in on the stadium, as did existing semipro teams. Even a midget-car racing outfit (competitions where cars could not exceed 1,000 pounds) sent a representative. Since the Rams were the first major professional sports franchise to arrive on the West Coast, few knew how other Coliseum tenants would react, or the commission itself.

One group entered the meeting with a very specific goal. The sports-writers and editors of all the major black newspapers in Los Angeles sought to persuade the commission to deny the Rams a lease until the team tried out or signed African American players, something no NFL squad had done since 1933.

The commissioners sat at the front of the room, in a semicircle behind an extended wooden desk similar to what would be seen at a city council meeting. Walsh spoke first. A squarely built man with a squat face, he had a perfectly straight part through his wavy brown hair. He held his proposal in hand and outlined it for the commission. He listed the dates the Rams wanted for home games the following fall and laid out a detailed plan for how the franchise and stadium would split gate receipts, radio revenue, television revenue (if any), and concession sales. He proposed a three-year agreement under which the Rams would get first dibs on Sunday dates for the length of the contract.

Soon after, Halley Harding, sports editor of the *Los Angeles Tribune*, rose to speak. Stocky but nimble, Harding moved like the athlete he'd once been. A three-sport star in college, Harding had played for the Detroit Stars and Kansas City Monarchs of the Negro National League and played briefly for the Savoy Big Five, a black all-star basketball team that predated the

Harlem Globetrotters. In Los Angeles, Harding was known less for his former athletic exploits, however, than for his quick wit and sharp pen.

He frequently called out racism and hypocrisy in the mainstream press and directly challenged individual writers. In many stadiums around the country, black reporters weren't allowed to sit in the press box. Food and coffee were often provided there, and Harding wasn't shy about yelling up to his white colleagues to pass down a sandwich or a drink. He also held his past athletic prowess in high esteem. One story swapped over chuckles among his peers was how Harding, when watching NFL legend Ernie Nevers practice kicking before a game, walked over and showed a startled Nevers the best form for kicking off.

Harding and the other newspapermen had read about the Rams' move days before and immediately understood the opportunity it presented. The Coliseum was Los Angeles's only centrally located stadium that sat more than 25,000 fans. Ticket sales drove most of a team's revenue, so being able to draw a large audience was crucial to a franchise's financial success.

The Coliseum was also publicly owned, and the black reporters believed that a ban on black players, unofficial or not, conflicted with rights of African American residents, whose taxes helped support the stadium. The group chose Harding to be their spokesperson given both his background as an athlete and his speaking skills. Harding studied oratory in college and, according to Brad Pye Jr., former sports editor of the *Los Angeles Sentinel* and colleague of Harding, "He was a loudmouth . . . When he was in the room everyone knew it."

Harding began by chronicling the achievements of black players in the early years of professional football. He traced the rise of Fritz Pollard, who served as player-coach for the Akron Pros in the early 1920s, and Paul Robeson, a famed end from Rutgers who also played for the Akron Pros and later became a lawyer, international theater star, and civil rights activist. As Harding walked in front of the commissioners, he looked at each one. He described the supposedly unwritten yet clearly effective agreement among NFL owners to bar African Americans from the league's rosters. He noted the last time a black man had played in the league was more than a decade before, and that since Joe Lillard and Ray Kemp had been cut by their teams before the 1934 season, no other black player had suited up for an NFL team or, to Harding's knowledge, even had a tryout.

Pivoting, Harding then described the heroics of black service members in the recently ended war. He talked of how proud these brave men made him to be American and about how much black soldiers had valiantly risked on the bloody battlefields of Europe and Asia to defend the nation's ideals of freedom and equality. How tragic would it be if those young men who'd fought racial demagoguery far afield returned only to still be treated as second-class citizens at home?

Decrying the unfairness of black players being shut out of the highest level of professional football, Harding turned again. He hailed the talent and skill of ex-UCLA star Kenny Washington, how Washington had put UCLA football on the map in the late 1930s and become the school's first All-American. Many of the commissioners and others at the meeting had witnessed and cheered Washington's spectacular play firsthand in the Coliseum itself. Harding revisited Washington's electrifying performances, then paused, letting the faces around him open up to the common memories of Washington's achievements.

He stopped in front of commission president Leonard Roach. It was "singularly strange," Harding said, furrowing his brow, that no NFL team had seriously considered Washington. How was that possible? As gatekeepers of the publicly owned stadium, the commission should refuse to host a pro franchise until that team had tried out black players such as Los Angeles's very own Kenny Washington.

Most in the crowd burst into applause as the commissioners nodded acknowledgment of Harding's appeal. Commission president Roach immediately decried segregation. Commissioner John Anson Ford praised the passion of Harding's speech and wondered how anyone would do that to "our Kenny Washington." Chile Walsh stood and replied with a promise of his own: "Any qualified Negro football player is invited by me at this moment to try out for the Los Angeles Rams." He added he would love to sign Illinois star Buddy Young once his college career ended—a rather empty gesture since Young was completing his military service and had several years of collegiate eligibility left.

Harding asked Roach to formalize a commitment to integration in any lease the pro teams would receive. Roach promised to do so. Skeptical of the lip service that was often given in such moments, Harding requested Roach draft and sign a resolution on the spot. Roach hesitated for a moment, then agreed.

"[The resolution] stipulated that no user of the stadium was to discriminate against anyone because of race, color, or creed, which was exactly our reason for being there," Harding later explained. "[Roach] assured us that the insert wasn't there just to fill out the page . . . the rest of the commission will stand back of that resolution."

When the meeting ended, Roach urged Harding and Walsh to meet again on their own and work out an understanding between them. A week later they did meet, at the Last Word Café, a jazz supper club on Central Avenue. "The Avenue" was the epicenter of black Los Angeles. Every type of business flanked the thoroughfare: stores, music venues, beauty salons, restaurants, insurance companies, newspapers, hotels, and more, many of them black owned. Across the street from the Last Word stood the Dunbar Hotel, named for black poet Paul Laurence Dunbar, and described as the most luxurious black hotel west of the Mississippi. Next door to the Dunbar was Club Alabam, which showcased the day's biggest stars: Louis Armstrong, Duke Ellington, Josephine Baker, Count Basie, and many more.

The nightclubs closed in the early morning, and musicians and revelers migrated to after-hours "basket houses," breakfast places where patrons brought their own bottles of liquor and ate chicken or pancakes. On nice nights, which were frequent, musicians might go around back of the clubs, turn over some milk crates, and continue playing. Members of the audience would sit out back and pass around a bottle of Ballantine's while playing cards until the balmy Southern California dawn.

That evening, Halley Harding sat inside the Last Word at the head of a full table. He saw the Rams men enter the club. While he continued his conversation with the men next to him, his attention remained on the three who had just arrived. He recognized the ruddy-faced Walsh and the taller, dark-haired Maxwell Stiles, the Rams' new PR director, who weeks before had been a sportswriter for the *Los Angeles Examiner*. The third, unknown to Harding, was Walsh's brother-in-law.

Other bar patrons also looked quizzically at the newcomers. White people rarely came to nightclubs on Central Avenue, but those who did were stars, such as Cary Grant or Mae West. No one could place these plain-looking, blandly dressed men in any movies or stage shows they'd recently seen. Losing interest, the clientele turned back to their companions or their drinks.

Unaware of the attention, the three men zigzagged between tables and scanned the room for Harding. They finally spotted him and, coming closer, noticed the men seated to his left and right. A who's who of black newspapermen in Los Angeles circled the table: Eddie Burbridge and Leon Hardwick of the *California Eagle*; Abie Robinson of the *Los Angeles Sentinel*; Herman Hill and J. C. Fentress, West Coast correspondents of the *Pittsburgh Courier*; and five or six more from other newspapers or local radio programs.

Harding stood and boomed, "Welcome, gentlemen!" He extended a hand to each in turn. Whatever introductions were necessary ping-ponged among the gathered parties. If the Rams men were surprised by the large reception, they didn't show it.

The men eased into their seats, and waiters arrived to take their drink orders. Dootsie Williams and his seven-piece orchestra started their set. After chatting about the team's prospects for the upcoming season, Harding clasped his hands together and fixed his gaze on Walsh. "So when will Kenny Washington get his tryout?" he asked, looking steadily at the smaller man.

With an apologetic shrug Walsh explained that the Rams had to honor Washington's current contract with the local semipro Hollywood Bears, so they could not pursue him. Nor could they pursue any other African American players currently under contract with semipro teams. Most top-level black players were tied to such clubs, their only playing options given their exclusion from the NFL.

Harding calmly considered the Rams general manager. When the AAFC formed, it had moved aggressively to sign away white NFL veterans, and the senior league responded with their own backroom deals to secure top college talent and star players returning from military service. Bidding wars erupted between the two leagues, and each often dismissed the validity of the other league's claims on players they wanted.

Harding considered how fortuitous this newfound deference to existing contracts was for the Rams as a way to avoid hiring black players. He tapped his index finger on the edge of his glass and leaned forward. "What if I could convince [Hollywood Bears general manager] Bill Schroeder and [coach] Paul Schissler to allow Washington a tryout, and to agree to release him if the Rams make him an offer? Would Kenny then get a tryout?"

The other newspapermen nodded their agreement toward each other, and at Walsh, who glanced around before looking back at Harding. Washington was the Bears' biggest draw, and his departure would surely weaken the team financially, Walsh knew. The Bears might allow a tryout, but would they agree to a transfer? Unlikely. Walsh glanced again at the men flanking Harding and nodded. "Yes, yes he would."

Harding leaned back slowly, his hand still on his drink. "Well, I've already talked with Mr. Schroeder and Mr. Schissler and they've agreed. So when will that tryout be?"

The following week, several black weeklies reported that the Hollywood Bears had agreed to a potential transfer of Kenny Washington to the Los Angeles Rams. Little was mentioned publicly for the next six weeks, but on March 21, 1946, the Rams held a press conference at the Alexandria Hotel in downtown Los Angeles to announce they had officially signed Kenny Washington.

White and black newspapers alike ran articles on the signing alongside photos of a seated Washington holding a pen over a sheaf of papers. Chile Walsh stood over one of his shoulders, and Chile's brother Adam, the Rams' head coach, stood over the other. Black newspapers claimed a major barrier had fallen in pro sports. White dailies emphasized that Washington's signing in no way set a precedent for the hiring of other African Americans. Events in Los Angeles and Cleveland would soon prove who was right.

AFTER KENNY WASHINGTON FINISHED HIS UCLA CAREER in 1939, Coach Paul Schissler signed him to headline a local all-star team. Schissler later signed him to the Hollywood Bears, an outfit in the Pacific Coast Football League, which included semipro squads along the West Coast. Kenny Washington dominated the PCFL each year he was in it, but the recently ended 1945–46 season was his most remarkable. In a 38–13 rout of the San Jose Mustangs, Washington ran for two touchdowns, threw for another, kicked a field goal, and nailed all five extra point attempts.

Prior to joining the Bears, Washington had never handled kicking duties. Knee injuries had kept him from kicking in college, and they also kept him from military service during World War II. Coach Schissler had two other players swap kicking responsibilities early in the season, but he wasn't happy with the performance of either one. He convinced Washington to try with his left leg, his weaker one. Washington proceeded to convert more than half of his field goal attempts and 26 of 28 extra points, both rates eclipsing those of nearly all NFL kickers at the time.

Washington's biggest PCFL battles were against the Bears' crosstown rivals, the Los Angeles Bulldogs, quarterbacked by future San Francisco 49ers star Frankie Albert. In their first matchup of the 1945–46 season, Washington led the Bears to a 9–7 victory, scoring his team's lone touchdown on a 34-yard scramble. The battle for city supremacy always drew large crowds by semipro standards, and more than 20,000 fans showed up the second time they played. The Bulldogs tallied first when Washington fumbled a punt that had initially sailed over his head. Shortly after, Washington found former UCLA teammate Woody Strode for a 41-yard touchdown. A few possessions later, he drove the Bears to the Bulldog 32-yard line. The center snapped the ball to the fullback, who tossed it over to Washington. End Ezzrett "Sugarfoot" Anderson, one of four black players on the Bears, ran downfield and looked back, only to see Washington running away from the line of scrimmage with defensive linemen in pursuit.

"Kenny's running around back there so I'm trying to stay open," Anderson said. "But he just waved me on, so I ran for the corner [of the end zone]." The 6-foot-4 end was at full speed with two defenders on his back when Washington hurled the ball from the far sideline. Anderson was running out of room as the infield dirt switched to grass. He reached high and plucked the ball from the air. He crossed the end line and veered to the dugout, where he sat down for a moment to catch his breath. The touchdown gave the Bears a 14–7 lead, which they would pad with a Washington field goal and a late defensive touchdown.

Fans and press debated how far Washington's pass to Anderson had traveled in the air. The line of scrimmage was the Bulldog 32-yard line, but Anderson caught the pass in the corner of the end zone, and Washington had not only backtracked to avoid rushers but ended up planting and throwing from the opposite sideline. Maxwell Stiles, then with the *Los Angeles Examiner*, walked off the pass from the spot he thought Washington threw the ball to where Anderson caught it. He estimated the ball traveled 65 yards.

Over the next several games Washington reinjured one of his legs and played sporadically. The Bears edged the Bulldogs for the league title, a championship powered mostly by Washington's passing and rushing. Washington topped the PCFL in scoring, even though none of his passing touchdowns counted toward his total. Those were credited only to the receivers at the time. He missed two full games and parts of several others yet finished second in both passing and rushing yards. He played once more with the Bears, an exhibition game versus a military-service all-star team on January 20, 1946, several days before Halley Harding met with the Rams at the Last Word Café.

Once the Rams signed him, Washington had his knees examined by an orthopedic surgeon. Soon after, he was admitted to Cedars of Lebanon Hospital for surgery. The surgeon reported that the "semilunar cartilage" in Washington's left knee had torn and required removal. From Washington's right knee the surgeon took out a "joint mouse," which seemed to be scar tissue from a previous surgery. Barring potential complications from infections, the doctor expected the joints would be as good as new in a few weeks. The *Los Angeles Tribune* ran a photo of Washington sitting up in his hospital bed, gown on, with papers on the tray in front of him. He held a pencil in his right hand while he studied the Rams' modern T formation offense, a system he had never before played in.

Media reactions to the Rams' signing of Washington were mixed. Few journalists directly spoke out against it, but Dick Hyland of the *Los Angeles Times* questioned whether Washington could succeed given the abuse his legs had already suffered. "Had Kenny Washington been signed by a National League team in 1940 he would undoubtedly have been, with one year's experience, one of the greatest of professional backs and a drawing card from one end of the league to the other," Hyland proclaimed. He then said that if he had to take only one player to play both ways for a full sixty-minute game, he'd choose Washington over Ernie Nevers, Red Grange, and Tom Harmon, citing Washington as a better defender than both Grange and Harmon, and a better passer than all of them.

But Hyland predicted that the knee injuries had sapped enough of Washington's speed that he would be catchable in the open field at the highest level of the sport. "Kenny Washington will work his head off to prove this prediction wrong, and I hope he does," Hyland added. Halley Harding shot back on the pages of the *Tribune* that while Washington didn't have a whole lot of years ahead of him in pro football, "We'll string along with him for our money's worth, never having been robbed yet."

CHAPTER 3

City of Angels

Lincoln Heights
Los Angeles, California

1920s, 1930s

Aweek after the Rams signed Kenny Washington, Halley Harding reported that Los Angeles was close to adding another black player. Abie Robinson of the *Los Angeles Sentinel* wrote it was Washington's friend and favorite receiver from college, Woody Strode. Four weeks later the *Pittsburgh Courier* confirmed the signing. The two players would team up for the city's first major pro football franchise. Both were native Angelenos, and fans had followed not just their college exploits but their successful high school careers as well.

Kenneth Stanley Washington was born in Los Angeles on August 31, 1918, and grew up in Lincoln Heights, an Irish-Italian neighborhood separated from downtown by railroad tracks and the Los Angeles River. In the mid-1800s Lincoln Heights was called East Los Angeles and was considered the first suburb of the city, before being absorbed by it. John Strother Griffin, a military surgeon who served in expeditions against Native American tribes during the California Gold Rush, was one of the neighborhood's most prominent early residents. So was Confederate general Albert Sidney Johnston, who was a close friend of Jefferson Davis and one of his best military commanders.

After the Civil War, the neighborhood was renamed for the victorious Union president. Over the following decades Southern California's aristocrats abandoned the rapidly industrializing area for enclaves farther west, leaving the neighborhood to the mostly Italian and Irish immigrants whose labor powered the region's growth in the early part of the twentieth century.

Like so many of their neighbors, Kenny Washington's family also came via the railroad. Kenny's grandfather worked as a cook on the trains and also ran a mess tent serving miners working in the San Gabriel Mountains. Like the brakemen and engineers on the railroad, the elder Washington settled in Lincoln Heights. People remembered the Washingtons as the only black family in the area at the time. Susie Washington, Kenny's grandmother, was a janitor at the Avenue Nineteen elementary school and a mother figure to many of the neighborhood kids. It was said that when boys were interested in dating one of the local girls, they had to get Susie's permission first. She had four children of her own, including Kenny's father, Edgar, known as Biscuits to his family and Blue to everyone else.

Blue was a precocious athlete who started boxing at fourteen under the name Kid Blue. By eighteen he was an up-and-coming pitcher for the Chicago American Giants in Rube Foster's Negro National League. When home in Los Angeles, Blue got bit roles in films—moviemaking, like Blue's family, was another recent transplant to the West Coast.

Many report Blue's first film role, uncredited as many of his were, was in D. W. Griffith's infamous *Birth of a Nation*, an ode to the then-defunct Ku Klux Klan, and a film partially credited for the group's revival. Washington got other movie gigs in the few roles open to black actors at the time: slave, ex-slave, Kenyan manservant, chauffeur. His later film career included partnering with a young John Wayne in the western *Haunted Gold* and an uncredited role in *Gone with the Wind*.

Shortly after his baseball and film careers started, Blue met Marian Lenán, who was from Kingston, Jamaica. They began a relationship as teenagers and soon married—or maybe they didn't. Some family members said the pair did legally wed; others weren't so sure. Either way, Blue didn't stay still for long. When he wasn't barnstorming with black baseball teams or shooting a film, he pursued popular vices of the day: womanizing, drinking, or gambling. Given Blue's well-known and prodigious appetites, on any given night he might have been indulging in all three.

Marian tired of Blue's frequent absences and separated from him when Kenny was two years old. She and Kenny stayed with the Washington family, though. Marian, barely an adult herself, was always around, but it was Susie Washington and Kenny's uncle Rocky (the first black Los Angeles police officer to become a patrol lieutenant) and aunt-in-law Hazel who raised him. At a young age Kenny took up Blue's first love, baseball. The Washingtons lived two blocks from the Downey Avenue Playground, and Kenny regularly shagged balls for the white semipro team that practiced there.

When he wasn't at the playground, Washington was often at a nearby Catholic church. Lincoln Heights had few other places to go besides school. An elderly Italian woman who lived next door took Kenny to early mass on Saturdays starting when he was five or six years old. He learned to say a prayer before meals, and though he was never baptized, he would later cross himself before big games.

Kenny first played football at the playground, but it was at Lincoln High that Washington blossomed as both a runner and a passer. As a senior he tossed long touchdowns almost weekly. He threw passes of at least 50 yards to ends Pete Torreano and Joe Garofalo in a game against Garfield High. He led the Lincoln Tigers to an undefeated regular season his senior year. Lincoln High faced Fremont High for the city championship at the Los Angeles Coliseum.

Fremont had won three of the previous five city titles, and with the ground muddy from steady rain, many expected the heavier Fremont team to win. But Washington won it for the Tigers. His rushing and passing accounted for 169 of Lincoln's 173 total yards, and he scored their only touchdown in the 13–9 victory. Local press named Washington to the first-team all-city, and the *Los Angeles Times* decided Washington's large hands and long fingers were the secrets to his passing success, something the paper would also note two years later when remarking on his achievements as a UCLA Bruin. They added, "Washington is what is aptly known as an unorthodox runner. He's not remarkably fast, but has a baffling change of pace . . . He has what is known in a motor car as 'pick up.' Washington can stop dead and then bolt away faster than ever."

The *Times* speculated that hordes of colleges were descending on the Washington household to woo the young star. Other observers said he was already committed to Loyola University (later Loyola Marymount), the Jesuit school that was the choice of his vocal Catholic neighbors. Washington favored Notre Dame, but the school didn't welcome black players. USC was the dominant force on the coast, but its coach, Howard Jones, rarely played African Americans. The last time Jones brought in a black recruit, Bert Ritchey, Jones stuck him on the bench. The USC coach later admitted he recruited Ritchey to prevent him from playing for one of the Trojans' opponents.

In stepped UCLA. In 1929, the school moved to its new campus in Westwood, and university directors wanted to build a competitive athletic program to garner the school national acclaim. The football team had typically faced minnows such as Occidental, Cal Tech, and Whittier. To gain the kind of attention the directors wanted, the team had to play USC, and the first Bruin squads to take on the Trojans got crushed. "What they lacked in size, they made up for in slowness," Woody Strode later joked. University leaders viewed recruiting players like Washington and Strode, who was a fellow prep standout, as a step toward beating USC.

Like Washington, Woodrow Wilson Woolwine Strode was a local schoolboy star, born and raised in Los Angeles. Strode's father, a brickmason, moved to Southern California from Washington, Louisiana. Shortly thereafter he bought a half acre of land near Fifty-First Street and Holmes Avenue in Furlong Tract, a mostly African American working-class development a mile from Central Avenue. Black home ownership was not unusual in Los Angeles at the time. In 1910 between 30 and 40 percent of the nearly 8,000 African Americans in the city owned their homes.

Strode's mother's family came from New Orleans. She, like her husband, followed a familiar path out of the mostly agrarian South. When slavery yielded only slightly to sharecropping and black codes, which required trumped-up charges to be paid off via forced labor, many African Americans left to seek better conditions elsewhere. While black migrants from the Southeast—Georgia, Alabama, South Carolina—often moved north to Chicago, New York, Detroit, or Cleveland, many African Americans from Louisiana and Texas headed to the West.

Woody Strode was born in the family's three-bedroom house in 1914. He remembered his mother raising chickens and growing vegetables in the family's yard, where white peaches and figs grew wild. "My daddy would buy a hundred-pound sack of potatoes, and Mama would bury them in the ground so they wouldn't rot," Strode recalled. "I don't know how they learned that stuff. It was part of their generation."

Strode experienced neither luxury nor great hardship as a youth, until the Great Depression. Several factors exacerbated the struggles African American Angelenos faced during the Depression. One was the timing of their arrival in the region. To understand how that impacted lives in the 1930s, it's necessary to quickly trace California's growth.

The first to settle in the current state of California were various Native American tribes. European expeditions explored the area from the sixteenth through eighteenth centuries, and Franciscan priests established missions along the Pacific Coast. In an 1819 treaty the United States ceded the region known as Alta California to New Spain. Three years later the newly independent country of Mexico annexed Alta California. After the Mexican-American War ended in 1848 the region became a territory of the United States.

That same year, miners found gold in the Sierra Nevada, which spurred an influx of nearly 300,000 people to the area. Many of the newcomers were Euro-American settlers or hired mercenaries paid by Eastern moneyed interests to lay claim to as much gold as possible. Spanish settlers had battled indigenous communities during previous decades, but the lust for gold triggered even greater violence against local tribes. Many of the new settlements brought or raised their own militias in order to grab and defend as much land as possible.

While the Gold Rush boomed, immigration rules were relaxed to enable the rail companies to import cheap Asian labor. Chinese immigrants cleared land and laid track for the transcontinental railroad. But once much of the work was done, the United States passed the Chinese Exclusion Act in 1882, prohibiting future Chinese immigration.

The expansion of railways was not limited to the United States. Mexico built lines running north from Mexico City, and that made travel to Texas, New Mexico, and Southern California easier and cheaper. The growth of the mining and agriculture industries near Los Angeles drew more Mexican newcomers to the area. The start of the Mexican Revolution in 1910 spurred another burst of immigration.

By the time significant numbers of black families moved to Los Angeles in the 1920s and 1930s, recent immigrants from Mexico, China, Japan, and elsewhere had already settled in large numbers in Southern California. When the Great Depression hit, the presence of established nonblack communities of color meant more competition for the types of jobs that black workers might have had in Northern cities but were rapidly disappearing everywhere as the economy shrank in the 1930s.

Franklin Roosevelt's New Deal programs helped many in Los Angeles, but not communities of color as much as they did whites. Woody Strode got a job with the Civilian Conservation Corps laying roads through Griffith Park. The CCC was one of Roosevelt's first large-scale jobs programs. Like many of the other New Deal efforts, such as the Works Progress Administration and the Federal Housing Administration, it promoted racial segregation. Unlike some of the others, though, it did hire black laborers, even if it then put them in segregated work camps.

Strode and other workers were paid in money and food, distributed at county stations. Despite the Conservation Corps work, the Strodes struggled. As a brickmason Woody's father had helped erect the city's iconic art deco buildings downtown, but he lost his job during the Depression and only found work sporadically during the early part of the 1930s. The family lost their home in Furlong Tract and moved to a one-room house at Thirty-Fourth Street and Central Avenue.

Woody Strode discovered football when he started high school at nearby Jefferson High. He saw a sign for team tryouts and decided he had to have one of the uniforms. The problem? While he was tall at six feet one, he weighed only 130 pounds. Jefferson High's coach, Harry Edelson, who had played under Howard Jones at USC, figured that end was the only possible position where he could put Strode, who was too slow at the time for the backfield and too light for line play. "I looked like a broomstick running around out there," Strode said. "But I was like a piece of wire; I just didn't have the weight."

Edelson had moved to Los Angeles from Jaffa, then a part of the Ottoman Empire, and changed his name to Edelson from Eidelsohn, which local sportswriters tended to misspell. "He was probably discriminated against [because of being Jewish]," said Kalai Strode, Woody's son. "My feeling is he saw something in my dad and helped him through, like a second father."

Edelson taught Strode all he knew about playing end. Strode's main role was to block the defensive tackle inside or out, depending on which way the running play was supposed to go. Soon Strode didn't even need a running back's help to turn the tackle, a sure sign of an effective end.

During football's off-season, Strode focused on track and field. He ran high and low hurdles and did the high jump and the shot put. Soon he gained muscle and speed. By his senior year he was all-state in track and all-city in football. At one track meet he high-jumped six feet five inches while barefoot, after a piece of his track shoe had broken off. He received five scholarship offers and agreed to play for UCLA.

There was a catch, however. He had to take most of his classes again to meet the university's admission requirements. If a football player lacked credits, the school normally sent him to a military academy to get his grades. This was true of many of Strode's Bruin teammates. But none of the military schools allowed African Americans, so Strode went to UCLA's extension program instead. During that time he lived with several Jewish members of the Bruin football team in an apartment in Bel Air, back when coyotes likely outnumbered people. Strode initially struggled to get the required credits. "I remember sitting in algebra class thinking I was flunking Spanish," he recalled. But he slowly progressed toward enrollment.

He competed in track meets on weekends to keep his physical skills sharp. He made money modeling for art classes and for painters who were enamored of his newly filled-out physique. Strode was asked to pose for a painter who was working on a collection depicting men in classic Olympic sports. Strode met the artist and agreed to five sittings, one each for different athletic events. Strode stripped to his underwear, and the bespectacled and besmocked man walked around him, measuring his limbs, his cheekbones, even his eyelashes. Strode ended up sitting for only two sessions: discus and javelin.

The painter, Hubert Stowitts, submitted his *American Champions* collection of nude male athletes to an art show that was part of the 1936 Berlin Summer Olympics. While the collection received critical acclaim overall, the depiction of virile African American and Jewish athletes offended Nazi sensibilities, and Alfred Rosenberg, one of the Nazi Party's primary racial ideologues, shut down the exhibit.

Stowitts told his friend German filmmaker Leni Riefenstahl about Strode. She marveled at the paintings and later sent a message to Strode asking to film him on the white sands of Carmel, California. Strode considered it, but his Jewish teammates urged him not to, given the anti-Semitic laws the Nazis imposed on Jewish residents and Riefenstahl's connections to the party's leaders. Strode declined her invitation.

In 1936 Strode completed his entrance requirements and became a freshman at UCLA as part of the same class as Kenny Washington. Strode was initially taken aback by the black kid who spoke with an Italian accent and preferred pasta and ice cream over steak and potatoes. Washington was the more gregarious of the two—friendly, charming, and outgoing. Friends later described Strode as a storyteller of the first order, but when he first got to Westwood, he was soft-spoken and, according to him, had a more Victorian attitude than his peers. He hadn't even drunk alcohol before college.

Washington took advantage of Strode's naivete to get back at his team-mate for mocking his accent. The afternoon before an evening football practice, Washington took Strode around to visit his friends in Lincoln Heights. He explained that it was common for his Italian neighbors to drink wine at every meal, and if offered a refill, you were expected to say yes. Saying no would be incredibly rude. Washington made sure his friends offered often. Strode didn't remember getting to campus, and he staggered to the field before the coaches dismissed him from practice. Teammates covered for him, saying he had a stomach ailment.

Many of Washington and Strode's UCLA teammates accepted them, but not all were comfortable with black players. The duo played on the freshman team their first year (NCAA rules prohibited freshman from playing varsity), so not until 1937 did Washington and Strode line up alongside upperclassmen.

At an early-season practice their sophomore year they heard talk that some of the upperclassmen didn't want to play with them. Celestine Moses Wyrick, a meaty Midwestern farm boy known as Slats, was the main agitator. Every time the coach inserted Strode in the line next to Wyrick, the terse lineman, who grew up in Texas and Oklahoma, stalked off the field. The coach told him to stay put. "I can't play next to a n— because my folks would disown me," Wyrick replied. Strode kept his face blank but seethed inside. The unspoken rule among Strode and his friends was that you'd swallow most verbal abuse, but if someone called you n—, you'd fight.

The coach paused, then motioned Strode to the defensive line, directly across from Wyrick. Both men put their hands on the ground and raised their eyes, glaring at the other. The whistle blew, and Strode launched himself into Wyrick, driving him backward and onto the ground. "You black son of a bitch!" Wyrick yelled. Strode rained punches on the cursing Texan, who swung back wildly. The coaches seemed to wait a few seconds as Strode landed more shots, then separated the two men.

The episode with Slats was the only racial incident with their teammates that Washington or Strode recalled publicly, but it wasn't the only one. The university commissioned a report on the football team after the 1937 season and a persistent issue it highlighted was "prejudice among some against the colored boys."

Bruins teammate Dave Gaston remembered fights between Wyrick and Strode as a regular occurrence, not a onetime event. "When we would scrimmage, many, many times they had to be separated," Gaston said. "It was all Slats. It was [his] being from Texas . . . he had a hard time adjusting to playing with black teammates."

Predictably, opponents were even nastier. Some targeted Washington and Strode for abuse, biting or slugging them under pileups, or grabbing a handful of the lye-based chalk used to mark the field and rubbing it in their eyes. Word got back to Washington and Strode that a Stanford football coach applied burnt cork—blackface—to the face of his scout-team half-back so that the rusher would, apparently, better simulate Washington in the team's practices before its game against the Bruins. Several opposing coaches were known to yell racist epithets at Washington or Strode when they neared the rival team's sideline.

Both men recalled their time in Westwood fondly, in general, and they were popular among the student body. Starring on the football team certainly came with perks. When Washington arrived, one of the athletic directors gave him a car, which was put in Strode's name since Washington was only seventeen. Strode remembered driving from his parents' place in South Central to Lincoln Heights to pick up Kenny in the morning and heading along Wilshire Boulevard on the way to campus. "We'd listen to Al Jarvis on the radio, and sometimes the music would be so good we'd stop the car and do a jitterbug right there," Strode remembered.

During Washington and Strode's time in high school and college, the demographics of Los Angeles were changing. It started in the early part of the century and accelerated through the 1940s with the spread of racially restrictive housing covenants. The covenants were boilerplate agreements included in real estate documents barring the sale of a property to "Mongoloids," blacks, and sometimes Jews and Catholics. They originated as municipal codes in the mid-1800s and were initially created to exclude Chinese railroad workers from setting up laundry businesses in white neighborhoods in the San Francisco Bay Area.

Restrictive covenants worked in two main ways. In some cases, real estate developers inserted covenants into titles for all parcels of a given tract of land before any individual properties were sold. Another type was separate from the title documents and required property owners to mutually agree to prohibit the sale of their properties to people banned under the covenant. This usually obligated neighbors to create homeowners' associations to organize and execute the agreements.

The latter was more common in already-developed and crowded cities in the North and Midwest—Chicago, Detroit, Cleveland, and St. Louis—while both types were prevalent in Los Angeles. Powerful real estate associations supported covenants because, they said, the agreements kept property values high. Title companies loved the covenants because they could charge $20 for the boilerplate agreement that cost them less than a dollar to execute.

Developers, real estate agents, and sellers weren't the only ones imposing racial restrictions on housing; municipalities did so, too. South Pasadena's city manager admitted in 1946 that he and the city attorney had been writing restrictive covenants into the deeds of all properties that passed into municipal ownership since 1941. Many towns and cities near Los Angeles also added restrictive covenants to deeds that came into municipal possession.

The federal government enforced covenants as well. As part of the New Deal, President Roosevelt pushed for more support for homeowners. The Federal Housing Administration was created as part of the National Housing Act in 1934, and the intent was to stabilize and broaden the ability of people to buy homes. Prior to the FHA's creation, most mortgages were short-term agreements with high penalties and they required large down payments. As the Great Depression set in, banks failed, unemployment soared, and many mortgages were foreclosed. The FHA's main role was to provide mortgage insurance to encourage banks to loan money to aspiring homeowners. This did work, but mostly for white mortgagees.

The FHA often *required* building developments or tracts to include racially restrictive covenants as a prerequisite for mortgage insurance on those properties. In providing mortgage insurance the FHA considered whether the property was in an area with "inharmonious racial groups." If so, the insurance was often withheld.

The FHA also used a color-coded system to denote which properties in a given city were good mortgage risks for banks. If a house sat in a green or blue area, home buyers found it easier to get an FHA-backed mortgage. Yellow areas were considered risky, and red the riskiest of all. In most cities the red sections on the map were the predominantly black neighborhoods. Thus the term *redlining* came to describe the practice of banks refusing mortgages to people seeking to buy in areas where the FHA wouldn't provide mortgage insurance.

This not only institutionalized the exclusion of black or mixed neighborhoods from economic improvement, but also gutted the values of homes in the redlined areas and thus gutted black wealth that had been built up via homeownership. This was especially devastating in cities such as Los Angeles where a relatively high percentage of black residents owned their homes in the early part of the twentieth century.

The rise of racially restrictive covenants in Los Angeles overlapped with the implementation of the FHA programs. So while the FHA crippled house values in mostly black neighborhoods, those were also the only places in Los Angeles where African Americans could buy property without being under threat of eviction.

In 1920, racially restrictive housing covenants covered roughly 20 percent of Los Angeles County. By 1946 some reports put the covenants as covering 80 percent of the county. In the early days, the agreements were inconsistently enforced, but by the early 1940s enforcement was much more frequent.

The process often went like this: Existing neighbors or outside agitators would try to convince or intimidate black newcomers to move out. Some real estate agents were rumored to be in league with the Ku Klux Klan, then resurgent in Southern California, and would ask the Klan to intimidate black families through cross burnings, eggings, or recurrent drive-bys after dark, all intended to terrorize the families into leaving.

If intimidation didn't work, then a member of the local white home-owners' association would take the black family to court, seeking an injunction under the terms of any applicable racially restrictive covenant. The county court often sided with the covenanters, and the African American family could appeal to higher state courts to get the injunction overturned. However, this took time, money, and legal resources. (Asian, Latino, and Jewish residents also lived under threat of eviction under the covenants, but black residents were the ones most often targeted and evicted.)

Between 1942 and 1946 more than two hundred covenant cases were brought to court in Los Angeles alone. That number didn't count the scores of residents who moved after legal action was threatened but before it was taken.

The city's most famous covenant case originated around the same time Kenny Washington and Woody Strode starred for UCLA. During the mid-to-late 1930s several prominent black professionals bought houses in unre-stricted areas of West Adams Heights. This neighborhood northwest of the USC campus was developed specifically for the social elite, with turreted mansions surrounded by well-groomed estates. At the beginning of the century, industrialists and university deans occupied the area.

But by the 1930s some had moved to the Westside. Others suffered heavy financial losses during the Depression and had to move out as well. Well-off African Americans who were part of Los Angeles's small but growing black professional class—doctors, dentists, and lawyers—along with black Hollywood stars, began buying houses in nearly all-white parts of the neighborhood. People started calling that particular region of West Adams Heights "Sugar Hill" after the affluent part of Harlem known by that name.

Some of the neighborhood was covered by racially restrictive housing covenants, but some was not. And the covenant that applied to many of the blocks was set to expire near the end of the 1930s. When black actress Hattie McDaniel, who is best known for her role as Mammy in *Gone with the Wind*, bought her place in West Adams Heights, she was told not to worry about the covenant as it was about to expire and wouldn't be enforced.

What wasn't divulged was that white residents who had recently moved into the neighborhood wanted to extend the covenant. Some of their older neighbors refused to join, but enough banned together under the West Adams Improvement Association to enforce a new covenant that would last until 2035.

On May 24, 1945, the homeowners' association served McDaniel and roughly thirty neighbors with injunctions demanding they vacate their homes. This began a short but critical case in the fight against racially restrictive covenants.

By the time McDaniel was served papers, Kenny Washington and Woody Strode had starred for the Hollywood Bears for several years and would soon sign contracts with the Los Angeles Rams. While they weren't in the same economic class as the top Hollywood stars, they were part of the black elite in Los Angeles. Numerous peers in the sports world, including boxers Jack Chase and Dynamite Jackson, were targeted by covenanters. In the mid-1940s, every week brought news of other black Angelenos being sued to leave their property, some in neighborhoods where covenants had long laid dormant.

CHAPTER 4

Moore's Ford Bridge

Banks of the Apalachee River
Walton County, Georgia

1946

Once WASHINGTON AND STRODE SIGNED WITH THE Rams, they had plenty to worry about on the field. Washington was rehabbing his knees through May and June, and observers debated whether he'd recover fully by the time the season started, and then what position he'd play in the Rams offense. After signing him, Los Angeles head coach Adam Walsh said, "We will use Kenny where his assets as a passer and runner will give us the strongest possible four-man [backfield] combination on the field at one time." To which Strode later commented, "In other words, Adam Walsh didn't know how he was going to use Kenny."

As the summer progressed, Walsh settled on slotting Washington in at backup quarterback. "I am going to try Washington at that position until I see how his knees that were operated on recently hold up," the coach said. "If Kenny's legs stand up under some rugged scrimmages in training camp, we could make more consistent use of his running ability."

Washington wasn't getting a shot at the starting quarterback job. Bob Waterfield, the incumbent, had led the Rams to an NFL title in 1945 when he was a rookie and the team was still in Ohio. With a league title on his résumé, and an NFL Most Valuable Player award, the starting quarterback wasn't going anywhere.

Waterfield grew up near Los Angeles, in Van Nuys, California, and followed Washington's exploits at UCLA while he himself was still in high school. Waterfield starred for the Bruins a few years after Washington did and led UCLA to its first-ever victory over USC in 1942 and its first Rose Bowl, where the Bruins lost to the Georgia Bulldogs. After a brief stint in the military, Waterfield returned to UCLA. The Cleveland Rams drafted him in 1944 while Washington and Strode played for the Hollywood Bears.

Some might have expected a frosty, competitive dynamic between Washington and Waterfield, but they became friends on and off the field. Waterfield taught Washington the finer points of playing quarterback in the modern T formation, including the play-calling system. Before the modern T, quarterbacks mostly called the plays in the huddle. But in the T the quarterback called out the play as the team came to the line of scrimmage. Because their opponents could plainly hear the call, quarterbacks started using codes. Washington likened it to learning Chinese. One time early in training camp Washington approached the line and barked out, "Ready seventy-five, fourteen, period, twenty-six, down, comma, semicolon, right!"—to the laughter of his teammates, many of whom were also playing in the T formation for the first time.

Even if Washington's knees did hold up for rushing duties, the Rams backfield was already crowded. Some of the logjam came from talent Los Angeles already had; the rest was part of a larger flood of pro and college stars returning from military service. Fred Gehrke started at left halfback, and he'd led the team in rushing during their championship run the year before. Former USC Trojan Jack Banta started at right halfback, and Los Angeles had drafted promising rookie Tom Farmer from Iowa.

The Rams also signed Tom Harmon, who played at Michigan when Kenny Washington was at UCLA. In 1939, Washington led the nation in total passing and rushing yards with 1,370; Harmon was second with 1,356, but in two fewer games. That season Iowa running back Nile Kinnick won the Heisman Trophy and Harmon finished second. The Michigan back then won it the following season. Besides Strode, Harmon was Washington's best friend on the team, and they would stay close long after both had retired.

While Washington's place in the lineup was unsure, Strode's seemed nonexistent. Jim Benton was the starting left end. The previous year he'd established an immediate rapport with Bob Waterfield and led the league in receiving yards. Steve Pritko returned as starting right end, and newcomer Bob Shaw was expected to get plenty of playing time as well. The modern T formation used two ends. Most players went both ways, playing offense and defense. In a few years a platoon system—different starters on each side of the ball—would become common across the NFL. But in the last years of the two-way era, Strode faced little playing time with potentially three ends ahead of him.

Strode may or may not have been a better receiver than Benton or Shaw, but he excelled where the other three did not: crashing the edge on defense. In this thankless task the end plowed into the opposing team's tackle and guard and occupied both to clog seams where ballcarriers might otherwise get through. But as with Washington, the Rams coaching staff seemed unconcerned with where they'd play Strode or how much they'd use him.

Strode suspected the Rams signed him to provide Washington a room-mate on the road rather than from a specific interest in him as a player. While both endured uncertainty about where and how much they'd play, some in the mainstream press were still debating whether they deserved a shot at all. Writers such as Vincent X. Flaherty of the *Los Angeles Examiner* said black players simply weren't good enough to make the grade in the NFL.

But Tim Mara, owner of the NFL's New York Giants, praised the sign-ings for the black fans it would bring to the league. "We can't lose on that move," Mara told the *Pittsburgh Courier* in late May. "Both are good football players and both will prove to be real attractions. I am sure we will get thou-sands of more Negro fans to attend the games at the Polo Grounds this year because they will have an added interest in the league." His support, while earnest enough, was likely also motivated by the arrival of a new AAFC franchise in New York competing for locals' attention.

Near the end of July, Washington's friends threw him a dinner party as a good-luck send-off before he and the rest of the players reported to training camp at Compton College. Dr. Charles Wesley Hill hosted the party at his home on Franklin Avenue in Hollywood. Reverend George Garner was the master of ceremonies, and Frank Roane and the Originaires, a Great Lakes Naval Base singing group who had been broadcast nationally during the war, entertained the guests. Kenny and his wife, June, were joined by Rams quarterback Bob Waterfield and his wife, actress Jane Russell, as well as Rams backfield coach Bob Snyder, opera star Caterina Jarboro, actor Clarence Muse, and others.

Days later, on July 25, a white mob lynched two black men and two black women near Monroe, Georgia. Roger Malcom, an African American share-cropper, had stabbed his white boss, whom he suspected of sleeping with his wife. Malcom was thrown in jail. His wife, Dorothy, summoned her brother George for help. George Dorsey worked for a white landowner who needed extra hands on his farm to prepare for the upcoming cotton harvest.

Dorsey convinced his boss, Loy Harrison, to post Roger Malcom's $600 bond in exchange for Malcom working off the debt in Harrison's cotton fields. Harrison drove Dorothy and George and George's wife, Mae Murray Dorsey, to bail out Roger. They stopped in town to run several errands, then went to the jail to pick up Malcom. On their drive back home they rounded a curve and saw several cars blocking their path across Moore's Ford Bridge. They slowed and more cars pulled up behind them.

About twenty white men exited the vehicles, several with shotguns and a few with handguns. They surrounded Harrison's car. One walked to the driver's side and put a gun to Harrison's head. A large man with a florid complexion standing a few yards away ordered the mob to grab Roger, and then George, and pull them out of the car. Harrison protested that they were his workers and he needed them in the field. The leader ignored him. He had Roger Malcom's hands bound together, and his men escorted Roger and George down the embankment toward the Apalachee River. As the car's male occupants—save for Harrison—were marched down the hill, one of the women in the car screamed the name of a man she recognized among the mob.

The leader of the group stopped and turned back toward the bridge. He pointed for his henchmen to pull the women out of the car and drag them down the riverbank next to the men. Dorothy and Mae braced themselves against the frame of the car as the men swung their guns at the women's arms to break their grasp. After a brief struggle they, too, were yanked down to the river. There the mob lined them up by some sweet-gum seedlings. A handful of the armed white men stood opposite the foursome. "One . . . Two . . . Three . . . Fire!" A volley followed. All four bodies slumped to the ground. The men lowered their aim slightly. Another count and a second volley. Then a third. Finally satisfied, the men climbed back up the embankment. The mob dispersed and Harrison drove home.

The immediate aftermath was typical of a lynching in twentieth-century America. An hour or two later the coroner arrived, a cursory inquest was held on the spot, and the bodies were removed. As fast as the coroner could label the deaths as "murder at hands unknown" the next morning, souvenir seekers showed up. A young white couple parked by the bridge and took their four-year-old boy to stare at the pools of dried blood beset by flies. A University of Georgia student on his way to Athens detoured to check out the lynching site and found a bullet-strafed piece of rope, likely the piece used to tie Roger Malcom's hands.

Before he could celebrate his find, another man grabbed it from him and took off. A woman posed for a picture while pointing toward the bloody dirt. Others peered closely at the sweet-gum trees, their trunks riddled with bullets at about four feet high. After the initial volley felled the four, the killers aimed down at the victims' heads and torsos. The coroner recorded sixty bullet wounds.

A white sharecropper who lived near the river talked with passersby and souvenir hunters on the loose-planked bridge. He recalled the sounds of the shooting but said he did not go down to the river and didn't see anyone suspicious passing through.

Newspapers across the country carried announcements of the grisly killings. All of the country's black newspapers, including those in Los Angeles and Cleveland, covered the lynchings and over the next two weeks reported on two more. On July 30, a black man in Mississippi was flogged to death by six white men who accused him of stealing a saddle. Barely a week into August, word came that two black men in Louisiana had been jailed for supposedly entering a white woman's house uninvited.

Local white men swarmed the jail, and the deputy released the black men to the mob. The horde dragged the two to a nearby bayou and attacked them with a meat cleaver and blowtorch. One of the men died. He, like George Dorsey, was a World War II veteran. The man who survived escaped during the night. When his attackers realized he was still alive and gone, they set about tracking him as he made his way north. Local black sharecroppers risked their own safety to shelter the victim while he fled his pursuers. A week later he'd made it far enough that some NAACP members could get him the rest of the way to New York City.

Until that summer, the number of reported lynchings in the nation had been trending slowly downward. The six in the summer of 1946 was the most the nation had seen in ten years.

Back in Los Angeles, the front pages of the black weeklies carried updates on the search for justice in Georgia, while their sports pages reported on Kenny Washington's and Woody Strode's progress in training camp and what the upcoming season might yield, on the field and off, for the first black men to play in the NFL in thirteen years.

The Los Angeles Rams opened their 1946 preseason with the College All-Star Game at Soldier Field in Chicago. Kenny Washington met with the

Rams brass to discuss his availability. His doctor said that playing on his recently operated knee was not likely to lead to further injury. The Rams said it was up to Washington to determine whether his knee felt strong enough. He thought it did and declared himself ready to go.

The Rams practiced for just a few weeks before boarding the train to Illinois. The pros were usually favorites against the college men, and the 1946 game was no exception. Promoters expected a big crowd, too. With World War II over and a return to a peacetime economy well under way, fans showed up in droves to sporting events for much-needed relaxation and entertainment. The College All-Star Game packed 97,380 fans into Soldier Field that day.

The college all-stars notched the first touchdown when Wisconsin halfback—and soon-to-be Chicago Rocket and later Los Angeles Ram— Elroy "Crazy Legs" Hirsch sliced through the Rams defense for a 68-yard scoring run. Los Angeles wasted several scoring opportunities with inaccurate passing and turnovers. Bob Waterfield hit on just seven of his 21 pass attempts, and the offensive line blocked poorly.

On the defensive side of the ball, the Rams failed to tackle well, or in the case of Hirsch, tackle him at all. He scored another touchdown in the second half off a long throw from Northwestern star Otto Graham, who was headed to the Cleveland Browns training camp after the game. The Rams continued to flail on offense, and the college all-stars led 14–0 by the fourth quarter. Coach Adam Walsh finally replaced Waterfield with little-used backup Albie Reisz, who was injured several plays later and had to be helped off the field. Kenny Washington came in at quarterback with the Rams on their own 20-yard line. On his first play under center with an NFL team, Washington dropped back to pass, found no one open, and scrambled for a 10-yard gain. He then threw an interception. With the Rams down two scores halfway through the fourth quarter, Washington had little choice but to throw and the collegians knew it.

Washington got one more chance with 45 seconds left, with the Rams again pinned deep in their own end. He bobbled the snap and backpedaled into the end zone, where he was tackled for a safety. Strode played little, and mainly on defense. The college all-stars had shut out the Rams, 16–0.

Washington and Strode's first trip as part of an NFL team went just as badly off the field. When the Rams arrived in Chicago for the exhibition game, they went straight to Soldier Field for practice and then on to the Stevens Hotel, where the team usually stayed when in the Windy City.

Either head coach Adam Walsh or his brother Chile filled in Washington on a looming problem, but Strode didn't know something was amiss until he saw the irritation on Washington's face after practice.

"What's wrong?" asked Strode.

"We can't stay at that stinking hotel," Washington replied. Strode was surprised. He had stayed at the Stevens for a track meet while at UCLA. Strode realized that the Bruin coaches or administrators must have pulled some strings behind the scenes to make sure he could stay with the team as the hotel forbade black guests.

"What do they want us to do?" Strode asked.

"They're going to give us a hundred dollars to go find someplace else to stay."

"What the hell. Let's be segregated."

The two headed across town to the Persian Hotel, said to be the nicest black hotel in the city. Count Basie was playing at the nightclub downstairs, so they grabbed seats at the bar and each ordered a Tom Collins.

At midnight Bob Waterfield walked in and weaved his way to the bar. "You crazy sons of bitches, what are you doing here this late at night?"

"Just sitting here enjoying this club," Strode replied while Washington chuckled.

"Look, we've made arrangements for you to come uptown with us and stay in the hotel."

"Forget that, boy." Strode laughed. "I'm going to be segregated, spend this hundred dollars, stay right here, and listen to the Count play his music."

"What the hell." Waterfield shrugged, pulled up a seat, and ordered a drink.

After the College All-Star Game, the Rams had little time to regroup before their charity game against the Washington, D.C., team at the Los Angeles Coliseum. In scrimmages, Coach Walsh had Kenny Washington and Bob Waterfield take turns leading the first-team offense, and the *Los Angeles Times* reported that Washington was hitting all of his passes. *Times* columnist Braven Dyer thought Washington impressed in his College All-Star Game cameo and claimed Walsh was considering nominally starting Washington against the D.C. team but swapping in Waterfield after a series or two, to wake up the veteran.

"Walsh has an idea that if Waterfield sits with him on the bench for a few minutes . . . Bob can then take the field with added confidence and full knowledge of what Adam wants done after viewing the setup," Dyer wrote. Walsh wound up starting Waterfield and played him for most of the game. Washington missed on the one pass he threw, though he did get an ovation from the hometown crowd when he entered the game. Another backup quarterback, ex-Trojan Jim Hardy, completed his only attempt. Los Angeles was satisfied to edge Washington, 16–14, in front of nearly 70,000 fans.

CHAPTER 5

Offside

Cleveland Browns Training Camp
Bowling Green, Ohio

1946

C LEVELAND RAMS OWNER DAN REEVES HAD CONSIDERED moving his team from Ohio to the West Coast for several years before he finally convinced his fellow NFL owners to approve the idea. Attendance had lagged during the war, as it had for many teams, and Reeves thought Los Angeles had a growing fan base ready for an NFL franchise. While he yearned for the greener pastures of the coast, he also knew the AAFC had big plans for Cleveland.

The new league launched in 1944 and had initially aimed to start play in 1945, but pushed it back a year because of war demobilization. The AAFC recruited well-heeled owners, many of whom had previously sought to start new NFL franchises but were turned down. The senior league had been wary of overextending its business when it was struggling to maintain financial stability. The NFL's loss turned out to be the AAFC's gain.

Mickey McBride, owner of the Yellow Cab Company in Cleveland, as well as numerous real estate investments across northern Ohio, had previously offered to buy the Rams from Reeves, but Reeves had said no. Through his early background in the newspaper business McBride knew Arch Ward, the Chicago reporter who launched the AAFC, and McBride quickly signed on as owner of the new Cleveland franchise.

He initially set his sights on hiring Notre Dame coach Frank Leahy. But the Catholic football powerhouse fought to keep him and Leahy decided to remain in South Bend. So McBride settled for his second choice, Paul

Brown, who had coached Ohio State to a national title in 1942. Brown had begun his head-coaching career at his high school alma mater, Massillon Washington High. He turned the Tigers into a high school juggernaut, going 80-8-2 and winning six state titles in nine seasons. He took over at Ohio State and continued his success there. Drafted into the Navy during the war, Brown coached the Great Lakes Naval Training Station service team that beat Notre Dame in 1945. The hiring of Brown as Cleveland's head coach was a success even before his squad took the field, as Brown's deep Ohio roots guaranteed strong fan interest from the beginning.

When McBride hired him in 1945, Brown immediately contemplated the signing of black players, according to the coach's autobiography. The same month Washington signed with the Los Angeles Rams, Cleveland's black weekly, the *Call & Post*, reported that Bill Willis, a middle guard who had starred at Ohio State under Brown, was up for a role on the new squad.

When weighing signing Willis, Paul Brown worried that publicity from the move could hurt Willis's performance or distract the team, and he loathed distractions. To avoid such complications, Brown later wrote, he planned to wait and ask Willis to try out after training camp was already in progress.

He didn't let Willis in on this idea, however. By the time Brown finally reached out to Willis, the ex-Buckeye had verbally agreed to play for the Montreal Alouettes, an expansion team in the Interprovincial Rugby Football Union, a forerunner of the modern Canadian Football League. Brown persuaded Willis to stop by Cleveland's training camp in early August on his way to Québec.

At least that was Paul Brown's version. Stories differed on what exactly brought Willis to Bowling Green. Paul Brown claimed Willis contacted him and Brown told the middle guard to stop by camp on his way north. Willis's sons say that their father did contact Brown that spring or summer, but not about a spot on the team. "He had no inkling that would ever happen," said Clem Willis, one of Bill's three sons. According to him, his father was applying to be head football coach at Wilberforce University and wanted a letter of recommendation from Brown. Only after a Cleveland-area sportswriter nearly goaded Willis into trying out did he decide to stop by the Browns training camp.

The evening Willis arrived in Bowling Green, Brown convinced the lineman to stay, saying, "I'll stake my reputation that you'll be able to make our team." Brown claimed that he had signed Willis before the Rams signed Washington and Strode, but newspaper reports proved that to be false.

Regardless of Brown's shaky claim to have beaten the Rams to the punch, on August 5, Bill Willis stepped into a scrimmage against Cleveland's starting offensive line. He lined up at middle guard, right across from the center. The middle guard's primary role, like that of a modern nose tackle, was to disrupt running plays and occasionally pressure the quarterback.

Across the line of scrimmage from Willis stood NFL veteran Michael "Mo" Scarry, who had played for the Rams before they moved to California. Willis dug his cleats in the dirt and planted both hands on the ground, like a sprinter but lower, head up. "He had a crouch almost like a frog," Clem Willis said. "He was spring-loaded in that position." The two men stared at each other across the line of scrimmage. At the snap Willis blew past Scarry and sacked quarterback Cliff Lewis. The whistle blew, and the players unpiled and walked back to their spots.

Scarry shook his head and lined up again. He put one hand on the ground and wrapped the other around the pigskin. After snapping the ball he stepped quickly to block Willis, but the middle guard was already at his hip. Scarry lunged and weakly redirected Willis, who charged into the back-field to take down Lewis again. Scarry jabbed the ground with his cleats and scowled. The third time Scarry snapped the ball he got his hands up faster, but Willis ducked under them and knifed into the backfield. The whistle blew. Scarry pointed at Willis: "He's going early."

Willis, walking back to the defensive side of the ball, stopped. The other players also stopped, unsure what to make of this accusation. They looked at the veteran Scarry, and then the newcomer Willis, who stood with his hands on his hips and a practiced blank expression on his face. Even the players going through separate drills yards away paused to look over.

Coach Brown walked into the scrimmage. "Run the play again," he demanded. He positioned himself down the line of scrimmage and crouched. The linemen sank into their stances. Seconds later they exploded at each other. Scarry struggled again. Brown didn't look up. "Again," he said. He had the play run several more times with similar results. Brown stood up. He looked at Scarry, then said to the group, "He's not offside."

The lesson was one that Browns' opponents would learn all too well. For years afterward, whenever a new referee called a Cleveland game, one of the Browns coaches would suggest the official watch Willis carefully because many people thought he was offside when he wasn't. When Brown asked Willis how he got such a quick jump, Willis explained: He went when he saw the center's fingers tighten around the ball.

Practices continued, and a week later Paul Brown invited Marion Motley to try out. Motley was a 6-foot-2 fullback and linebacker who, like Willis and many of the new Browns, had past ties to the head coach. When Brown coached the Massillon Tigers in Ohio, Motley had played for their archrivals, the Canton McKinley Bulldogs. After high school Motley briefly played for South Carolina State, then followed his former high school head coach to the University of Nevada at Reno. Motley starred for the Wolf Pack for several years before injuring a knee, then joined the Navy in 1944. He was sent to Great Lakes Naval Training Station and was recruited to play on the base football team, coached by none other than Paul Brown.

Great Lakes was where Coach Brown tinkered with many of the new ideas he had for the game, including updating the T formation system. In Motley he had the perfect multiskilled player to make his version of the T work. Motley was not only talented but also huge by the standards of the era. Motley so intimidated other players with his size and power that when future Minnesota Vikings head coach Bud Grant arrived at Great Lakes as a nineteen-year-old would-be fullback, he took one look at Motley and switched positions to end. Motley quickly adapted to Brown's flavor of the modern T offense and led Great Lakes to a 39–7 victory over Notre Dame. Motley had planned on returning to college in the fall of 1946 but instead came back to Canton, Ohio, to work in a steel mill to support his family.

When he heard that Paul Brown was going to coach Cleveland's new AAFC team, Motley wrote him a letter asking for a tryout. Brown replied that he had enough fullbacks. Why did Brown change his mind and invite Motley in August? Maybe other fullbacks got injured. Or, as Motley suspected, perhaps Brown wanted a black roommate for Willis. Or Brown simply changed his mind. In any case, Motley was on his way to Bowling Green.

Shortly after he arrived, so did rookie quarterback Otto Graham. The former Northwestern star was drafted by the Detroit Lions of the NFL but agreed to terms with the upstart Browns after meeting with their head coach. Graham missed the beginning of training camp because he had been in Chicago for the College All-Star Game. Upon arriving, Graham had to contend with Willis. "Our backfield coach was curious to see how I'd handle a hard-charging defense and especially Bill Willis," Graham said.

According to the talk around camp, Willis had jumped clear over Scarry at one point to tackle Cliff Lewis as the quarterback pivoted away from the center. Graham didn't know whether to believe that, but as he lined up, he tried not to let Willis distract him with his shifting from one center gap to the other. Scarry hiked the ball. Graham turned his hips, stepped back, and hit the ground, followed by an avalanche of bodies.

In an effort to get a jump on Willis, Scarry had retreated so quickly that he had stepped on his quarterback's foot. Because of Willis's speed, Coach Brown realigned Graham's stance, changing it from parallel and square behind center to staggered, with his left foot farther back than his right. This also helped Graham get into his drop faster. The staggered quarterback stance was one of many ways large and small that the Cleveland Browns, and particularly their black players, changed modern football.

Several teammates remembered Coach Brown telling the team in one of their preseason meetings that Willis and Motley were there to help the team win, and if anyone had a problem with their presence, they could leave. "[Bill and Marion] weren't welcomed with open arms," said William Willis Jr., one of Bill's sons. "I'm sure when my father reported to camp, there was a certain percentage of guys who were in awe, others who were probably jealous, others who for whatever reason were uncomfortable initially." Willis and Motley tried to get along with almost everyone, and soon had numerous allies on the team.

"Once they got to a point that they were functioning as a team, there were a number of guys on the team who were his protectors when they would go and play other teams," Clem Willis said. "[They said to my father,] 'If someone bites you in the leg, or someone kicks you in the back getting up from the pile, let me know and I'll retaliate.'"

Neither Willis nor Motley reported being treated differently from white players in camp, where players had their days planned out to the minute by their obsessive head coach. But they certainly couldn't avoid racism. Discrimination constrained the public lives of African Americans in the North almost as much as it did in the South.

The campus of Bowling Green State University in northwestern Ohio hosted the Browns camp, and each week the players were given free time on the weekend. Groups of players went into town for dinner or a movie. Usually one of the players would pick the restaurant, another the film, and many on the team would go together. That is, except for Motley and Willis. "He and Motley . . . they just knew they weren't accepted at these places," Clem Willis said. "It was enough of a struggle to be accepted on the team, play, do well, and everything else. They weren't trying to be the first ones to sit in the front row of this theater or what have you. They picked their battles."

Some of their teammates may have called ahead to see if a restaurant or theater prohibited black patrons, but for the most part their white teammates likely didn't think about it. The white and black players tended to socialize separately off the field, and many white players would have prioritized the comfort of their white teammates over including Motley and Willis.

In interviews years later, several white players said they didn't purposefully exclude black teammates from plans, but assumed that black players preferred not to risk being turned away in front of them. Several black players from that time also remembered how they hadn't wanted their teammates to witness their being refused service and also knew nearly all their white teammates would bow to the racial standards of the day rather than stand up for them off the field.

This was true for Kenny Washington and Woody Strode in Los Angeles as well. "We had this cleavage on the Rams football team," said Rams teammate Jim Hardy in the documentary *Forgotten Four: The Integration of Pro Football*. "There were guys who grew up in an entirely different social environment where blacks worked for you or did the menial work. There were a bunch of [guys] on the team who didn't cotton to Kenny and Woody."

Black sportswriter Brad Pye Jr. put it more bluntly: "On the field you were a star. But once you walk off of that field, as Muhammad Ali said, you are still a n—."

In Cleveland, Motley and Willis dealt with the situation by staying in the Bowling Green dormitory on the weekends and playing cards, sometimes with Paul Brown's young son, Mike, then an eleven-year-old kid and later the owner of the Cincinnati Bengals. Their favorite game was Dirty Hearts. All the cards would be dealt, and the goal was to avoid getting a heart. The queen of spades was the worst because it counted for thirteen hearts.

"Motley would always let Mike Brown sneak the queen of spades on him and then just fall out, 'You got me! You got me!'" Clem Willis said, laughing. "Mike Brown idolized those guys."

Like the black press in Los Angeles with Washington and Strode, the *Call & Post* covered Willis's and Motley's signings and their progress from week to week. Writers on the sports page scoffed that such skilled players needed to "try out" for the Browns and speculated where on the depth chart each would end up.

THE FRONT PAGES OF THE *Call & Post* reported on the lack of progress in identifying the murderers in the Monroe quadruple lynching and also briefed readers on escalating tensions much closer to home, at Cleveland's Euclid Beach Park, a popular amusement park on the city's far east side.

In the summer of 1946 an interracial group of twentysomethings launched a protest of Euclid Beach Park over its long-standing policy banning black parkgoers from the dance pavilion, the roller-skating rink, and the bathing area on the edge of Lake Erie. Black Clevelanders had protested the exclusionary policies at Euclid Beach before, referencing the Ohio Civil Rights Law of 1894, which banned racial discrimination in public accommodations.

Past protests at Euclid Beach had usually been one-off events or intermittent, but that changed in 1946. Activists sustained protests through the summer and the fall. Their demonstrations were straightforward. Black couples entered the park, bought tickets, and proceeded to the areas where African Americans were barred. The private security firm that policed the park promptly threw them out. The protesters would return the following week, sometimes with white allies, and repeat the process.

On July 21 several black couples and white couples stood together at the amusement park's front gates. The group walked between the castlelike spires at the entrance and over to the city-block-sized dance pavilion, one of the park's main attractions. They bought tickets and approached the door. But when they handed their passes to the staff, the ticket takers told them that African Americans were not allowed in the pavilion.

A security guard appeared a moment later and told the group that "no sitting, no talking, no mixing of any kind, is allowed between the races in this park." The couples asked why, citing the 1894 law. Several additional guards arrived and reiterated that mixed couples were not allowed on the dance floor. One of the women countered that the couples themselves were not mixed. One of the white protesters, a man, demanded to see the park manager.

A phalanx of security personnel escorted the demonstrators to the office of H. C. Shannon, the elderly white manager of the Humphrey Company, which owned the park. He said that close contact between the races was not allowed, regardless of state law. Eight guards then pushed the handful of men and women out a back gate.

When reached by the *Call & Post*, Shannon explained that the policy was not a result of racial discrimination but of business necessity. "Negro patrons of the park are free to participate in any of the activities open to the public at Euclid Beach with the exception of dancing, swimming, and skating," he said. Management had resisted previous efforts to open those areas to African Americans because they believed that if they did, white patrons would leave en masse. Shannon said people had suggested he try full desegregation and see what happened. "But none would guarantee that no friction will result," he said. When asked what he would do if the park-goers sued under the state law, Shannon shrugged. "We'll meet those suits when we get to them."

On Sunday August 3, members of United Negro and Allied Veterans of America along with the Ohio chapter of American Youth for Democracy gathered at the Ivanhoe Union Hall to finalize their picketing plans before heading to the streetcar entrance of Euclid Beach Park. Their goal was not to physically prevent people from entering the park but to raise awareness and support for changing the park's policy.

One hundred protesters marched in an oval in front of the entrance. Some carried signs that read WE WENT TO NORMANDY BEACH TOGETHER— WHY NOT EUCLID BEACH? A military veteran in uniform boomed an indictment of park practices through a megaphone while picketers distributed handbills. Handfuls of people gathered to watch. A trolley conductor parked in front muttered that the policy had been consistent for years; he didn't know why people were upset about it now.

A group of white teens briefly countered with pro-segregation chants. One took a handbill, wiped his shoe with it, and threw it away, laughing. Police passed by but did not intervene, and onlookers were mainly silent, though a few joined the protest. The demonstration began at four in the afternoon and ended ninety minutes later, as the organizers had planned.

Civil rights demonstrations continued the following week in Cleveland. Led by church groups and the local chapter of the NAACP, five hundred participants marched through downtown decrying the lynchings in Georgia and the discrimination at Euclid Beach. They demanded a federal anti-lynching law and took up a collection for a national fund that had been created to help prosecute the Monroe murders.

Local civil rights groups and other community leaders differed on what to do about both the Euclid Beach discrimination and the lynchings. Some of the city's African American leaders had argued against the march, claiming that protesters risked attack from sympathizers of the lynchers. "No such thing happened," Sidney R. Williams wrote in the *Call & Post*. "And if it had, Cleveland would have been better off. For then we would have known what we had to deal with right here in Northern Ohio. All of us are sure of certain elements of the South, but none of us know exactly what the score is today up here North of the Line."

CHAPTER 6

Assault

Euclid Beach Park
Cleveland, Ohio

1946

WHILE EQUAL ACCESS TO AMUSEMENT PARKS MIGHT seem like a low priority in the long fight for integration and equal rights, it was a crucible in the battle for racial equality, and these were some of the most bitterly defended spaces by those who sought to preserve segregation.

What people fought for at amusement parks was the same as what they fought for at movie theaters and restaurants, in buses and at hotels: equal access and use of public accommodations. The legal system interpreted public accommodations to include entities public and private that were commonly used by the public, including inns, restaurants, courthouses, libraries, parks, stores, and schools. In the first half of the twentieth century, ending segregation in public accommodations was one of several primary targets of civil rights advocates—the others being voting, housing, and employment.

During and shortly after the Civil War, Congress passed and the states ratified three amendments to the Constitution. The 13th Amendment abolished slavery. The 14th defined national citizenship and declared all citizens to have equal protection under the law. The 15th prohibited federal and state governments from denying a person the right to vote based on race, color, or previous condition of servitude. These measures, collectively known as the Reconstruction amendments, were intended to protect the civil rights of black people in the immediate aftermath of the war.

The legislators who penned the Reconstruction amendments sought to reinforce the federal government's power to ensure the equal treatment of black Americans. Massachusetts senator Charles Sumner codrafted the Civil Rights Act of 1875 with John Mercer Langston, cofounder of the Howard University School of Law and great-uncle to poet Langston Hughes. The bill specifically provided for equal treatment in use of public accommodations, public transportation, and jury service, regardless of race. The bill passed and was signed into law in 1875.

It survived in its intended form for only eight years. In the aftermath of the passage of the Thirteenth, Fourteenth, and Fifteenth Amendments, many Southern and some Northern states rushed to pass laws to ensure continued disenfranchisement and second-class status for black Americans.

The judicial branch approved those moves. The U.S. Supreme Court's 8–1 ruling in *Civil Rights Cases of 1883* neutered much of Reconstruction-era law. The decision declared the specific public accommodations passage in the Civil Rights Act of 1875 unconstitutional, claiming that Congress lacked the authority under the enforcement provisions of the Fourteenth Amendment to regulate the actions of private businesses, whether they served the public or not. Congress could only bar discriminatory action by government bodies, what was referred to in the legal system as "state action."

The Supreme Court didn't hear a case challenging that decision until thirteen years later. The famous *Plessy v. Ferguson* case emerged from New Orleans, where black and Creole residents traveled by train to Gulf Coast resorts, the Southern coastal version of places such as Euclid Beach. When Louisiana passed the Separate Car Act in 1890, requiring black and white riders to be seated in separate railcars, a group of black and Creole residents who opposed it created the Citizens' Committee to Test the Constitutionality of the Separate Car Law.

They drafted Homer Plessy, who was one-eighth black and often passed for white, to challenge the separate-accommodations requirement in intrastate travel. The Citizens' Committee notified the railroad that they'd hired a detective to arrest Plessy when he refused to move from the whites-only car.

Plessy's lawyer then filed suit that he had been denied equal protection under the law as defined by the Fourteenth Amendment, which stated, "No State shall make or enforce any law which shall abridge the privileges or immunities of citizens of the United States; nor shall any State deprive any person of life, liberty, or property, without due process of law; nor deny to any person within its jurisdiction the equal protection of the laws."

The Supreme Court disagreed, ruling that the Equal Protection Clause did not exclude separate accommodations and separating the races did not brand "the colored race with a badge of inferiority." The Plessy separate-but-equal ruling spurred a subsequent binge of segregationist laws.

It also coincided with a nationwide boom in amusement parks. The success of the 1893 Chicago World's Fair and New York's Coney Island, along with technical advancements such as electric trolleys and mechanical rides, spurred business interest in building more amusement parks, particularly at a time when cities were growing and urban dwellers were seeking more leisure opportunities. The companies that ran the trolley lines built amusement parks around the ends of lines to lure riders and increase profits. Steamboat operators on the Great Lakes and Midwest rivers also capitalized on the new interest in beaches and boardwalks.

Soon Cincinnati had its own version of Coney Island; Cleveland had Euclid Beach; Youngstown, Ohio, had Idora Park; and Pittsburgh had Kennywood Park. By 1910, most major Northern cities boasted large trolley parks or boardwalks. Since the rise in amusement parks coincided with segregationist campaigns regarding public accommodations, most amusement parks—North or South—were never completely integrated.

The majority of white parkgoers doggedly supported segregation, especially at attractions where teens were likely to flirt or cavort, such as dance floors, roller rinks, and bathing beaches or swimming pools. The fear of interracial flirting, and thus interracial relationships, drove much of the seething resistance to integration in these gathering places.

Those fears were shared by Dudley Humphrey, who had purchased Euclid Beach Park in 1901. He opposed the drinking and gambling he felt were prevalent in the park before he bought it and vowed to make it a respectable, family-friendly place of recreation. To Humphrey this meant excluding black Clevelanders from various parts of the park.

Only on a few specifically allotted days would the Humphrey Company open the dance hall or roller-skating rink to African Americans. By 1934 some racial liberals in Cleveland had begun to protest this policy. When the park banned African American schoolchildren from the dance hall during a series of school picnics, the Cleveland School Board passed a resolution that schools would not use the park until all the children were "accorded the full and equal enjoyment of the accommodations."

In 1936 two black high school students filed lawsuits after they were refused admittance to the dance pavilion. The Humphrey Company set up a slush fund to settle such lawsuits. Just a few years after that, the private guards at Euclid Beach beat a young black man, and in 1943 nine members of the NAACP Youth Council filed suit against the Humphrey Company for barring them from various attractions. They received a settlement, but the company remained committed to banning black customers.

The 1946 protests were the brainchild of several youth-run groups. American Youth for Democracy and the National Negro Congress organized the July 21 action. Both organizations had ties to Depression-era leftist or communist organizations. AYD formed as an evolution of the Young Communist League and appealed to those who agreed with the fight for racial equality, but not under an explicitly red banner.

The National Negro Congress had been founded at Howard University during the Depression and advocated for the working rights of African American laborers and industrial workers. Many unions excluded black workers from membership or shunted them off to nonvoting auxiliaries. The labor movement's racial bias in the first half of the twentieth century gave management a convenient way to break strikes—hire African Americans as strikebreakers, since black workers had little reason to support unions that excluded them. This notable area of friction between labor and civil rights groups was one reason civil rights organizations remained skeptical of the intentions of predominantly white leftist labor groups.

For a short time the National Negro Congress succeeded in bridging this divide by advocating for black unions and the opening of white unions to African Americans. But the NNC's national influence would soon wane. This was initially due to the NNC leaning more toward Communist ideology, exacerbated by the rise in red-baiting during the later 1940s.

In Cleveland, the actions initially planned by AYD and the NNC would be continued by a relatively new group, the local chapter of CORE, Congress of Racial Equality. CORE would become one of the "Big Four" civil rights organizations in the 1960s, but it began in Chicago as a small tangent of an antiwar group dedicated to nonviolent direct action.

Unlike many of the other civil rights groups in the 1940s, CORE was less concerned with negotiating or persuading recalcitrant companies or individuals to desegregate and more interested in pressuring them to do so. CORE's first large-scale action targeting public accommodations was a long-standing protest of the exclusion of African Americans at the

White City Roller Rink in Chicago in 1942. Later that year one of CORE's founders—George Houser—moved to Cleveland and started a chapter there. By the summer of 1946 Cleveland's chapter was one of the most active in the Midwest.

On August 23, 1946, twelve members of CORE, some black and some white, entered Euclid Beach at eight forty-five P.M. with plans to integrate the dance pavilion. The group initially stopped by the Skee-Ball area but didn't get much farther. Eight to ten uniformed guards approached the group fifteen minutes after they entered the park. Without asking them any questions, Lieutenant Alexander Campbell told them they had to leave. When one couple asked why, Campbell replied, "You know why." He added, "We've been expecting you since six . . . We knew people were coming to look for trouble."

Two of the guards grabbed one of the black CORE members by his arms, shoved him backward, and hit his legs with a nightstick. Another guard grabbed one of the other black men by the back of his collar and pushed him toward the exit. Yet another sneered, "We don't want any n— lovers here," to one of the white men in the group, while another guard grabbed one of the black women by her arm to force her through the gate.

Albert Luster arrived at Euclid Beach not long after. Luster, a black transit worker and CORE member, had come to meet up with the rest of the protesters. He later reported that as soon as he entered the park, he felt that he was being followed. He walked around the main thoroughfares of the park but did not see any of his colleagues. He found a pay phone and called the home of one of the people he was supposed to meet. The person who answered told him they had already been to the park, were assaulted by guards, and were thrown out. As Luster heard the recounting of the events earlier in the evening, he looked through the glass wall of the booth. Just across from him, on the other side of the pane, a park guard was staring at him.

When Luster left the booth, the guard approached him. They exchanged a few words and the guard swung his billy club at Luster. Another guard rushed him from behind and hit him across the back of the head. A swing at his face opened a gash in his lip. Two hours later Luster reached the house of the person he had called. He wore a bandage across the bottom third of his face and another on the back of his head and had bruises all over his upper body.

Parkgoers had called the police after finding Luster beaten and bloody. The officers who arrived sent Luster to a medical clinic and asked the park's security personnel why they had set upon the 145-pound man. The guards claimed that a patron had reported a black man wandering around who looked suspicious because he had his hands in his pockets. The security guards said they confronted Luster and he then insulted them, calling them Nazis.

"It didn't happen in Monroe, GA ... it happened in Cleveland, OH where a civil rights law has been on the statute books since 1894," led the *Call & Post*. Their coverage outlined some of what had happened that evening at Euclid Beach. In the week before the August 23 protest the organizers had contacted city police to let them know they were planning an action on Friday and wanted police there in case the guards got violent. Instead, the officers only showed up when summoned after Luster's beating, while the guards knew when the activists planned to arrive.

A week after the assault, Luster's lawyer revealed his client had suffered a fractured skull. Luster pressed charges against the guard who first hit him, Julius Vago, for using excessive force. Luster's was now one of at least five lawsuits against the Humphrey Company over the actions of their security personnel during the recent protests. CORE activists called for another action, and it, too, would be met with violence.

The same issue of the *Call & Post* that updated the city on Euclid Beach also reported disturbing news on the Georgia lynchings. Investigators uncovered that Loy Harrison, the white farmer who drove the Malcoms and Dorseys to pick up Roger, hadn't bonded Roger Malcom out of jail so he could help with Harrison's cotton harvest. Or, at least there was no record of his having done so. Also, the deputy who signed out Malcom to Harrison was the brother-in-law of the man Malcom had stabbed. Soon, Loy Harrison would be added to the growing list of locals suspected of planning and carrying out the lynchings.

MEANWHILE, BROWNS TRAINING CAMP WOUND DOWN, AND Paul Brown finalized his starting lineup. Bill Willis would start at middle guard and Marion Motley would be a backup at fullback. The team's schedule was released as well. Their last tune-up for the regular season would be a September 6 scrimmage against the Brooklyn (football) Dodgers at Akron's Rubber Bowl. But the Browns' opponent for their regular-season opener—and the host of one of their last games of the year—drew the most attention.

The Browns would open the inaugural AAFC season at home against the Miami Seahawks, the only franchise in all of pro sports in 1946 located in the Deep South. Miami's owner and head coach stocked the team exclusively with white Southern players, or white men who had starred at Southern universities. Like George Preston Marshall's Washington team in the NFL, the Miami Seahawks were built and marketed as the team of the South, in hopes of nurturing a broad regional fan base.

Black fans and press circled December 7, the day the Browns would play the Seahawks, this time in Miami. Florida state law banned interracial sports competition, which meant that black and white athletes were not allowed together on the same field. What would happen when the Browns showed up with Willis and Motley? No one really knew.

However, people did have a glimpse of what might happen. The Brooklyn Dodgers baseball team had signed Jackie Robinson to a minor league contract in the fall of 1945. High minor league affiliates often joined their big league brethren for spring training. So Robinson, like many of the other Montreal Royals, joined the Dodgers in Daytona Beach, Florida, in March of 1946, the same month the Rams signed Kenny Washington. The Dodgers did not yet have their own spring training facility, so the players stayed at local hotels. That is, except for Robinson and Johnny Wright, the second black player Branch Rickey had signed to the Royals. They had to stay with friends of friends or strangers since the hotels where the white players stayed barred black patrons.

The Royals scheduled games with other minor league teams at local baseball fields, but arrived to find the gates closed. Posted signs claimed electrical issues, plumbing problems, or similar conditions for the sudden closures, troubles that were always "fixed" for the next scheduled game. Jacksonville took the extra step of padlocking its stadium's gates and fences against the Royals. Branch Rickey's lobbying finally convinced Daytona Beach to go ahead with a Dodgers-Royals intrasquad contest on March 17, 1946. In the subsequent month the Royals managed to play only a handful of additional games before traveling north to open their International League season.

Paul Brown didn't tell Willis or Motley what he planned to do in December when the team traveled to Miami, and he might not have known himself. The team focused on their immediate challenge, the tune-up with the football Dodgers. The preseason game was uneventful, except for one altercation. On one play a Brooklyn ballcarrier attempted to swing wide, then cut back between the end and the tackle. Motley, playing linebacker on defense, came up and met him in the hole, driving him back three yards onto the turf. The Dodger jumped up and seemed ready to take exception to the play. Bill Willis put a hand on the man's arm, and several players on the Browns bench rushed in before the knot of players dispersed.

The *Call & Post* noted the tension and observed that Paul Brown appeared to use Motley mainly as a blocking back for the smaller backs in his backfield. "Professional grid foes of the Browns will rue the day when they take it for granted that Motley will block and tackle only, for the big Canton, Ohio, lad is one of the best open-field runners in the country," the paper warned.

Cleveland fans eagerly awaited their opening contest. The game against Miami drew 60,135, including 10,000 African American fans. Black fans, having followed Willis's and Motley's progress via their local black newspapers, traveled from Chicago and other cities across the Midwest to see them play. Black hotels in Cleveland reported they were at capacity and that rooms for that weekend had been booked weeks in advance.

Before the game, Paul Brown met Miami's principal owner, Harvey Hester, on the field. The jocular Floridian said he felt sorry for Brown that his team lacked the big Southern boys Hester had on his squad. "How do you expect to win?" he asked a stone-faced Brown. During warm-ups Cleveland players noticed the Seahawks quarterback squatting low to take the snap from center. They chuckled at how he would soon be struggling to get out of there with the ball. "We knew Bill Willis would devastate them much as he had us earlier in training camp," Coach Brown said.

And devastate them Willis did, as did the rest of the squad. On the Seahawks first drive their quarterback fumbled the ball away under pressure. Paul Brown started Cliff Lewis at quarterback for the first drive since Lewis had starred at nearby Lakewood High. The Browns got the ball first at Miami's 29-yard line. After a couple of rushing plays netted 10 yards, Lewis fired a touchdown to left end Mac Speedie.

The Seahawks stalled on their next drive and punted to the Browns, who took over near midfield. After two rushing plays, Otto Graham found Motley on a short pass on third and long. Motley caught the ball in the right flat and sped downfield. A would-be tackler tried to bring him down at the Miami 35-yard line, but Motley shook him off. Finally, the big fullback was pushed out of bounds at the 25. After a few short runs the Browns called on rookie placekicker Lou Groza.

This was the first time for many fans to see Groza's unusual kicking ritual. He brought out a three-foot-long piece of athletic tape and lined it up behind the ball in a straight line pointed toward the goalposts. Groza explained later that he kept his head down the whole time while kicking and looked at the tape to make sure his kick was straight. After kicking, Groza usually wouldn't look at the outcome until he had snapped the tape up from the ground. In 1950, artificial kicking aids such as Groza's tape were ruled illegal by the N F L.

But here in 1946, in the AAFC, his tape was legal and his aim was true. The Browns led Miami 10–0. Undoubtedly all of the Browns wanted to win, but some likely wanted to beat the Southerners emphatically. Cleveland piled on another 17 points in the second quarter under the direction of Graham, while Miami's offense went nowhere. The stout Southern boys of the Seahawks netted zero yards through the first half, gaining 15 yards in the air while losing 15 on the ground. Paul Brown cycled in numerous backups in the second half, and the Browns barely slowed down. Cleveland crushed Miami by a final score of 44–0.

Willis and the defense held the overmatched Seahawks to minus 1 yard rushing and 27 yards total. The Browns offense rolled up almost 400 yards, with Motley serving as backup to Gene Fekete at fullback. The *Call & Post* boasted of the play of Willis and Motley: "For their play in this opening game of the All-American Conference is seen as a fitting tribute to race gridiron stars and a definite acknowledgement by the nation's top grid coach, Paul Brown, that Negro athletes can make the best teams in the sports world." There were no public reports of racially motivated foul play during the game.

That wasn't the case the following week when the Browns traveled to Chicago to take on the Rockets. Motley made his first start in place of the injured Fekete and stole the show, as well as the starting job. He rumbled for 122 yards on 12 carries and scored the game's first touchdown on a 20-yard run. Paul Brown loved running a particular trap play with Motley. If the planned run was going to the left, then at the snap the right guard would pull out and cross behind the center and in front of Motley. That way the guard was the first to hit the line and could clear a lane for the fullback.

If the block worked, Motley would often have only one linebacker to avoid to break into the secondary. And with his power and speed, who knew if the opposing defensive backs would catch him. Would-be tacklers pinballed off Motley whether he was hitting a hole between the tackle and the guard or rushing outside around the line. Many hadn't realized how fast he was for a big man, faster than all but Elroy Hirsch of the Rockets defenders.

Cleveland scored 13 more points to take a 20–0 lead. Tired of losing and the beating Motley was giving them, Chicago went after him in the fourth quarter. Rockets players hit him well after the whistle and piled on at the end of tackles, a time-honored place to get in a few cheap shots before the referee pulled everyone apart. The first time the Rockets hit Motley late, the referee promptly called a 15-yard unnecessary-roughness penalty . . . on the Browns, who had done nothing. After another Rockets late hit, Cleveland's Ernie Blandin retaliated by jumping on a Chicago player, and the Browns were flagged for another unnecessary-roughness penalty, this one more deserved.

The Browns pounded out the 20–6 win over the heavily favored Rockets. Besides Motley's rushing, the *Cleveland Plain Dealer* praised the Browns defensive line for bottling up Hirsch, Chicago's exciting rookie halfback, who left the game in the third quarter with a likely concussion. Next for Cleveland was a trip to Buffalo to face the Bisons.

CHAPTER 7

Second Quarter

Cleveland Municipal Stadium
Cleveland, Ohio

1950

THE FIRST QUARTER OF THE 1950 NFL Championship Game had
shown the two sides of the Los Angeles offense, the quick strike of
their first touchdown and the ability to gouge out five to ten yards
at a time and drive over from short yardage with their oversize backfield.
Meanwhile, Cleveland had done what it had done throughout the year:
protected Otto Graham enough so his intermediate-to-long passes could
find their targets. Opening the second quarter down 14–7, the Browns
offense went back to work.

This time, Paul Brown sent the halfbacks wide and kept ends Mac
Speedie and Dante Lavelli in tight. The goal was to stretch the Los Angeles
defense laterally and have the ends work over the middle between the Rams
defensive halfbacks Tom Keane and Woodley Lewis.

The Browns succeeded at getting the ball out wide and quickly progressed
down the field to the Rams 35-yard line. Graham had time to find Lavelli
streaking diagonally down the field. At the time Graham threw the ball,
Lavelli had just a few inches on his defender. But Graham led his receiver
perfectly, and Lavelli stretched to grab the ball at the eight-yard line and
bolted into the end zone. Cleveland trailed by one, 14–13.

The Browns lined up for the extra point attempt. Though teams executed
the banal-looking play all the time, it required the completion of a perfectly
timed sequence of events to work. The center needed to make a good snap.
The holder needed to catch the ball, bring it down to the right point on the

ground, and tilt it the right way. The kicker would have started his run-up just after the snap, so by the time the holder got the ball down, the kicker was upon him with his kicking leg at the top of its backswing and coming forward. If any piece of the sequence was more than half a second off, the whole thing crumbled.

That's what happened on this play. The center's snap was low. Holder Tommy James bobbled the ball for a second while Groza had to stop midapproach or potentially kick his holder instead of the pigskin. Most teams had a code word like "Fire!" that the holder or kicker would yell in the case of a botched field goal attempt. This would alert the linemen who were facing away from the kick to block for a rushing play or run out for a possible pass. James or Groza yelled whatever Cleveland's signal was and James grabbed the ball and spun away from the line. As James rolled right, he didn't see much room ahead of him. He spotted lineman Tony Adamle rumbling to the end zone. James fired a pass toward Adamle, who leaped even though the throw wasn't that high. The ball bounced awkwardly off his forearm and to the ground. He smacked his hands together in frustration. Instead of tying the game, the Browns still trailed by one, 14–13, just a few minutes into the second quarter. Above the field one of the panels in the manual scoreboard moved. The official scorer peeked out through the opening and surveyed the field and the crowd. A moment later his fedora disappeared and the panel moved back in place.

The teams exchanged possessions, and Los Angeles marched to the Cleveland seven-yard line only to have the Browns defensive halfback Ken Gorgal snatch a Waterfield pass and return it to midfield. The Rams wasted another scoring opportunity later in the quarter when Waterfield knocked a 16-yard field goal attempt wide.

Like many squads at the time, the Rams had their quarterback do the kicking, punting, and placekicking, in addition to quarterbacking. This was a vestige of the single-wing offense, the most common system in college and pro ball before the modern T. In it the best athlete on the team usually did the majority of the rushing, passing, and kicking. The Rams starting quarterback, Waterfield, was a good kicker, better than most in the NFL, but it wasn't his top priority or his best skill.

Unlike most coaches, Paul Brown had players who specialized in kicking, and that gave his club a crucial advantage. His Browns teams eventually carried two specialists: Groza, a placekicker, and Horace Gillom, a punter.

Both played on offense and defense, too, either as starters or second-string options. But Paul Brown emphasized their kicking duties. This enabled Groza to spend more time practicing field goals and extra points. During the regular season Groza topped the league in both field goal percentage and total field goals converted, connecting on 13 of 19 attempts, while Waterfield hit 7 of 14. Gillom ranked third in the NFL in yards per punt, while Waterfield ranked 10th.

But that wasn't the only way to measure a punter's value. Gillom excelled at two other aspects of punting. He was known for his hang time, which was the length of time the kick was in the air. The longer the hang time, the better chance his teammates had of tackling the punt returner soon after he caught the ball. The other was directional kicking. Not many teams focused on that, but Gillom could angle his kicks either to take advantage of which way the wind was blowing or to give his punt-coverage team a better angle at the returner. All of these skills collectively helped the Browns keep their adversaries farther away from the end zone.

Having Bill Willis in the middle of the defense also helped keep opponents from scoring. Though solid and powerful, the former Buckeye weighed at least twenty pounds less than the typical NFL player lining up in his position. His relative lightness would have been a liability if all Willis did was line up over center and try to drive his opponent back, but it wasn't. Willis was quick enough to slice between linemen to get into the backfield or to track ballcarriers laterally, or to drop back and cover backs running routes as receivers.

When an opponent tried to rush wide, Willis often took a step back so he could run behind the other linemen and meet the running back at the end of the line when the ballcarrier was looking to turn upfield. Many running backs would string along behind the line of scrimmage looking to get to the edge or to cut back through a gap between the defenders, but with Willis in pursuit there were rarely gaps, and the back would run out of room at the sideline with the Browns defensive backs coming up to help out. When Willis wasn't making the tackle himself, he often chased rushers into teammates' tackles.

Initially, Willis's speed surprised opponents. But that's because they didn't know his history with the sport. Growing up in Columbus, Ohio, Willis idolized his brother Claude, who was eight years older than Bill. Claude went out for his high school football team and quickly earned a reputation as a bruising running back. Years later, Bill also wanted a spot in the backfield. But the legend of his older brother preceded him. "Everyone kept asking him, 'Are you going to be like your brother? Are you going to be like your brother?'" Claude Willis explained decades later. "So he got tired of being asked that and he switched to tackle. I think that might have been one of the reasons he was so quick on the line, because he had played in the backfield."

Willis's ability to cover the field laterally enabled right defensive end Len Ford to focus on getting upfield after the quarterback. Paul Brown would eventually tailor his front line around Ford's pass-rushing skills, making him the forerunner of the modern pass-rushing defensive end. The coach then sometimes moved linebackers behind the two ends and dropped Willis back a few steps in an early version of a 4-3 defense. Having only four linemen rather than five meant Ford could line up closer to the quarterback. In the next four seasons, Ford would be named All-Pro.

But in 1950, Brown used a base defense with Ford on the right side of a five-man front, Bill Willis at middle guard, and George Young at left defensive end. Early in the 1950 title game Waterfield had completed quick passes over the oncoming Browns linemen. To keep Los Angeles from scoring, Cleveland needed its defenders to tighten coverage on the receivers and to get more pressure on Waterfield.

Midway through the second quarter, with the score still 14–13 Rams, Los Angeles took possession at the 50-yard line. This gave the Rams an excellent chance to extend their lead. Waterfield immediately hit Elroy Hirsch in the middle of the field. The flanker evaded Willis and weaved between another two tacklers for a 25-yard gain.

That's when Len Ford took over. The Rams handed off to Vitamin Smith, but Ford sliced through the line and tackled Smith 10 yards behind the line of scrimmage. Second and 20. Waterfield went back to pass. Five-foot-nine halfback Glenn Davis tried to block the six-foot-four, 260-pound Ford while the Rams left guard scrambled to help. Davis initially went low, but Ford rushed outside, and the left guard ran into Davis. Davis dove desperately at Ford's midsection as the Browns defensive end reached over him toward Waterfield's back. Davis's momentum was pushing Ford past the Ram quarterback, but Ford grabbed Waterfield's shoulder pad and yanked him down for a 12-yard loss.

Third and 32. Waterfield backpedaled again as if to pass, but went for a late handoff to Davis. Ford and left defensive end George Young were already barreling upfield. As Waterfield spun to feed Davis the ball, he had his back to Young, who hit both quarterback and halfback as Davis got the ball. Young knocked Davis to the ground 11 yards behind the line of scrimmage. End of drive. Shortly after, the second quarter ended with the score still 14–13 in favor of the Los Angeles Rams.

Len Ford's demolition of that late second-quarter drive, and his performance during the rest of the game, was all the more notable given the injuries he had suffered in a home game against the Chicago Cardinals earlier in the year. Many didn't think Ford would be able to return during the 1950 season, or possibly play ever again.

Ten weeks earlier, on October 15, the Browns trailed the Cardinals 24–10 halfway through the third quarter. The game had already been chippy, with both teams committing fouls. At one point Browns defensive back Cliff Lewis tackled Chicago end Bob Shaw around the neck on an incomplete pass. Shaw grabbed Lewis as he walked away from the play. Other players exchanged words after questionable altercations. "The Cards began to taunt us a little when they got that fourteen-point lead. You should have heard some of the conversation," Paul Brown said after the game. "I guess the boys didn't like it and went to work."

On the Browns' next drive, Graham backpedaled to throw. He heard Dante Lavelli's alto-pitched "Otto! Otto!" as he saw the end waving frantically. Lavelli had maybe a half step on his defender. Graham hit him in stride, and Lavelli stumbled into the end zone for a 29-yard touchdown. (That Lavelli yelled or waved urgently was no surprise; his teammates insisted that the all-star end always thought he was open.)

The Browns defense stopped the Cardinals, and Cleveland got the ball back, trailing 24–17. Graham again hit Lavelli for a touchdown, this one a 26-yarder. The game was tied. On the next series, Ken Gorgal intercepted a Chicago pass and took it to the Cardinals 19-yard line. The drive culminated in a Groza field goal, and Cleveland took its first lead, 27–24. Motley added a two-yard rushing touchdown shortly after.

During the whole game but especially during the Browns second-half comeback, Len Ford beat the Chicago blockers and harassed Cardinals quarterback (and ex-Ram) Jim Hardy. Chicago fullback Pat Harder resorted to using his elbows and forearms against Ford and other Browns linemen. Now near the end of the game, with the Browns likely to secure the victory, Ford got around Harder and leveled Chicago's backup quarterback. On the next play Harder clocked an unsuspecting Ford flush across the face with a forearm. Ford staggered and slumped to the ground. The head linesman threw his flag at the prone Ford, called a 15-yard unnecessary-roughness penalty against him, and ejected Ford from the game.

While Cleveland players howled in protest at Ford getting punished for Harder's shot, the Browns team doctor helped Ford into the training room and looked at his injuries. Ford's nose was bent to the side, his mouth was bloody, and half of his head was swelling up. When reporters were allowed into the locker room, Ford's face was already wrapped in towels, and the team doctor was preparing to take him to Charity Hospital. In the visitors' locker room Pat Harder dressed hurriedly and left the stadium without talking with reporters. His Chicago teammates insisted to the press they'd been at the receiving end of illegal blows from Ford all game.

Several days later, *Cleveland Plain Dealer* reporter Harold Sauerbrei wrote that he had seen the game film and it showed that Ford was the victim. "The pictures clearly showed plenty of flagrant use of the elbows and forearms and all of it was employed by Fullback Pat Harder of the Cardinals. In defending Harder's apparent slugging action against Len Ford which put the Browns' end in the hospital with serious facial injuries, Chicago players and officials working the game said the incident grew out of Len's conduct throughout the contest," Sauerbrei wrote. "Unless the pictures are deceiving, Ford is not guilty. On the other hand it would have been excusable for Ford if he had resorted to such tactics—it would have been in self defense."

While Ford was still at the hospital having his face put back together by a plastic surgeon, NFL commissioner Bert Bell wired the Browns a $30 fine for Ford slugging Harder on the play. Paul Brown called Bell and got the fine rescinded. The final damage to Ford was a broken nose, fractured jaw, fractured cheekbone, two missing teeth and several others chipped. Though angry about Harder's play, Paul Brown downplayed the overall roughness of the game. "You know Len just likes to unload on the passer," Brown said. "He just kept getting past the guys that were supposed to do the protecting for Hardy, and they didn't like it."

The *Pittsburgh Courier*, one of the nation's leading black newspapers, had a different take on what transpired. The week after the game, the paper's Ohio edition ran a piece titled BROWNS, CARDS IN NEAR RACE RIOT ON FIELD. The *Courier* article claimed the Cardinals yelled racist epithets at the Browns' black players throughout the game and threatened fistfights. Cleveland's *Call & Post* immediately followed up with interviews of Willis, Motley, and Cleveland's other black players.

The players termed the *Courier* article "utterly without foundation" according to the *Call & Post*, and the Cleveland paper insisted it would ask the *Courier* for a retraction in the interest of "preserving Cleveland's reputation for excellent race relations." Black fans who were at the Cardinals game wrote the *Call & Post*'s office and called the *Courier* article a "race-baiting distortion."

Harder's shot at Ford may have been racially motivated, but even if so, why was this situation pitting two black newspapers against each other with the *Call & Post* rushing to claim no racial animosity from Chicago's side?

The dynamic is best understood by looking at how racial violence was framed in general and who was likely to be blamed for it. In Atlanta in 1906, after months of a gubernatorial campaign where the challengers strove to top each other in racist invective in order to curry favor with poor white voters, a mob of hundreds of white men attacked black workers and residents near downtown Atlanta.

For several weeks prior, white newspapers had printed vague and sensational reports of black men assaulting white women. One claimed a black man had been caught trying to break into a woman's bedroom in a house near downtown. Another article claimed that large groups of black men left saloons in African American neighborhoods to seek white women to rape or kidnap. No one claimed to see these groups of men, and the specifics of each story changed wildly day by day such that they seemed clearly fabricated. The only constant was that the reports got progressively more gruesome the more often they were told. As the days passed, white men gathered at bars and talked of revenge.

On September 22, large groups of white men rampaged through Atlanta's historic black neighborhood of Sweet Auburn, stabbing, beating, and shooting people while lighting wagons and houses on fire. Only when residents brought out rifles and started shooting at the mob did the horde temporarily back away. W. E. B. Du Bois, then a professor at Atlanta University, bought a Winchester double-barreled shotgun and sat on the front steps of his nearby house, ready to defend his home against attackers. The mobs rampaged for three days, leaving anywhere from twenty-five to forty black residents (estimates varied) and one white man dead. One white woman died, but from a heart attack, possibly from seeing the mob outside her house.

A similar scenario happened in 1921 in Tulsa, Oklahoma. On May 30, a story began circulating about a supposed altercation or possible assault involving a young black man and a young white woman in an elevator in a building downtown. A clerk at a store in the building heard a woman scream, and when he got to the elevator, he saw a black man run away. The police were called, but after a short investigation it appeared they did not think that an assault had happened. The woman declined to press charges. Years later, investigators speculated the young man might have tripped while getting onto the elevator and grabbed the woman's arm and she screamed.

But the newspapers got hold of the story, and the *Tulsa Tribune* (a white newspaper) claimed he raped the woman and urged townsfolk in a headline to NAB NEGRO FOR ATTACKING GIRL. The young man was arrested, and the night after the newspaper had hit the streets, several hundred white men gathered near the Tulsa County Courthouse where he was being held.

Hearing of the young man's arrest, about thirty black men armed with shotguns and other weapons walked to the courthouse to defend him from a possible lynch mob if necessary. The gathering of whites had swelled to nearly a thousand and upon seeing the group of armed black men, many went home to get their weapons.

Shortly thereafter a shot was fired in the vicinity of the courthouse. It wasn't determined by whom or whether it was a warning shot or aimed at someone. Other shots followed and a rolling gunfight ensued that drove the black men back toward the Greenwood District. Over the next two days, mobs of white men attacked various parts of Greenwood while the residents either hid or fired back. Someone lit some buildings on fire. When the city fire department approached to put out the growing blaze, armed white men turned them back. The fire raged for hours. The governor called in the National Guard to quell the "Negro uprising," and most of the bloodshed ended a few days later.

The Greenwood District, known as the Black Wall Street, was burned to the ground. Thirty-five city blocks were destroyed, most of them in Tulsa's black neighborhoods. Reports of the death toll varied widely, from between 55 to 300 black residents and 10 to 80 white ones. Significantly, these events were almost universally called a Negro uprising or a race riot, although those who initiated the violence were almost always white. The events could more accurately be called mass lynchings, as that was the intent of the mobs and often the outcome.

Throughout the first decades of the twentieth century, dozens of smaller versions of Atlanta and Tulsa erupted in towns and cities across the country. Black residents knew that any racial violence in their cities would be blamed on them, no matter the origin. That's why the *Call & Post* immediately refuted the *Pittsburgh Courier*'s labeling of the Cardinals-Browns game as a "near race riot." The *Call & Post*, the black players, and Cleveland's black fans knew they would ultimately be blamed for any fallout from real or perceived racial animosity the Cardinals may have directed toward the black Browns.

Willis and Motley were stars, but their positions must have felt tenuous nonetheless. They had seen their talented peers released after speaking out on such things as equal pay or equal treatment. As black players on one of the blackest teams in the league, they commented carefully on the game.

Defensive halfback Emerson Cole, one of the black players more recently signed by the Browns, denied he was called any names. Bill Willis did the same. "[Motley] pointed out that the [*Courier*] story, in addition to its potential for wrongfully inciting riots among the Browns fans, also causes suspicion to fall on the Browns Negro players," the *Call & Post* reported. "It was a rough game," conceded Motley. "Probably a little rougher than we are accustomed to, but it was by no means the roughest game in which I have ever played ... I heard no threats from either Cardinal players or from spectators during or after the game and neither did other players with whom I talked."

A few days later, *Call & Post* reporter John Fuster visited Len Ford in the hospital. Ford's head was almost entirely encased in plaster. His mouth was still swollen and his right eye was opening for the first time since the game. Commissioner Bert Bell had rescinded the fine for Ford's supposed punch, but he had offered no apology or expression of concern for the injured player. Funster asked Ford whether any of the Cardinals had called him names or singled him out for abuse because of his race.

"I don't remember anybody calling me any names, but Willis, Motley, Gillom, Cole, and I always seemed in trouble during the game," Ford replied. "I know a lot of those guys [on the Cardinals]. Some of them played with me on the Los Angeles Dons, and Fred Gehrke and I used to go swimming together out on the coast." Ford paused. "I do know, though, that I was dodging elbows on almost every play." He paused again. "But football is a rough game and every team we play really wants to beat the Browns."

CHAPTER 8

Black Lightning

Los Angeles Memorial Coliseum
Los Angeles, California

1937, 1946

WITH THE 1946 REGULAR SEASON ABOUT TO start, many Los Angeles football fans wondered how Washington and Strode would fare in the pros. Most of the local sportswriters and fans remembered when the two players burst into the college spotlight on the very same Coliseum turf nearly nine years prior. Both were first-year starters and Washington presaged the sport's upcoming passing fixation with his own aerial show against the USC Trojans.

Southern California fans had hotly anticipated the December 4, 1937, USC-UCLA matchup, although both teams had stumbled through their respective seasons. Both the Bruins and the Trojans had been so inconsistent that "there is no sane reason to make either team the favorite," the *Los Angeles Times* concluded.

Sophomore Grenville Lansdell led the Trojans, subbing for injured star quarterback Ambrose Schindler. Washington was hurt, too, which UCLA hid from the press. He was so beat-up his sophomore season that he spent weekends at Hollywood Hospital getting glucose drips in his arm, his teammates ribbing him for having to tolerate the ministrations of the nurses. Washington told Strode that week, "If we weren't playing USC, I wouldn't be playing."

Seventy thousand fans came to the game, a fifth of them black. With Washington and Strode leading the Bruins, UCLA had quickly built a large following among African American Angelenos. Though the matchup was touted as Washington versus Lansdell, the offensive and defensive lines were more likely to determine the outcome. The Trojans had a decided advantage in both weight and experience on the line.

The Bruins got the ball first, but Washington misfired on their first drive, and USC went on offense. Lansdell squirted around the right side for a 15-yard gain. But after several more short gains USC had to punt. Washington completed his first pass, a five-yarder to Hal Hirshon, but the offense stalled again and the Bruins punted right back. Who scored first might determine the winner in what was shaping up to be a defensive battle.

On the Trojans' next drive, USC's Bill Sangster burst through the right guard and rumbled 50 yards, to the Bruin 19-yard line, where Washington knocked him out of bounds. Lansdell slammed into the line on three successive plays, grinding out 11 yards. The Trojans had a first down on the Bruin eight-yard line. Lansdell hit the right side for three yards and Sangster followed for two. On third and goal Sangster scrambled for another two yards. Fourth and goal at the one. Lansdell called for a run up the middle. Sangster got the ball and catapulted himself over center. The Bruin line rose to meet him and knocked him to the turf inches short of the goal line. Nervous UCLA fans exhaled.

Sitting on their own half-yard line, the Bruins kicked the ball back to USC to get better field position, a common practice in an era of low-scoring games. The USC offensive line knocked the Bruins defense back and bulled inside the five once again. UCLA battled the Trojans to a fourth and short, but this time Lansdell ran the ball in himself and scored. The conversion was good and USC led 7–0. The Trojans kicked off and the Bruins had made it back to their 39-yard line when the first quarter ended.

Lansdell was dominating the supposed duel with Washington, running for 54 yards and the only touchdown. Washington had tallied just three yards on the ground and completed a single pass. The Bruins could take solace that they weren't further behind, but they were getting pushed around all over the field.

UCLA started the second quarter strong, stringing together several good runs and crossing midfield. But then Washington was dropped for losses on consecutive plays and they punted. Luckily for the Bruins, the Trojan ends struggled to hold on to Lansdell's passes, and UCLA got the ball back on its own 15-yard line. They managed to craft a longer drive this time. Rushes by Washington and Walt Schell netted a first down. Washington completed a 15-yard pass near midfield, then a 12-yarder to the Trojan 43-yard line.

The Bruins had momentum and their offense was starting to click. Perhaps they'd be able to tie the game. Washington dropped back to throw again. He didn't see anyone open, so he pulled the ball down and raced around right end to the Trojan 20-yard line. The Bruins were called for illegal motion in the backfield, however, and penalized five yards. The USC defensive line promptly sacked Washington, quelling the drive. Neither team generated much offense in the waning moments of the first half.

If UCLA made substantial adjustments to their strategy during halftime it wasn't evident in the third quarter, as both teams played sloppily. The Trojans continued to threaten on UCLA's side of the field but couldn't get back to the end zone. The Bruins continued to commit penalties that crippled drives. At one point Slats Wyrick got into a fight with a Trojan lineman. USC started using more misdirection plays against the tiring UCLA line. They ran several reverses to get close to the end zone. Then Lansdell ran four yards off right end for a touchdown. The point-after attempt failed, and USC led 13–0.

Lansdell and his ends were finally clicking in the passing game, while the Bruins still struggled. USC blocked a UCLA punt and recovered the ball on the Bruin 27-yard line. Several plays later Lansdell tossed a touchdown. Again the extra point attempt failed: 19–0.

The UCLA offense had mustered only 26 total yards through the third quarter. If they didn't score soon, the game would be out of reach. The Bruins stalled again on the first drive of the fourth quarter, and the Trojans got the ball back. Then an odd thing happened. The Trojan center shanked the snap. The ball caromed off the fullback's head, and Bruin tackle Larry Murdock recovered it on USC's 44-yard line.

A few plays later Washington backpedaled. He looked left and right, then saw right halfback Hal Hirshon racing toward the goal line. Washington rifled the ball just past the lunging defensive halfback and into Hirshon's arms. Touchdown! The Bruins converted the extra point, and USC lined up to kick off, their lead trimmed to 19–7.

Yes, that's right: UCLA had just scored but the Trojans were kicking off. USC had the option to either kick or receive after their opponent's score. Choosing to kick was a common strategy at the time since teams rarely scored quickly, and field position was considered more important than possession. Clearly, USC thought the quick strike was a fluke. When UCLA got the ball back, Washington and the Bruin coaches wondered if USC would expect them to go deep again.

"I was calling signals," Washington recalled. "Hirshon told me he could get behind the safety man again just like the time we scored our first touchdown. So I said, 'Okay, Hal, you just keep running and I'll stall around back here as long as I can.' Well, that Radovich or some other guy took a shot at me, and when he missed, I had plenty of time." Washington rolled right to shake the rush.

Hirshon, a high school sprint champion, just ran. "I was pretty tired, but Kenny told me to run as far as I could," he said. Defenders sagged off as Hirshon passed the 40-yard line, then the 30. "Only a goof would go back that far to defend against passes," the Los Angeles Times observed.

Near his own 15-yard line, Washington angled upfield, planted his front foot, and let rip. The pigskin spiraled into the darkening sky. Hirshon looked up and initially calculated it would sail beyond his grasp. He churned his legs as the ball arced downward, all eyes tracking where the ball and the man might meet. Hirshon stretched and the pass hit his arm. He bobbled the ball momentarily before clutching it to his chest. Hirshon's defender had given up several strides back, and the Bruin halfback jogged into the end zone. The UCLA sideline erupted, while the Trojans sank against their bench. UCLA's team doctor had to physically restrain an assistant coach who was screaming and jumping all over the sideline. In only 26 seconds of game time, the Bruins had scored twice to climb within 6, 19–13.

Spectators wondered how far Washington had retreated before throwing. Did Hirshon make the catch on the 23-yard line or the 12? The questions weren't purely academic. Washington might have just thrown the longest airborne pass completed in a college football game. The previous record, as far as anyone could tell, was 53 yards.

With no instant replay in 1937, people could only speculate. Film companies often shot major college football games so they could include highlights in the ten-minute sports reel that ran before feature films. Fox Movietone News was shooting the game, but it would be two or three days before the film was developed. Meanwhile, the invigorated Bruins prepared to kick off, down one score with five minutes left in the game. Would this finally be the day that UCLA upset their oft-dominant rivals?

The Bruins immediately pinned the Trojans and forced a punt. Hirshon caught it at UCLA's 22-yard line and lateraled to Washington, who sliced to the 43. Several plays later Washington called a pass to Wyrick, a tackle who lined up as an eligible receiver on the play. USC never saw it coming. Washington hit Wyrick on the numbers, and the big Oklahoman lumbered for a touchdown. The Bruin faithful went wild. But as their screams left their throats, their hearts plummeted. The referee was walking in the opposite direction and pointing to the turf. Wyrick's knee had touched the ground at the USC 31-yard line.

UCLA regrouped and punched the ball forward seven more yards. Washington found a receiver at the 14-yard line to convert a fourth down. Two minutes to go. The Bruins managed two completions but lost yardage. On third and 11 Washington called his own number. Hirshon took the snap and Washington charged down the field, uncovered. He turned back as he crossed the goal line. Hirshon's pass wobbled toward its target, but Washington slipped and lunged for the ball in vain.

The Bruins plodded back to the huddle. What could they do on fourth down? They had already thrown every play at the USC defense. Washington took the snap and backpedaled, looking for Strode in the end zone. The tall end was alone and Washington snapped off a throw. "It came at me like a bullet," Strode said, "And like a bullet it went right through me." Incompletion. The Trojans took over on downs and ran out the clock.

USC celebrated the victory, relieved to have held on. The Bruins barely moved, they were so exhausted and emotionally spent. The most popular postgame topic of conversation was Washington's brilliant fourth quarter: six completions for 144 yards and two touchdowns. And how long was his second touchdown pass? Some said 72 yards; others estimated 60. Washington said after the game that when he let it go, he didn't think it was longer than 50. The debate fueled many a late night at bars across the southland.

The next day local papers splashed photos of Washington across their pages. One series showed his grip on the ball from several angles—readers could try to solve the secret of his long, accurate throws for themselves. Another picture in the *Los Angeles Times* showed the nineteen-year-old in a suit with a caption reading, "The well-groomed colored boy is interrupted in his studies by a literal flood of telegrams." The sophomore would have his work cut out for him, sportswriters at mainstream newspapers speculated. No longer would Washington catch a defense underestimating his skills.

NONE OF THE MANY FANS WHO SAW Washington's near triumph in 1937 expected his transition to the NFL in 1946 to necessarily be easy. But they did hope he'd get a chance to show off his arm. The Rams opened the regular season hosting the Philadelphia Eagles on September 29. Los Angeles jumped out to a 14–6 lead before Bob Waterfield injured his side.

Coach Adam Walsh put in backup Jim Hardy at quarterback rather than Washington, saying after the game that he preferred Hardy because the ex-Trojan had run the modern T formation in college. Hardy later explained that at USC they weren't really taught the modern T but simply ran the single-wing offense out of a T formation alignment. Hardy struggled mightily against the Eagles pass rush. Of Hardy's trouble Halley Harding wrote, "You can't take the ball out of the center's hand, run back ten strides, and wheel to throw a pass through an opposing lineman's crotch or under his armpits; that is, you can't with any commendable accuracy."

The Eagles took control in the second half. They scored 17 unanswered points with a field goal and two touchdown passes. Heading into the last half of the fourth quarter, Los Angeles trailed by nine points, and that's when Coach Walsh put Kenny Washington in at quarterback.

Washington faced the same situation as he had in the College All-Star Game: his team behind late in the game, and everyone in the stadium knowing he had to throw long. Washington completed one pass to Jim Benton for 19 yards. In the final minute Washington took a safety, stepping out of bounds in the end zone while being chased by Philadelphia defenders. According to Harding's contacts, Washington's left leg hurt so much during the game he could barely walk afterward.

Woody Strode finally saw meaningful action on offense, playing end for several series and catching one pass from Hardy. Black and white sportswriters alike began wondering if the Rams had signed Washington and Strode to boost ticket sales rather than to win games. Indeed, an estimated 20 percent of the 30,500 fans at the Coliseum that day were black.

"The scam to advertise names to hustle the chumps and then letting the names be only numbers in the program (25 cents please) seems to be an accepted practice with the pro promoters," wrote Gordon Macker in the *Los Angeles Daily News*, a mainstream newspaper. "Well this town won't go for it."

Overt racial animosity from opponents didn't make Washington's or Strode's situations any more comfortable. In one early-season game, Washington made a block and ended up on his back as the play went in the opposite direction. The opposing left end, also out of the play, ran at Washington's prone body. Washington saw him at the last second and jerked out of the way as the defender swung a leg through the spot where Washington's head had been. Jim Hardy saw the play from the bench and asked Washington about it after the game. "It's hell being a Negro, Jim," Washington said as he shrugged out of his jersey and pads.

The Rams' next games were in the Midwest, at Green Bay then at the Chicago Bears. Rams coaches kept Washington back in Los Angeles to convert him to fullback, a curious move. Limiting Washington to blocking and line plunges wasted his best skills, namely the dual threat to run or pass. But over the next several weeks Washington duly learned the fullback role in the Rams offense.

Coach Walsh rarely played Strode on offense despite rotating through numerous potential starters on the right side across from left end Jim Benton. Walsh preferred to send Strode in on defense to bang with opponents' tackles. They usually outweighed Strode, but he held his own. "I think the Rams' brass was hoping I'd get killed out there," Strode wrote later. "I survived."

Walsh kept Strode on the bench for the first two quarters against the Bears in their October 13 tilt. Heading into the locker room at the half, Strode was stopped by the Bears' Fred Davis, who had played with Strode on a military-service team during the war. "Woody, what the hell are you doing on the bench?" Davis asked, incredulous. "I didn't know how to answer," Strode recalled. "That's the first time I really felt bad about not playing."

In the third quarter Walsh looked for a defensive sub to disrupt the Bears offensive line, one of the biggest and strongest in football. One of Chicago's signature plays had the offensive line position themselves about a yard apart from each other along the line. At the snap they'd all pull around and trample the outmanned defensive end on the side the run was going toward. For the defense, the goal was for the end to hold up long enough for the linebackers to help drive the Bears blockers back. This strategy sometimes worked, but usually after the defensive end had been pulverized by the wave of bodies. Strode compared this task to lining up across from the skyscrapers in Times Square.

But in Strode went. At the snap the linemen pulled, but Strode had gotten a jump and knifed through them to tackle the ballcarrier in the backfield. On plays where the Bears offensive linemen held their positions and blocked straight up, Strode hit his man and got into the backfield. Five times Strode battered Bears left halfback Dante Magnani, tasked with blocking Strode on pass plays.

The sixth time Magnani flinched, and Strode streaked past him, heading for Sid Luckman. The Bears quarterback was looking downfield for a receiver, and Strode lowered his shoulder and drilled him in the middle of the back, dropping the future Hall of Famer for a 10-yard sack. The Rams and Bears battled to a 28–28 draw.

Washington's first test at fullback came the following week at home against the Detroit Lions. The Rams jumped out to a 21–0 lead, and Jim Hardy came on to give Waterfield a breather behind center. Washington logged 49 yards on eight carries, nearly half of the Rams' rushing total. He caught one pass for 20 yards. Late in the third quarter Los Angeles held a 28–14 lead and recovered a Detroit fumble on the Lions' 14-yard line. Three times Waterfield took the snap, spun, and handed off to Washington. The third time he bulled into the end zone for his first touchdown in the NFL.

Los Angeles beat Detroit 35–14 for a 2-1-1 record and second place in the Western Conference. But the team struggled to put together consecutive strong performances and were sabotaged by their turnovers. The Chicago Cardinals clobbered Los Angeles 35–10 when Waterfield had another off day, hitting only 13 of 44 passes and tossing several interceptions. Four of his completions were to Washington coming out of the backfield. "Kenny gave the home club more fits than Jim Benton did," wrote the *Los Angeles Times*, referring to the Rams' All-Pro end.

With a spurt of receptions since being moved to fullback, Washington was second only to Benton in total catches through two games, all the more reason to wonder why the Rams weren't giving Strode a shot opposite Benton. Backfield coach Bob Snyder compared Washington to the Chicago Bears' George McAfee, an all-purpose back used as a rusher, receiver, kick returner, and punter.

But if Washington or Strode was going to make a bigger mark on the season, they needed more playing time. Neither Washington nor Strode played in the Rams' 41–20 beating of the Lions in Detroit. Washington was ostensibly held out to rest his left leg before the game against the Chicago Bears the following week. The Bears held the edge in the conference with a 4-1-1 record, and the Rams were a game behind at 3-2-1. Nearly 70,000 fans flooded the Coliseum, and they saw a close but sloppy game.

The Bears and Rams tallied 31 penalties, with one nullifying a Los Angeles touchdown and one on Bears owner-coach George Halas for arguing a call. Bears quarterback Sid Luckman got the best of Waterfield in a 27–21 win. Waterfield tossed four interceptions, and Washington only got the ball three times for four yards.

The Rams' seesaw season continued with a solid win over the Chicago Cardinals, followed by a loss to the previously winless Boston Yanks. The Rams did win their final two games to salvage a better-than-.500 record, but it was a letdown given they had won the NFL title the year before. It was also a disappointment for Washington and Strode. Washington never got much of a shot at quarterback, and even his time at fullback shrank as the season progressed.

For Strode it was a completely frustrating year. He had suspected he was signed to be Washington's roommate, and his remaining on the bench even as the team sought a second end to complement Benton confirmed it for him. Strode caught four passes all season and was generally sent in to handle the most thankless defensive assignments.

CHAPTER 9

Backlash

Courthouse
Monroe, Georgia

1946

THE DAY AFTER THE MONROE LYNCHINGS, Walter White, executive secretary of the NAACP, contacted the press and President Harry Truman, demanding the federal government help bring the killers to justice. He called the NAACP's Atlanta office and told them to hire a white investigator to go immediately to Walton County and look into the lynchings, and also to keep tabs on local law enforcement, including what they did with evidence and how they treated witnesses.

White was a veteran of such violence. He was thirteen years old when the Atlanta Race Riot of 1906 erupted. He and his family lived between downtown and Sweet Auburn, the neighborhood the mob targeted the second night of the attacks. White's father was a mail carrier, and Walter was helping his father on his route the first evening white hordes stormed downtown. He and his father saw the crowd run down and kill a man mere yards from their horse-drawn cart, and they barely escaped the swallowing mass of people.

Late the next afternoon a neighbor warned them that another mob was forming and likely headed their way. White's father got some guns from a friend and turned off their lights early and bolted the doors, as did their neighbors. They sent the women to the back of the house. White's father stood at the edge of one of the front windows and stationed Walter at the other. This evening's mob was larger than the last, and it pushed its way through the streets armed with any number of weapons, including knives and torches.

Many residents who saw the White family didn't realize they were black because of their light skin and Walter's blue eyes. But as the crowd swelled toward their house, the son of a grocer they regularly traded with screamed, "That's where that n— mail carrier lives! Let's burn it down!" Walter's father looked out the window, his eyes glancing over the crowd to find the man who'd yelled. He turned to Walter. "Son," he said quietly, "don't shoot until the first man puts his foot on the lawn, and then—don't you miss!"

The mass of bodies lurched closer. Walter raised his gun and fixed his aim on the few men at the very front. A volley of shots rang out. But not from Walter's gun, from a neighbor's house. The men in front stopped, perhaps realizing now how exposed they were if residents decided to defend themselves. They hesitated, then the crowd melted back toward the corner and surged down a different street.

Walter White never forgot that evening and years later joined the NAACP as a field investigator, using his ability to pass as white to get information on lynchings from white men. In 1931 he was named executive secretary. He continued the group's work in advocating for civil rights and augmented it with the organization of a legal department, believing it was time to push the issue of equality more aggressively in the courts.

After the Monroe lynchings, though, he and other national NAACP leaders decided the most effective role for the organization was as a catalyst to keep public pressure on the case. In the immediate aftermath of the murders that wasn't hard to do, as thousands of individuals and civic groups sent letters and telegrams to Attorney General Tom Clark and President Truman and demanded federal action. Outgoing Georgia governor Ellis Arnall ordered an inquiry into the lynchings by the Georgia Bureau of Investigation.

Most Walton County residents didn't expect such a reaction. To them the murders were a local issue, to be handled by the sheriff's office. That the lynchings included two women made the case more notable than most, but few whites in town openly decried the killing of the two men. Several days after the lynchings a white reporter from the *Louisville Courier-Journal* talked with E. S. Gordon, sheriff of Walton County, in front of the courthouse eight miles from the site of the quadruple murder.

While they talked, a large man walked over to the journalist and the lawman and said, "This thing's got to be done to keep Mr. N— in his place. Since the court said he could vote, there ain't been any holding him. I just come from Atlanta and ninety-eight percent of the policemen and a hundred percent of the streetcar men voted for [Eugene] Talmadge, because they come in contact with the n— and know what he's doing. Gene told us what was happening and what he was going to do about it. I'm sure proud he was elected."

"They hadn't ought to kill the two women," Sheriff Gordon replied, edging away. Another man, loitering at the courthouse entrance, added, "The sight of that long line of n—s waiting to vote put the finishing touches to it."

Georgia's Democratic primary election was held on July 17, eight days before the lynchings. It was the first primary election in nearly fifty years in which African American Georgians could vote. In the Jim Crow South, where Republicans rarely had a shot in the general election, the real race was in the Democratic primary. When the 15th Amendment guaranteed black American men the right to vote in 1870, Southern state and local governments moved to circumvent the law. In 1891 the Georgia General Assembly decreed that the state Democratic Party, not the state or local government, would set the rules for party primaries. The party primaries were viewed by some as a separate part of the electoral process from the general election and thus not covered by the 15th Amendment.

A host of additional barriers went up to effectively bar African Americans from voting. In many areas poll taxes were implemented; these may have looked to be color-blind on the surface, but weren't. The catch was that men whose grandfathers had been eligible to vote were exempted from the tax (thus "grandfathered in"). This excluded almost all white people from the tax and ensured almost all black people had to pay—as most of them were the grandchildren of slaves. Even if a black citizen was able to pay the poll tax, he would be otherwise discouraged.

Another common tactic was the literacy test. In many Southern towns, black would-be voters were required to prove not just an ability to read and write, but also demonstrate a nuanced understanding of federal or state law. In Georgia, the state Democratic Party oversaw the execution of the primaries and could choose who had to take the literacy test and determine who had passed.

In 1944, the U.S. Supreme Court ruled in *Smith v. Allwright* that the right to vote in a primary election was guaranteed by the Constitution, and black citizens could not be denied that right. But due to the tactics described, this removed few barriers to voting. Many African Americans in the South worked as sharecroppers for white landowners. White bosses threatened to fire black workers who registered to vote or bribed them not to vote. Often the same white families who owned the land and employed the field hands ran the county political apparatus. So even if no one admitted to registering or voting, the bosses of would-be voters would know who had either tried to register or who had gone to the polls.

White farmers knew that threats and bribes would work to keep some of their black workers from voting, but they worried that black veterans returning from World War II, like George Dorsey, might be emboldened to resist their efforts at control. Southern white landowners both feared resistance from black locals and feared their leaving, too. As the 1930s and 1940s progressed, many Southern towns were losing black residents at a 10 to 30 percent clip, most heading north or west. As much as white overseers may have resented or hated their black workers, they also needed them to keep their businesses running.

Despite all of these obstacles to black voting, organizers in Atlanta and around the state fanned out to register African Americans in the wake of the Supreme Court's *Smith v. Allwright* decision. By July 1946, the number of black registered voters in Georgia had jumped to 135,000, by far the most of any Southern state.

That summer's gubernatorial primary pitted former governor and white supremacist Eugene Talmadge against moderate James Carmichael. Talmadge had served three terms as governor before and during World War II. After he lost the statehouse to moderate Ellis Arnall in 1942, he ratcheted up his already-incendiary rhetoric to win back the position.

He also played numerous dirty tricks on his opponent to feed racist fears. He paid African Americans to sit in the white area of audiences at Carmichael's speeches. He hired a man who looked like Carmichael to drive around in a car full of black men.

The majority of voters in Monroe itself supported Carmichael. In the eyes of numerous merchants in town, becoming the site of violence and controversy was bad for business. They were generally less threatened both by black voting and black flight than were rural farmers, the backbone of the Talmadge vote.

In the July 17 primary, Carmichael won the popular vote by 16,000 votes, but Talmadge won the election. Georgia ran on a county-unit voting system, similar to the electoral college that governs national elections. Fulton County, which included much of Atlanta, had sixteen times the voting population of Walton County. But Carmichael got only six county-unit votes for winning Fulton County, while minuscule Walton County delivered two for Talmadge, who swept the rural regions.

Talmadge's campaign also exploited a detail in Georgia law that allowed any citizen to challenge a registrant's right to vote. Talmadge volunteers were given challenge forms to enter the name of a person whose vote they wanted to silence. The recipients would receive a notice to appear in court to defend their right to vote or be stricken from the rolls. Tenant farmers usually couldn't afford to take a day off work to go to the nearest courthouse to address the challenge. And if they did, they were asked arcane questions about the country's supposed democratic voting process, all in service of blocking their right to vote. They were generally marked as failing the test and removed from the list of eligible voters.

In many counties, more than three-quarters of black registrants were challenged. The elections registrar of Walton County also disqualified hundreds of black voters' ballots as improperly marked. The day before the primary, a black man was severely beaten in what many construed as a warning for African American voters not to go to the polls. Many didn't.

Vote suppression in Democratic primaries exploded all over the South that summer, the first major election cycle after the *Smith v. Allwright* decision. Democratic Party organizations fought to limit black voting not just in Georgia but in Mississippi, Florida, and South Carolina as well. Although the Monroe lynchings came after Roger Malcom's stabbing of his white boss, many local black residents saw the murders—and the other two lynchings in the summer of 1946—as revenge for the recent, modest civil rights gains.

The Monroe sheriff's office made little progress in identifying members of the lynch mob, though it also wasn't clear how hard they tried. Loy Harrison still insisted he hadn't recognized anyone in the group, and few others admitted to being anywhere near the bridge the day of the lynchings. Meanwhile, President Truman and Attorney General Tom Clark acquiesced to the avalanche of public pressure. A week after the lynchings, Clark ordered FBI agents to Monroe.

As African Americans struggled to exercise their constitutionally protected right to vote in the South, black residents in Los Angeles battled escalating barriers to living in their own homes. A peculiar difficulty in fighting racially restrictive housing covenants was that pro-covenant advocates often didn't live in the neighborhoods they canvassed, so residents had a hard time figuring out where the opposition was coming from. Real estate firms paid solicitors a commission to go door-to-door to sell the covenant agreements. This led to surreal neighborhood meetings such as one in Ocean Park, a Santa Monica neighborhood bordering Venice that was referred to as the Coney Island of the Pacific because its growth coincided with the rising popularity of the beach boardwalk built on its land.

In 1945 the Property Owners Association of Ocean Park circulated a petition to keep out "lowly Negro characters" and Jewish residents, though they conned several Jewish homeowners into signing it by downplaying the anti-Semitic angle. Signers were told that the petition was to keep a black nightclub out of a residential area, but in reality it was to keep out African Americans, period.

Locals gathered to discuss the petition and question a man named Bluett, who had organized the signature drive. He said he was not intolerant of African Americans; he knew an African American cop when he was on the force, and while the man was a fine fellow, Bluett wouldn't want to socialize with him.

What Bluett didn't know was that members of several civil rights organizations had received mailings about the meeting and came to protest the covenant effort. So when Bluett opened the floor for questions, he got an earful from representatives of the Anti-Defamation League and B'nai B'rith, who said their organizations would fight the covenants tooth and nail. A veterans group also criticized the petition. A woman defended the covenants but was reminded by a neighbor that not long ago she had had a NO JEWS ALLOWED sign in her store window. She sat down.

Then several self-identified communists stood and spoke. When Bluett asked what they were doing there, given that they didn't even live in Ocean Park, one of them replied, "The whole world is too small a place to live in as long as there is a single fascist in it," and noted that Bluett was one such fascist.

Bluett disagreed, arguing he was a good Irish Catholic and was not discriminating, merely fighting for the rights of the property owners to prevent African Americans from living next to them. Another participant asked Bluett if he lived in the area, and he admitted he didn't. It was later revealed that Bluett was being paid to recruit members to the covenant drive and got $10 for each signature.

Then sometimes the covenanters did live next door. This was true for

Pauli Murray, a Howard University School of Law graduate and activist who had moved from Washington, D.C., after finishing her LL.B. (equivalent to a bachelor's degree and commonly offered at law schools at the time. J.D.s became prerequisites for practicing law in the 1960s). Murray and her sister had heard Los Angeles offered good defense-industry jobs, and Pauli was seeking short-term work before she started classes at Berkeley's Boalt Law School in the fall of 1944. The sisters also sought to escape the constant oppression of Jim Crow in the nation's capital. When they arrived in Los Angeles, they struggled to find housing, like most newcomers moving to Southern California. They finally found a flat on South Crocker, in an industrial area of South Los Angeles. After moving in, Pauli Murray discovered they lived half a block over the dividing line between the white and black parts of South Crocker. Two hundred neighbors hurried to finalize a covenant, and shortly thereafter the sisters received a typed, unsigned letter from the Southside Property Owners' Protective Association saying they had seven days to vacate the flat or else legal action would be taken.

Murray wrote in a first-person account in the *Baltimore Afro-American* newspaper that "so long as white citizens use vigilante cowardly methods, not having the courage to even sign their names to a veiled threat, we have an enemy which we cannot see." "One thing is clear," she vowed. "We do not intend to move."

After arriving in Los Angeles, Pauli Murray had secured a part-time reporting gig with the *Los Angeles Sentinel*. There she met publisher Leon Washington Jr. and his cousin, and the paper's cofounder, Loren Miller. Murray, who had finished first in her class at Howard University School of Law, turned to Miller for assistance fighting the South Crocker covenant efforts. Two white neighbors filed lawsuits against Murray and handfuls of other black residents. Murray covered the clash in the *Sentinel* and she and her black neighbors filed a petition with the city council to put a moratorium on the covenant restrictions. The groups battled to a standstill.

Not long after, Murray moved to the Bay Area for school. She then passed the California bar, and in 1946 state attorney general Robert Kenny hired Murray as a temporary deputy attorney general. Several of Kenny's staff were still in the armed services and he was able to hire temporary deputies with the understanding that those who returned from military duty could reclaim their positions when they got back.

With war demobilizing in full swing Murray didn't serve in the attorney general's office for long. But one of her early cases was that of the gruesome deaths of a family in Fontana, California, east of Los Angeles. A black man, O'Day Short, had bought a plot of land in 1945 without realizing it was in a white neighborhood across the invisible boundary from a black neighborhood. The lot was empty and O'Day Short and his wife and children camped there while they built the house.

Several times after they began building, local law enforcement and city officials came around to warn them that they needed to leave because the property was in the white part of town. The house was their dream, though, so they stayed. After a visit from the sheriff telling them to move, the Shorts had gone into Los Angeles and asked the FBI for protection. The FBI said that it had no jurisdiction.

"They were building the house little by little," Murray described, ". . . and they had an oil drum to keep them warm and a lantern for light. Well, this lantern exploded and there was a flash fire and every single one of them was burned to death. The circumstances pointed toward murder, really. And the investigation of this case fell into the attorney general's office and was assigned to me. That was my first case."

The local police department quickly ruled it an accident, claiming the mother had knocked over the lantern and that had started the fire. An arson investigator hired by the local NAACP found evidence the fire started elsewhere in the house and ruled it intentional. "I recall writing up the case and . . . pointing the finger at the failure of the law enforcement officials, who should have been protecting the people, but rather were warning them to get out," Murray said. "In some ways, it was a cause célèbre because it indicated the intensity of racial prejudice." Despite both the local NAACP's belief and Murray's that locals murdered the Shorts, they couldn't sufficiently prove it and the case was closed. Around that same time in 1946, service members began returning from the war and Murray had to give up her position in the attorney general's office.

She'd remember her work with Loren Miller fondly later in life, and they indeed had a lot in common. They both loved journalism, and their writings consistently challenged the status quo. They'd both spent chunks of their early adulthood working in labor or socialist politics and activism. Miller had come out to Southern California a decade before Murray, but, like her, started as a writer. During most of the 1930s Miller was an avowed Marxist and regularly criticized the NAACP for what he saw as an incrementalist approach to civil rights and a willingness to compromise too often with the powers that opposed them. Back then he had little reason to believe that in a few years he'd collaborate with some of the very individuals he'd spent a decade critiquing.

In Los Angeles, as in many cities, far-left African American activists and more moderate community leaders distrusted one another. In Los Angeles this came out in the opinions and editorials of the three major black weeklies—the *California Eagle*, the *Los Angeles Sentinel*, and the *Los Angeles Tribune*—whose publishers and editors disagreed on many political and social issues. Charlotta Bass, publisher of the *Eagle*, had shifted from Republican to Democrat to Progressive, and editorials of the other two papers sometimes speculated she was a communist.

Almena Lomax wrote for Bass's *Eagle* in the late 1930s before launching the *Los Angeles Tribune* in 1941 with a $100 loan from her future father-in-law. Under Lomax's direction the paper covered racism in Hollywood and police violence in black neighborhoods. A staunch supporter of the Democratic Party, Lomax warned her readers not to fall for Republican promises on civil rights issues.

Leon Washington Jr., publisher of the *Sentinel*, also started out at the *California Eagle* before launching his own newspaper. The *Sentinel* wrote with a pro-entrepreneurial bent and covered economic equality issues while focusing more on specifics going on along Central Avenue. But the paper also occasionally supported Democrats for local offices.

Local black elites accepted Miller more than they did his Marxist peers, partly because of his wife's work and reputation. Juanita Ellsworth cofounded the Los Angeles chapter of the Delta Sigma Theta sorority, the first chapter of the Howard-founded sorority in the Far West. Sorority alumnae groups and social clubs were the backbone of middle-class black women's social, and often political, lives. Ellsworth also financially supported Miller with her social-worker salary while he struggled to make money writing. Miller soured on Soviet Communism once Stalin signed the Nonaggression Pact with Adolf Hitler in 1939 and committed himself, begrudgingly, to the profession he'd trained for but had resisted practicing: law.

He opened his first office in the late 1930s, several blocks from the Last Word Café on Central Avenue. His work was the bread and butter of most urban black lawyers whose clients were the Great Migration families resettling north or west: probate, divorces, and small-scale business disputes. He opposed the forced evacuation and internment of Japanese Americans that President Roosevelt initiated with Executive Order 9906, and which Roosevelt signed two months after Pearl Harbor was attacked.

Miller was one of only a few local lawyers to support the American Civil Liberties Union in challenging the constitutionality of the internment of Japanese Americans, though the black weeklies also opposed the internment in their editorials. Many civic groups either agreed with the forced imprisonment or refused to take a stand. Some said recent immigrants were reasonable targets for suspicion, while others noted that Americans of German or Italian descent were not being forced into camps.

Other immigrants' rights groups likely stayed quiet to reinforce their own patriotism, which could be the next to be called into question. Miller partnered with A. L. Wirin, counsel for the Japanese American Citizens League, in fighting the internments. The two later collaborated on housing-covenant cases.

By the early 1940s most of Miller's work involved housing covenants. To get local judges to overturn the injunctions, Miller often had to prove that the conditions of the neighborhoods had changed since the time the neighborhood associations had initiated the covenants. This might be done by showing that a few black families had moved into the broader neighborhood and the covenanters hadn't kicked them out. It might include demonstrating that other people of color had been allowed to stay.

Sometimes Miller won cases on missed deadlines or other bureaucratic details. California had a more complicated process than most states did for filing and updating housing covenants. If Miller spent enough time digging up title documents or sales records of surrounding properties over a long enough period, he would sometimes find an unsigned form or missing filing that would render a covenant void. In all his covenant cases, he looked for any workable angle for attacking the covenants.

However, he yearned to defeat the covenants not on what some saw as technicalities, but by striking at the legal rationale for them. One argument he used regularly, but that had been rejected by other state courts, was that using state courts to enforce covenants was an example of state action under the Fourteenth Amendment. When he argued the Sugar Hill case in front of California Superior Court judge Thurmond Clarke, Miller claimed that any evidence submitted for the covenanters would make the court an agent in enacting discrimination.

The homeowners' association in the Sugar Hill case argued that they had a right to enforce the covenant because the influx of black residents, whether Hollywood stars and doctors or not, cratered their home values, and that black neighbors were ruining the neighborhood. Judge Clarke figured he'd see firsthand what horrible damage Hattie McDaniel, Louise Beavers, and others were doing to the neighborhood. The next morning he joined Loren Miller and the homeowners' association counsel on a walking tour of West Adams Heights. The next day Clarke threw the injunction out of court, citing the Equal Protection Clause of the Fourteenth Amendment. He wrote in his decision, "It is time that members of the Negro race are accorded, without reservations or evasions, the full rights guaranteed them under the Fourteenth Amendment to the Federal Constitution. Judges have been avoiding the real issue too long."

CHAPTER 10

Champions

Cleveland Municipal Stadium
Cleveland, Ohio

1946

C LEVELAND SHOT OUT TO A 3-0 RECORD in the inaugural AAFC campaign of 1946, following its poundings of Miami and Chicago with a 28–0 shutout of the Buffalo Bisons. With Motley's dominant performance against the Chicago Rockets he had secured the starting full-back job, though it would be several weeks before it would be clear that the change was permanent. Against the Bisons, Motley caught a screen pass from Otto Graham and took it 33 yards for a touchdown. The Browns hosted the two New York teams, the uncreatively named Yankees and the Brooklyn (football) Dodgers, beating both Eastern visitors by similar scores, 24–7 and 26–7.

Five games into the season Motley led the league in rushing yards and yards per carry at eight yards a pop. On a short trip east, the Browns nearly lost to the Yankees and probably should have, given that Cleveland gained only 67 total yards. They got half of their total yards, and all of their points, from a 33-yard Graham pass to Lavelli in the third quarter. Cleveland only mustered five first downs in the rainstorm, but the Yankees, who nearly quadrupled the Browns' yardage total, turned the ball over five times and didn't score. The game ended with New York on the Browns' 16-yard line.

Cleveland found its offensive touch again in its matchup against the Los Angeles Dons. The teams were an interesting contrast on the field as the Dons wore bright red pants and helmets that looked like tomatoes, while the Browns wore white pants and brown jerseys with their white helmets.

Both teams struggled in the first half, and Los Angeles held a 7–3 lead at intermission. The Browns would have been scoreless except for a mammoth boot from Lou Groza to nail a 48-yard field goal. The score would stay 7–3 until just a few minutes left in the third quarter. Over the next 14 minutes the Browns scored four touchdowns.

The first was a Graham two-yard rush. Next came a touchdown pass to Mac Speedie. The rest was Marion Motley. The big fullback scored on a 49-yard run early in the fourth. Just a few drives later he burst through the line and ran over the middle linebacker en route to a 68-yard score, sealing the 31–14 victory. After the game Dons coach Dudley DeGroot visited the Cleveland locker room. He asked for permission to talk with Motley. While Paul Brown was comparing Motley to legendary Army fullback Felix "Doc" Blanchard to the press, DeGroot found Motley in front of his locker. DeGroot looked him over, then held out his hand. Motley shook it. "Yep, you're quite a bundle," DeGroot said, and left.

Cleveland loved its new team, but the Browns' undefeated 7-0 record and dominance were almost too much for the league. Midway through the season, few teams had even challenged the Browns, prompting Bob Yonkers of the *Cleveland Press* to boastingly plead, "Break Up the Browns—They're Ruining the League!"

Of course, Cleveland then stumbled. They fell behind the San Francisco 49ers early in their game and trailed 20–6 at the half. The teams traded blows until former Los Angeles Bulldog (and Washington's and Strode's nemesis in the semipro PCFL) Frankie Albert led the 49ers to a 34–20 win in front of 70,000 Browns fans. The Browns hurt themselves with five turnovers, one a fumble by Motley. (Motley's occasional fumbles bothered Coach Paul Brown more than anything else about his star back. After one game in which Motley had fumbled, Brown gave him a ball with a handle attached to it and insisted he carry it around the rest of the day.)

Next the Browns flew to the West Coast to play the Dons and the 49ers again. The matchup with Los Angeles was the second straight game in which the Cleveland linemen played poorly, particularly in the first half. That combined with a sluggish rushing game hindered the Browns, and the Dons beat them, 17–16, on an 11-yard field goal with 18 seconds left. Bill Willis sat out the Dons game because of a throat infection, Motley had a bruised shoulder, and half the Browns were in the trainer's room during halftime.

The loss was the Browns' second in a row and meant that San Francisco trailed them by only a game in the standings with their rematch coming up. Blustering winds wreaked all sorts of havoc in the Browns–49ers battle. On a Cleveland punt, the 49ers returner misjudged the ball. He couldn't gather it in, and Bill Willis recovered the fumble. In the second quarter, with San Francisco facing fourth down at the Browns' 14-yard line, Willis shot through the middle and sacked Frankie Albert.

Later in the game, Otto Graham backpedaled to flick a screen pass to Motley, in what was becoming one of their signature plays. The defenders closed in faster than Graham expected. With the hand of an onrushing lineman in his face, Graham tossed the ball to where he expected Motley to be, in the flat behind the lineman. The fullback caught the pass and took off down the sideline. The Browns withstood a late push by the 49ers and won, 14–7.

The Browns cruised through the next two games, crushing the Chicago Rockets and the Buffalo Bisons. Against Buffalo, Motley scored on a 76-yard burst through the line. Buffalo's fastest player, the 180-pound George Terlep, gave chase from his defensive-back position, but the burly Motley pulled away.

Up next was a game with significance beyond the standings. The Browns would travel to Miami to face the Seahawks. As reporters and fans had noted when the Browns' schedule came out, the state of Florida barred black and white players from competing together on the same athletic field. Would Paul Brown challenge the law by playing Motley and Willis?

According to Otto Graham, the players firmly sided with playing the two. The argument against it was that the Browns didn't need the win to make the playoffs, and cellar-dwelling Miami looked like an easy win even without the team's black stars.

The *Call & Post* favored bringing Motley and Willis to Miami: "It seems useless to lose a race without making some effort to run . . . The least [Paul Brown] could do would be to take Willis and Motley to Miami and have them ready for regular play. Let the southern folks expel the players from the field. Let them be shown up as a contemptible group of so-and-so's . . . There is everything to be gained by taking the lads to Miami."

Brown made up his mind the week before the Miami trip. He told Willis and Motley they would stay in Ohio. Later Brown informed the pair that letters mailed to team headquarters included threats to kill Willis and Motley if Brown sent them on the field. The threats were certainly plausible, though the letters were never verified.

Some believed the Cleveland coach preferred to acquiesce to the law, that he was invested in the success of the AAFC and may not have wanted to show up the struggling Miami franchise, which the league was trying to salvage. Had Brown felt he needed Motley and Willis to win, he would likely have chosen differently.

In his autobiography Brown simply wrote, "Not every situation was under our control. When we went to Miami to play the Seahawks in 1946, neither Willis nor Motley accompanied us because it was against the law in Florida at that time for blacks and whites to compete against each other." Years afterward, both Otto Graham and his wife, Beverly, recalled that the Browns took their resentments out on the Seahawks, walloping them 34–0 before an audience of 9,083 white fans.

Neither Willis nor Motley had time to dwell on the Miami game for long, as they were one game away from the inaugural AAFC championship contest. In front of only 13,000 fans at Brooklyn's Ebbets Field, Cleveland throttled the Dodgers, 66–14, in what a Cleveland sportswriter gleefully dubbed "A Spree Grows in Brooklyn."

The Friday before the AAFC title game five inches of snow cloaked Cleveland. Reporters predicted decent footing, though, as the grounds crew tried a new approach to keeping the field from freezing: putting a tarpaulin over it. The day before the game the AAFC announced the Miami Seahawks had been put out of their misery—potentially to be replaced by a squad in Baltimore—and the AAFC draft picks were announced. The Browns had chosen Iowa fullback Dick Hoerner, who would ultimately sign with the NFL's Los Angeles Rams.

For the league's inaugural title the Browns faced the East Division–winning New York Yankees, who sported one of the league's stingiest passing defenses. Cleveland wasn't sure it would have the services of kicking ace Lou Groza since he was still recovering from a sprained ankle sustained in the game against Brooklyn. The Browns had not struggled to score from distance during the regular season, though. Ten different players had tallied touchdowns of at least 40 yards long.

The Yankees were expected to leverage their league-leading ground game. They ran the single wing, putting them in the minority in a league in which most teams had transitioned to the modern T formation. New York scored first on a short field goal. Cleveland put together a 70-yard drive in response, and Marion Motley dove over for the touchdown. The Browns doubled the Yankees' yardage in the first half but struggled to get on the scoreboard and entered the break with a slim 7–3 advantage.

New York took the lead on an 80-yard drive in the third quarter. Lou Groza had two short field goals blown wide by fierce winds, one after a 41-yard run by Motley set up the Browns deep in Yankee territory. In the fourth quarter, the Browns relied on Motley to power the team down the field. The fullback finished with 98 yards on 13 carries. Once Motley had chewed up some yardage, Graham tried his luck passing in the wall-like winds.

The clocked ticked down to five minutes left and the Browns trailing 9–7. Cleveland dialed up a play that had helped them score the winning touchdown in a previous meeting with the Yankees. Graham threw to Dante Lavelli in the end zone, but this time the wind was so stiff that the receiver had to come out of the end zone to snag the ball. Lavelli battled back in for a touchdown, though, pushing the Browns ahead, 14–9.

Graham also contributed a one-handed interception on defense, and Cleveland withstood two last scoring attempts by New York before the clock ticked to zero. Forty thousand fans leaped to their feet, and the players hoisted Coach Paul Brown in the air. The Browns were AAFC champions.

AFTER PARK GUARDS FRACTURED ALBERT LUSTER'S SKULL at Euclid Beach, the protest organizers regrouped. They met to raise money for Luster's legal fees and pressed the mayor to support the integration efforts. Activists also planned to return to the park. Juanita Morrow was one of the Congress of Racial Equality activists leading the effort. Morrow had recently succeeded George Houser as president of the local CORE chapter and was one of those ejected from Euclid Beach the same night Albert Luster was beaten. Morrow's account of a third incident at Euclid Beach on September 21 ran in the *Call & Post*.

> Six of us, two white couples and one Negro couple, drove out to Euclid Beach Park about 9pm. We knew the policy of the park and were prepared to be thrown out as soon as we entered. Strangely enough, no one molested us as we bought tickets and went to a concession stand to buy frozen malteds. We even walked the length of the park to the ping-pong concession, and were not bothered.
>
> Four of us, two whites and two Negroes, played together and had a hilarious time. Other people who were playing paid no attention to us, except to graciously retrieve our balls. We learned later, though, from

other individuals at the park, that our every move had been watched. Nevertheless, for 45 minutes we were ordinary patrons of Euclid Beach Park and felt like normal human beings. It was not until we decided to dance that the feeling of tenseness which had pervaded the park since our entrance came out in the open and swallowed us up.

Two members of our party, Margaret Abbott and Carl Miller presented their tickets and were admitted to the dance floor. When Wilk Peters presented tickets for himself and for me, I saw a phalanx of park guards move up. With Lt. Campbell, whom I had met before, as their spokesman, we were told flatly that we couldn't dance. His tone indicated that we should be well aware of the fact. "Park policy" was the phrase constantly used to block all our questions on our rights as citizens, our protection under the civil rights law of Ohio.

The portly, white-haired Lieutenant became extremely annoyed. "We don't follow the civil rights law," he informed us. "It's public opinion that we go by." By that time Carl and Margaret had returned to the party. "Why can't these people dance?" asked Carl. "You can dance if you want to," the Lieutenant told them and Reverend and Mrs. C.F. MacLennan. "But these people are our guests," they protested. That made no difference. A huge crowd had gathered and watched the proceedings with interest, but with almost no comment. Curtly we were told to move. We were blocking the entrance. Carl Miller paused long enough to ask several of the crowd if they minded if Negroes danced. They said, "No." Guards began to shove the group toward the outside of the pavilion. I had the honor of being pushed by the Lieutenant himself.

By that time two Negroes in plain clothes came up and asked the cause of the disturbance. At first they were told it was none of their business. One guard said, "You're just part of the gang anyway." Finally they disclosed that two Negroes wanted to dance. "What was wrong with that?" the two men wanted to know. "Mixed couples are not allowed to dance out here," they were told. The two men showed their badges. They were city patrolmen Lynn Coleman and Henry Mackey.

They asked me who my escort was. I pointed to Wilk Peters, a Negro. "Why these aren't mixed couples," Coleman told the guards. Lt. Campbell gave his definition of mixed couples: blacks dancing on the same dance floor with whites. The patrolmen told him that his refusal to let the Negro couple dance violated the laws of Ohio. That was none of the patrolmen's business, according to park guards, and besides they were off duty. The patrolmen told the guard that city policemen were on duty 24 hours a day.

One of the guards grabbed Mackey's lapel. Mackey slapped the hand down. Three guards rushed Mackey, and one reached over and hit him a resounding thud over the right eye. It was only a matter of minutes before an enormous, discolored lump had appeared over Mackey's eye. Coleman came over to Mackey and told the guard who hit him that he was under arrest for assaulting a city policeman. By that time, both Coleman and Mackey had drawn their guns, keeping them pointed at the floor. They remained calm and in complete control of themselves.

I saw at least six guards rush toward Coleman and force him to one knee. Carl Miller testified that he saw a man in plain clothes take one of Coleman's arms, and a park guard grab the other arm. The gun went off and the crowd stumbled back. Before we could see what had happened, a guard yelled defensively, "He shot himself with his own gun!" Meanwhile, guards continued to surround Coleman, beating him with their fists and swinging their clubs. Somebody in the crowd yelled, "Kill him!"

The atmosphere of waiting had become charged with apprehension. I had no idea what might happen next. I fumbled through my pocketbook for a nickel and rushed for a telephone booth to call police. "We'll be right over," someone said when I told them there had been a shooting at Euclid Beach. I made the call because, although I had informed the police department that morning of our trip, up to that time I had seen no one whom I'd recognized as a city policeman.

When I came out of the telephone booth I saw Coleman lying on a bench in front of the dance pavilion, his head on his wife's shoulder. I saw Lt. Smythe talking with Mackey, his back to the man I later found out to be Julius Vago. Vago was brandishing a gun wildly and he told me to get down "before you get hurt." I asked one of the guards where the rest of my party had gone. "They've been put out of the park," he told me, "and you'd better go, too." I asked Lt. Coleman if I had to get out. He said, "No, you can stay as long as you behave yourself."

A crowd had gathered around Coleman and his wife. I heard one girl ask a man who these people were. He told her he thought we were members of the NAACP and expressed sympathy for our position. The police had not yet arrived to take Coleman to the hospital and I lingered since no one was paying any attention to me. I asked several people in the crowd for change for a half-dollar so I could contact the Community Relations Board. Finally, one girl searched her pockets until she found forty-seven cents. I made the call and walked out of the park, catching the street car since the others had left in the car.

CHAPTER 11

Shots Fired

Euclid Beach Park
Cleveland, Ohio

1946–47

THOUGH YOUNG, CORE LEADER JUANITA MORROW WAS not a newcomer to activism. She'd attended Howard University in the early 1940s before returning to her hometown of Cleveland. While in Washington, D.C., she'd joined several other Howard University women at sit-ins at segregated restaurants and stores near campus. She and her mentor Pauli Murray, who'd later fight housing covenants in California and serve as one of the state's temporary deputy attorney generals, founded the Civil Rights Committee at Howard to pressure local businesses to integrate.

"We actually opened up a restaurant on the edge of campus in one week," Morrow explained in an interview decades later. "I never had such a quick victory, [chuckle] never since that time. It was just a sort of a greasy-spoon restaurant, but it was a heady victory for us. We had a picket line; we had a sit-in; lots of people agreed with us, and [the owner] capitulated."

Morrow applied what she'd learned from Murray and others to her continued activism with the CORE Cleveland chapter. After the September 21 protest where Officer Coleman was shot, Morrow learned that her CORE colleagues had been ejected from Euclid Beach Park, and that the guards had picked out five of the six protesters almost immediately, supporting her suspicion that the guards had been told the protesters were coming and had been watching them since their arrival.

An editorial in the *Call & Post* reported that in the conflict between the guards and the African American cops, the police department had taken the side of the park guards.

"This is one reason why we must register our unqualified disgust over the antics of high ranking police officers who seem to have devoted most of their investigation to attempts to 'make a case' against these Negro officers, rather than against the unwarranted violations by the Euclid Beach police guards.

"We look with askance upon tactics which permitted the Euclid Beach guards, who were ordered arrested by the Negro policemen, to secure their release without even being charged or held for investigation. Such action by police officials in connection with assaults against members of the force, are virtually without precedent. There can be no other explanation than that there are some queerly distorted sympathies within the ranks of the police department, and some who must evidently be looking at the incidents at Euclid Beach Park through the same prejudiced tinted glasses as the park management."

The week after the Coleman shooting, Cleveland mayor Thomas Burke called a meeting with the Humphrey Company and told them to shut down the amusement park for the season. The city safety director relayed orders from Burke for a complete police investigation and shared a statement with the press that the Department of Public Safety "approved the conduct of the two Negro police officers."

The head of the police race relations unit took numerous statements from witnesses to the incident. The chief police prosecutor reported that no warrants had been issued by the Wednesday after the shooting, but he anticipated that to change once the police had concluded their investigation.

Morrow had contacted Cleveland's acting police chief the morning of September 21 to inform authorities of plans for a peaceful demonstration. The police sent two white detectives—Lieutenant George Smythe, head of the race relations unit within the police department, and Lieutenant John Ungvary—to the park as observers. Smythe and Ungvary said they arrived at the park an hour before the incident, and they must have suspected any protest would occur at the dance pavilion as that had been the center of the nonviolent actions all summer. But the detectives didn't intervene until after Coleman was shot and then did not take Coleman's gun from Vago, the park guard who had beaten Albert Luster several weeks before, even though Vago was seen waving Coleman's gun around after the officer was shot.

Neither Coleman nor Mackey seemed to know the other two police officers were there. Coleman, his wife, and Mackey were eating popcorn and candy on a nearby bench when they noticed the commotion at the dance pavilion. They walked over, showed their badges, and asked what was going on. When Lieutenant Campbell of the park guards explained that he was preventing "mixed couples" from dancing, Mackey asked the crowd whether they minded if the black couple danced. "Only two hoodlums said they did, and when I asked for their names, they refused to comply," Mackey reported. He continued:

Park police No. 33, whom I later learned to be Andrew Curry, then struck my hand and knocked my badge down. I told him to stop the rough stuff. He then told the two hoodlums that they didn't have to tell me anything and started shoving me around. I again reminded him I was a policeman and he shoved me again. I slapped him in the face. Coleman asked Lt. Campbell for his private police commission number. In violation of the rules, Campbell refused to comply.

Then Lt. Campbell grabbed me by the arms. While struggling, Curry struck me on the right forehead with his nightstick. I tore myself free and pulled my gun. Coleman at the same time pulled his gun and I placed Curry under arrest. Coleman assisted me in taking Curry towards the phone so I could call the police wagon.

At that time we were jumped upon by the crowd of about ten or twelve park police. In the struggle Coleman was separated from me and, to free my hands, I replaced my gun in my holster and started fighting the special police off.

Looking in Coleman's direction I saw Vago struggling with Coleman and wrestling Coleman's gun away. While they were struggling I heard a shot go off in the direction where Coleman was fighting. At that time I did not know it was Coleman's gun but thought it was one of the park policemen's guns as I had seen several of them with guns which they'd had in their pockets.

After the shot went off, I walked towards Coleman and told him, "Let's get away." The crowd had scattered and several park guards ran away after the shot. Coleman stated he couldn't leave because he was shot and showed me his leg. I then gave a young lady the police number to call.

Only after the violent scuffle did Smythe and Ungvary of the race relations unit approach their fellow officers. Ungvary told Mackey to cover up his gun and keep quiet. Mackey asked Ungvary to get Coleman's gun away from Vago, who was waving it around angrily. Ungvary suggested leaving Vago alone for five or ten minutes to let him calm down.

Several other Cleveland police officers showed up. Coleman and his wife were taken by squad car to the hospital, and Mackey was treated for his injuries. The park guards were taken to a police station to make statements. Both Coleman and Mackey pushed to have Vago and Curry charged with assault. But Lieutenant Smythe's superior officer ordered the pair released, an unusual move for men accused of assaulting police officers.

"Under ordinary circumstances, when a special police is arrested by a city patrolman, he's confined to jail until released on bond," Mackey said. "I don't know under what circumstances Curry was released without my being consulted or advised."

In the aftermath of the shooting, the *Call & Post* uncovered that the guards at Euclid Beach were not special police or formally associated with the police department at all, despite their claims to the contrary. According to the mayor's office, the park guards were never licensed by the city or bonded, and thus, according to the safety commissioner, not allowed to carry guns. Meanwhile, Coleman remained hospitalized after a two-hour operation to remove the bullet in his leg. He kept his gun next to his bed for the duration of his hospital stay.

HEADING INTO THE 1947 SEASON, PAUL BROWN pondered how he could improve his championship team. One of his moves was adding punter/end Horace Gillom, the third African American player signed by Brown. Gillom had played for Brown at Massillon High in the late 1930s. Brown claimed he initially considered signing Gillom in 1946, but decided against it once he'd landed Marion Motley.

Gillom followed Brown to Ohio State in 1941, but he joined the military in 1942. He served three years in the Army, fought in the Battle of the Bulge, and earned three Bronze Stars for exemplary conduct in ground combat. After his discharge, Gillom spent a year at Nevada-Reno with Motley's former high school coach, just as Motley had previously. Before the NCAA more strictly regulated player movement, athletes, particularly

African Americans, often followed their coaches to new universities. The alternative was to wait and see who the replacement was and hope they'd give equal consideration to black players.

Gillom was renowned for the height of his punts as well as their distance. He was one of the first punters to emphasize hang time. Gillom was also the first punter to drop back fifteen yards from the line of scrimmage on his kicks. Most punters at the time stood only ten yards back, some twelve yards. But Gillom felt that the few yards he sacrificed in distance were worth the extra time and space in the face of onrushing defenders.

Unlike the NFL, the rest of the AAFC followed Paul Brown's lead in hiring black players. In the 1947 season, the Los Angeles Dons, co-tenants with the Rams at the Coliseum, signed three: Ezzrett "Sugarfoot" Anderson, who had played with Kenny Washington and Woody Strode on the Hollywood Bears; Bert Piggott, who'd played at Illinois; and John Brown, formerly of North Carolina Central. Buddy Young signed on with the New York Yankees, Bill Blass the Chicago Rockets, and Elmore Harris the Brooklyn Dodgers.

Besides signing Gillom, Brown worked to improve his team by expanding its passing repertoire. Brown coached his ends to come back to the ball more and worked with Graham on timing his passes so as to arrive as the end entered his cut, not when he'd turned around. Cleveland did a lot more passing in 1947. In their first season, Browns quarterbacks had thrown an average of 17 times a game, completing nine. In 1947, the Browns made 21 attempts per game and completed 12 of them. Graham threw for nearly 1,000 more yards in his second season, pushed his completion percentage up, and increased his touchdown count from 17 to 25, leading the league in both yards and touchdowns.

Another dangerous twist in the passing game was Motley's coming out of the backfield as a receiver. Paul Brown liked to run screen passes to Motley at key moments in games. Defenders struggled to knock Motley out of bounds on those plays. Most players when racing down the sidelines would either step out to avoid a big hit or be bumped out by a defender angling over from the middle of the field. But when Motley burst in the clear along the sideline and a defensive back angled toward him, the big rusher often would veer a step or two inside to meet the would-be tackler with a lowered shoulder. "He wasn't going to run from you," explained his grandson, Tony in the documentary *Forgotten Four*. "He was going to run at you. And it was going to take a couple of people to stop him."

At first, defenders were caught off guard by this move. After being bowled over more than once, tacklers often aimed to catch Motley a bit behind him to make it easier to push him out.

Motley caught on to this tactic. Sometimes he ran at just under top speed, and then when the defender was about to push him, he'd speed up and elude the opponent altogether. This cat-and-mouse game opened up a play that normally went for small to moderate gains to something that could turn into a long touchdown. On one memorable occasion, a small defensive back tried to tackle Motley from behind on a sideline run. Motley just kept chugging, with the smaller man hanging off his back like a cape.

The Browns started 1947 as they had 1946, reeling off a string of dominant victories. Cleveland beat Buffalo (now renamed the Bills), Brooklyn, and the Baltimore Colts by a combined score of 113–21. Marion Motley scored five touchdowns over the three games, including a 48-yard interception return and a 51-yard run. If anyone thought Motley's success the first year was a fluke, his second-year performance quieted those doubts.

Before the opener versus the Bills, much of the buzz surrounded the quarterback showdown between Otto Graham and Buffalo's George Ratterman. But as Graham later said, after the game all the talk was about Horace Gillom's soaring punts and their five-second hang times. Two games later Gillom rocketed punts of 68, 74, 63, and 65 yards in a 28–0 shutout of the Baltimore Colts, the franchise that replaced the impotent Miami Seahawks.

In between handling Buffalo and Baltimore, the Browns crushed the Brooklyn Dodgers, 55–7. Graham would remember the game not because of the lopsided score, but for a new play that he and Motley stumbled into. Graham started the play, a sideline pass to the left, by dropping back. Motley's assignment was to either stay in and block or flare out as a second passing option out of the backfield, depending on the rush. But Graham tripped as he turned. "Seeing Motley crouched nearby ready to block and knowing I would be pummeled before I could regain my balance I stuck the ball in my fullback's gut as I stumbled by," Graham said.

Motley reacted a second late to the unexpected handoff, and by then the defenders had passed him and were on top of Graham. Motley bolted upfield for a sizable gain. When the offense returned to the sideline, Coach Brown told Graham to run that play again in the second half. By the following week it had been added to Cleveland's playbook, and the draw play was born.

The following week Cleveland dispatched the Chicago Rockets and returned home to host the New York Yankees, their opponents from the previous year's title game. This time, though, the Yankees boasted Buddy Young, the small but electric Illinois back that the Los Angeles Rams had supposedly eyed before the 1946 season.

Buddy Young and Marion Motley both wore #76, but they were otherwise a complete contrast in size and style. Young stood five feet five inches and was listed at 175 pounds, though he was likely closer to 160. Motley stood nine inches taller and weighed at least sixty pounds more. Motley had the speed to run past most defenders, but he didn't have the sprinter speed and cutting ability of Young. That said, Motley boasted better receiving skills and was the best blocking back in the league.

The showdown between Eastern and Western Conference leaders brought 80,067 fans to Cleveland Municipal Stadium, including 15,000 African Americans, who were there to see both the Cleveland stars and also Young. In the first half, Coach Brown had the defense pressure the shorter passing routes more, guessing that with the speed of his defensive halfbacks they could recover to defend longer passes if need be. It worked, and Cleveland shot out to a 17–3 lead in the first half.

Lou Groza would ultimately notch a game-sealing 43-yard field goal in the fourth, but he admitted after the game that his main concern was keeping kickoffs out of the hands of Young. Cleveland managed to bottle up the speedy #76, keeping him to 20 yards on six rushes in the 26–17 victory.

The Browns suffered their only regular-season defeat, to the Los Angeles Dons, the following week. Cleveland moved the ball well and dominated in total yards, but they committed four turnovers, two of them fumbles by Motley. Graham went on a tear the next three games, throwing seven touchdown passes and exceeding 250 passing yards in each contest. When Cleveland throttled San Francisco 37–14 to go to 10-1 on the season, they clinched a spot in the title game. The New York Yankees, who led the Eastern Conference and would be the Browns' likely opponents in the championship tilt, were their next opponent.

New York's rushers ran around and over the Browns defense in the first two quarters. Spec Sanders rushed for three touchdowns and Buddy Young added another to power the Yankees to a 28–0 lead, helped by two interceptions of Otto Graham. The Browns scored once before halftime to nudge closer. Early in the second half New York looked to extend their lead with first and goal at the Cleveland one-yard line. They ran consecutive plays and the Browns defense repelled them. Then Graham and Motley took over. The Cleveland quarterback found his fullback for a 12-yard touchdown pass, and on the very next Browns drive Motley pulled the Browns within 7 points with a 10-yard touchdown scamper.

The Browns drove 90 yards to tie the game in the fourth. The Yankees had a chance to win but couldn't get off a field goal try before time expired. Cleveland and New York tied, but in the competition between the NFL and AAFC the younger league won the day. More than 70,000 fans filled Yankee Stadium to watch the Browns take on the Yankees. Meanwhile, only 28,000 witnessed the New York Giants tie the Green Bay Packers at the nearby Polo Grounds.

Cleveland wrapped up the Western Conference with victories over the Dons and the Baltimore Colts in their last two regular-season games. Graham emerged as a premier passer that season, easily topping the AAFC with 2,753 passing yards and 25 touchdowns. He matched the NFL touchdown leader, Sammy Baugh, though Graham played in two more games than the Washington quarterback. Graham was more efficient, however, as he averaged 10.2 yards per pass attempt, while Baugh was nearly two yards below that. Motley held his own with a 6.1-yard-per-carry rushing average, and the Browns defense dominated. They snared a phenomenal 32 interceptions and held opponents to 1,707 total yards, the fewest allowed by any team in the league.

The Browns again faced the Yankees in the AAFC Championship Game at Yankee Stadium. Motley and the defense carried Cleveland. The thundering fullback wore down the Yankees with 109 yards on 13 carries. His 51-yard rumble set up Graham's quarterback sneak for the Browns' first touchdown in the 14–3 win.

Future pro football writer Paul Zimmerman was at the game, sitting in the upper deck above home plate. Many years later he recalled the moment and wrote, "My binoculars caught Motley coming right at me, 51 yards on a direct handoff over the middle, the last ten or so with the Yanks' Harmon Rowe riding his back and slugging him in the face. The papers next day had a quote from Motley, answering a photographer who asked him to smile. 'I can't,' he said. 'My teeth were knocked out,'" later clarifying that it was an elbow to the head earlier in the game that has knocked them out.

CHAPTER 12

Third Quarter

Cleveland Municipal Stadium
Cleveland, Ohio

1950

THE BROWNS AND RAMS TRUDGED INTO THEIR locker rooms at halftime of the 1950 NFL Championship Game with Cleveland's bobbled snap on the extra point attempt the only thing separating the two teams on the scoreboard. Caldwell High School's thirty-five-piece band marched onto the field to entertain the fans, who were huddled in their seats trying to stay warm. In the press box, Red Grange pushed back his chair and stood up. He was doing commentary on the game for ABC television, and despite being sixteen years removed from his last game, the Galloping Ghost was still one of the most famous athletes in the country.

Many considered Grange to be the best back of his generation. He burst onto the college football scene in 1924 when he scored four touchdowns for Illinois in 12 minutes (and six for the whole game) against the favored Michigan Wolverines. Grange was a dominant rusher in an era when running was king. As a result, his struggles in the passing game were forgotten. Players were recruited for their running ability first, and their passing skills second or even third (behind kicking or defense). Many college and pro teams of Grange's day ran a single-wing offense where the primary halfback was expected to do the majority of the running, passing, and kicking. This meant chucking six or seven passes a game, not the 20 or 30 that came later.

Coach Glenn "Pop" Warner devised the single wing in 1906 as a way to open up outside rushing lanes. In the old T formation that predated the single wing, linemen stood hip to hip and three backs lined up behind the quarterback, who could not run with or pass the ball. The backs struggled to get around the defense to the outside, so most offenses simply pounded the ball over the middle for a couple of yards.

Warner asked himself, Why not move more blockers ahead of the ball-carrier before the ball is snapped? As the quarterback did little more than hand off the ball, Warner moved him close to the line, behind the tackle. One of the halfbacks stayed in the backfield and took a direct snap a few yards behind the center. Often the other halfback shifted up but split wider than the quarterback, becoming what was called a wingback. A fullback stayed in the backfield for the occasional line plunge.

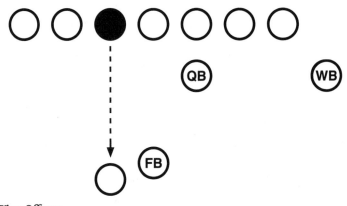

Single Wing Offense
Unbalanced line, direct snap to halfback or fullback. The wingback and quarterback mainly blocked.

By bringing two additional blockers to the point of attack, the single wing gave the runner a better chance to get down the sideline or cut back inside to the open field. Warner brought his new formation to the Carlisle School, where he took the head coaching job in 1907. The single wing was a perfect fit for Carlisle, whose opponents often outweighed them by 30 or 40 pounds per man. Warner continued to develop the scheme, adding reverses and other misdirection plays to take advantage of his squad's speed and superior ballhandling skills. Carlisle exploded to a 10-1 record in 1907, and 10-2-1 in 1908, several years before the supremely talented Jim Thorpe joined the team and brought it even more national attention. The Eastern football elite took notice of Carlisle's success, and many schools adopted the formation, tweaking it to their liking.

The year 1906 saw another big change in football with the legalization of the forward pass. The college game had been in crisis, with fans and university officials blaming constant line plunges for the gruesome injuries and periodic deaths that plagued the sport. At the behest of President Theodore Roosevelt, a consortium of rule makers, a precursor to the NCAA, changed the rules to open up play and make it safer. Included was the forward pass.

The change had little impact initially, and no wonder. At various points, incompletions were penalized 15 yards, passing down the center of the field, or beyond 20 yards was illegal, and incompletions in the end zone were ruled touchbacks.

Another problem was actually throwing the thing. The balls used in early football were fat and difficult to hold with one hand. Teams experimented with the aerial game for years, with passers holding the ball overhead with both hands and lobbing it end over end toward stationary receivers surrounded by blockers. Many football coaches, including Pop Warner himself, considered passing ridiculous.

A few teams adopted the new play with abandon and one was St. Louis University. On September 5, 1906, Bradbury Robinson connected with Jack Schneider for what's often considered the first recorded legal forward pass in college football. St. Louis coach Eddie Cochems added a wrinkle to the new offensive ploy. He worked with Robinson on throwing hard, straight passes at receivers on the run. This gave their ends and backs the best chance of eluding defenders and gaining more yardage. Robinson tried all sorts of grips and motions to master the awkward task.

Whatever Robinson did to throw the ball one-handed with velocity and accuracy worked. St. Louis crushed its opponents that year, outscoring them 407–11. The highlight of the campaign was the school's shocking 31–0 thrashing of Iowa, which purportedly included four touchdown passes in 10 attempts. But unlike with Warner's single wing, St. Louis's success did not generate a flood of copycat efforts. The traditional powers paid no attention to a small Jesuit school on the banks of the Mississippi. The coastal behemoths only perked up in 1913 when a different small Catholic school upset an Eastern heavyweight.

In the years after 1906, many of the arcane restrictions placed on the forward pass were lifted. In 1913, the University of Notre Dame exploited these softened passing rules. The Catholics (the moniker Irish and Fighting Irish were adopted in later decades) had racked up impressive records against minor competition, but in 1913 they scheduled away games with some of the top teams in the country. Passing would be their secret weapon.

Notre Dame ran a version of the single wing with the extra blockers balanced on both sides and the quarterback taking the role of the halfback in the traditional single wing. It fell on diminutive quarterback Gus Dorais, who stood five feet seven inches, to execute the daring game plan. That summer he and one of his ends worked as busboys at a resort on the shores of Lake Erie. They spent their breaks on the beach, practicing routes and honing their timing.

The beach work paid off. Notre Dame outscored their first three opponents that season 169–7. Next up was Army. The Indianans started slowly, as Dorais missed his first two attempts and Notre Dame punted twice. But on their next series Dorais found his summertime co-worker, Knute Rockne, for a touchdown.

Army scored on their next drive, but in the second quarter Notre Dame executed a drive that set the tone for the rest of the day. They ran for five, and then Dorais completed a 30-yard pass to a back, followed by a 35-yarder to Rockne, followed by a 10-yarder to Rockne. Notre Dame ran it in from the five.

This put Notre Dame up 14–13 at the half, and they pulled away after intermission. "The Westerners flashed the most sensational football that has been seen in the East this year, baffling the cadets with a style of open play and a perfectly developed forward pass, which carried the victors down the field thirty yards at a clip," the New York Times reported.

Dorais finished 14 for 17 for 243 yards and three touchdowns, and Notre Dame won handily, 35–13. Though the strategy was an extension of St. Louis's, this game took place in the country's largest media market and against a top Eastern opponent. "The press and the football public hailed this new game," Rockne later said. "And Notre Dame received credit as the originator of a style of play that we simply systematized."

When Rockne took the head coaching job at Notre Dame in 1918, he continued that work. By the dawn of the 1920s, almost every team boasted some minimal version of a passing game with ends running routes and passers throwing overhand.

The next passer to rattle football's run-first orthodoxy was a Jewish kid from Cleveland whose early childhood dream was to become a world champion strongman. Like Dorais, Benny Friedman was small, five feet eight inches and 172 pounds. But he was solid muscle. He lifted weights regularly at a time when weight training was considered detrimental to physical well-being. In high school he switched his focus from strength events to football. He played well at East Technical High (later known as Jesse Owens's alma mater) but didn't overly impress most Big Ten coaches. He decided to enroll at Michigan despite no promises he'd get any playing time.

Friedman rode the bench until the fourth game of his sophomore year. That game saw Illinois hammer Michigan 39–14 behind Red Grange's six total touchdowns. Friedman was thrown in for a few minutes near the end of the blowout. He impressed the coaches enough to start the following week. Friedman didn't disappoint, throwing a 62-yard touchdown to beat Wisconsin, 21–0. But Friedman would truly blossom the following season.

The muscular Ohioan threw on first down as well as third down. He threw when Michigan was ahead and when it was behind. He would throw from deep in his own territory, whether his opponent expected it or not. Friedman tossed 11 touchdown passes in 1925, leading Michigan to a 7-1 record. In 1926 Friedman was named the Big Ten's Most Valuable Player. Like Bradbury Robinson before him, Friedman tinkered frequently with his grip. He read that baseball pitchers would squeeze and release a tennis ball to strengthen their wrists and forearms. He bought a grip ball that he took with him everywhere. During lectures he'd busily work the ball in his coat pocket.

Once he jumped to the pros, Friedman led the fledgling NFL in touchdown passes for four straight years, amassing 20 in 1929. From 1927 to 1930, he threw for 5,653 yards, the most in the league. The second-most prolific passer collected just 3,770 yards.

Sammy Baugh kicked passing into another gear when he hit the NFL in the late 1930s. As a single-wing halfback Baugh was the opposite of Red Grange. He was an excellent passer and punter but a mediocre runner. So he threw more.

The NFL began its transition away from the single wing in 1940 when Sid Luckman and the Chicago Bears, running the new-fangled modern T formation, dismantled Baugh's Washington team, 73–0. Because the modern T eventually led to a much more prominent role for the quarterback and passing, many assume Luckman and the Bears chucked the ball all over the field as a tactic. They didn't. The Bears scored seven rushing touchdowns and capitalized on eight Washington turnovers, returning three interceptions for scores. Luckman tossed one touchdown pass. The Bears dominated the game, indeed, but they didn't actually throw the ball that much.

Otto Graham and Kenny Washington were part of the last generation of players who starred as single-wing halfbacks in college and then converted to modern T formation quarterbacks or running backs when they hit the pros. When Graham arrived at Northwestern, he didn't even plan on playing football; he was there on a basketball scholarship. But his arm got noticed in an intramural game and he joined the football team. One of the few single-wing halfbacks who excelled at both passing and rushing, Graham made his mark for the Wildcats as a sophomore when he led Northwestern to a 14–7 upset over Paul Brown's heavily favored Ohio State Buckeyes. He'd ultimately win two Big Ten Most Valuable Player awards and finish third in Heisman Trophy balloting in 1943.

Paul Brown never forgot Graham's performance against his Buckeyes. Graham joined the Navy Air Corps near the end of the war and Brown eyed him for Cleveland when he finished his service. Brown convinced the ex-Wildcat to sign with his new team and Graham picked up the modern T almost immediately, a transition many quarterbacks found rough going. Legend has it that it brought Sammy Baugh to tears when Sid Luckman was teaching it to him in the early 1940s.

In the 1950 NFL Championship Game, Graham faced one of the few other quarterbacks known for excelling in the modern T in Bob Waterfield. It wasn't immediately clear when the teams emerged from the locker rooms for the start of the third quarter whether Graham would be able to return to the field. He'd taken a crunching hit to his lower back at the end of the first half, but miraculously his back hadn't stiffened yet, and the Browns quarterback headed out for the last thirty minutes of the title game. The Browns still trailed the Rams by a point, 14–13.

Early in the third quarter, the Browns got the ball at their own 22-yard line. Graham faked a handoff to Motley to the right and looked for Horace Gillom in the left flat. While Gillom concentrated on punting, he was also a reserve end and had come in to replace Mac Speedie after Speedie tweaked an old leg injury. On this play Gillom feigned a block but let his man through. He then darted into the space vacated by the defender. Graham tossed him the ball five yards behind the line of scrimmage, and Gillom turned upfield with fellow kicker Lou Groza rumbling from left tackle to run interference. Left guard Weldon Humble nailed the first Rams defender, and Gillom sliced inside that block and accelerated downfield. Right as Gillom hit full speed, a Los Angeles defender lunged at his ankles and brought him down, but not before a 30-yard gain.

A few plays later the Browns had a first down on the Rams 39-yard line. Graham went back to pass and escaped a sack when Motley dove to cut off a

Kenny Washington passes to Woody Strode during a UCLA practice. The original caption of the September 14, 1937, photo said the sophomore duo was "expected to write Bruin history during the coming season." HERALD-EXAMINER COLLECTION/LOS ANGELES PUBLIC LIBRARY

Woody Strode blocks a defender while Kenny Washington carries the ball during the November 4, 1939, matchup between UCLA and California. Washington ran for 141 yards and led the Bruins to a 20-7 victory, keeping UCLA undefeated and on a collision course with USC to determine who would play in the Rose Bowl. JACK BURRUD, HERALD-EXAMINER COLLECTION/LOS ANGELES PUBLIC LIBRARY

Woody Strode, Jackie Robinson, and Kenny Washington stand together. In 1939 they led UCLA to its best season yet. At a time when few colleges had more than one or two black players, these three, and reserve Ray Bartlett, made the Bruins one of the "blackest" non-HBCU teams in the country. BETTMANN/CORBIS/AP IMAGES

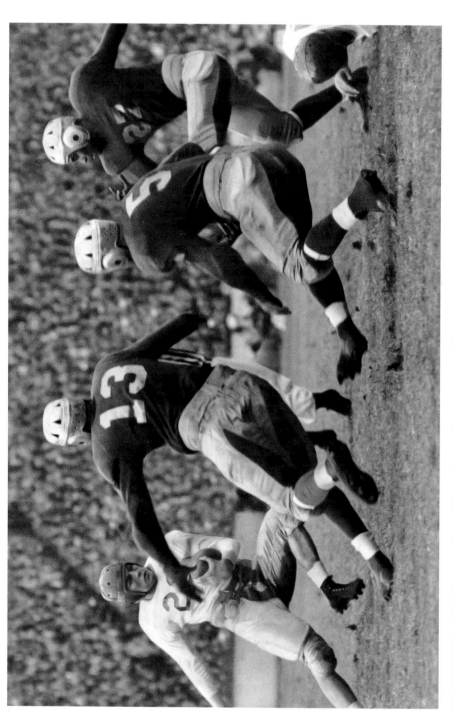

Kenny Washington (13), Bill Overlin (5), and Woody Strode (27) converge on USC's Bob Robertson on an attempted reverse. The December 9, 1939, game marked the first time both teams entered their showdown nationally ranked and undefeated.

TOP: In 1946 Halley Harding was the sports editor of the *Los Angeles Tribune*, one of three major black weeklies in Los Angeles. Harding and his peers at the *Los Angeles Sentinel* and *California Eagle* pressured Los Angeles Rams management to sign Kenny Washington, breaking the NFL's color barrier. HALLEY HARDING AT THE PIANO, WALTER L. GORDON, JR./WILLIAM C. BEVERLY, JR. COLLECTION (COLLECTION 2270). LIBRARY SPECIAL COLLECTIONS, CHARLES E. YOUNG RESEARCH LIBRARY, UCLA

BOTTOM: Black athletes and sportswriters eat dinner in an undated 1940s photograph. Boxer Dynamite Jackson (Ernest Bendy) sits at the head of the table. Third from left: Abie Robinson, *Los Angeles Sentinel*. First from right: Paul McGee, *Los Angeles Sentinel*. Next: Eddie Burbridge, *California Eagle*, then Halley Harding, *Los Angeles Tribune*. SPORTSMEN SITTING AT A TABLE, WALTER L. GORDON, JR./WILLIAM C. BEVERLY, JR. COLLECTION (COLLECTION 2270). LIBRARY SPECIAL COLLECTIONS, CHARLES E. YOUNG RESEARCH LIBRARY, UCLA

Club Alabam was one of Central Avenue's legendary nightclubs during the 1940s. Cousins Leon Washington Jr. and Loren Miller sit at the front left table. Washington ran the *Los Angeles Sentinel* and Miller would argue many of the city's biggest racially restrictive housing covenant cases.

In this January 20, 1946, photo of the semipro Hollywood Bears, Kenny Washington is the first player from left in the back row. Also: Ezzrett "Sugarfoot" Anderson (23), Chuck Anderson (22), Woody Strode (17), and Jack Jacobs (27), a top Native American (Creek) pro football player of the era. DAVID ESKENAZI COLLECTION

Supporters rally at Henry and Anna Laws's house on Ninety-Second Street. They'd been forced from their home due to a racially restrictive housing covenant. Such covenants were used regularly to bar black (and sometimes Mexican, Chinese, Japanese, or Jewish) families from purchasing or living in houses covered by the covenants. DEMONSTRATORS PROTEST DISCRIMINATORY HOUSING, LOS ANGELES DAILY NEWS NEGATIVES. LIBRARY SPECIAL COLLECTIONS, CHARLES E. YOUNG RESEARCH LIBRARY, UCLA

Pauletta Fears and Dolores Laws rest inside the home of their parents, Henry and Anna Laws, while picketers demonstrate against restrictive covenant laws outside. Fighting the covenants took a huge toll on families and worsened the wartime and postwar housing crunch for black-residents of Los Angeles. DEMONSTRATORS REST DURING A DISCRIMINATORY HOUSING PROTEST, LOS ANGELES DAILY NEWS NEGATIVES. LIBRARY SPECIAL COLLECTIONS, CHARLES E. YOUNG RESEARCH LIBRARY, UCLA

Pauli Murray graduated from the Howard School of Law and moved to Los Angeles where she battled racially restrictive housing covenants. She served as temporary state attorney general and then continued her studies and civil rights advocacy. She coined "Jane Crow" to describe the challenges black women faced from racism and sexism.
PAULI MURRAY PAPERS, SCHLESINGER LIBRARY, RADCLIFFE INSTITUTE, HARVARD UNIVERSITY

Loren Miller was a journalist, activist, and lawyer. He became a nationally renowned expert on racially restrictive housing covenants. He partnered with Thurgood Marshall to craft the legal strategies for the *Shelley v. Kraemer* case which Miller, Marshall, and others argued in front of the U.S. Supreme Court in 1948.
LOREN MILLER SEATED AT DESK, MILLER PAPERS BOX 21 (6), THE HUNTINGTON LIBRARY, SAN MARINO, CALIFORNIA

Kenny Washington met June Bradley while both were in college and they married in 1940. Their daughter, Karin Cohen, chuckled at this photo because helping with the dishes wasn't something her father actually did. Karin's older brother, Kenny Jr., played baseball at USC and in the Dodgers organization. KARIN COHEN COLLECTION

Kenny Washington shows his passing form posing for photographers while at UCLA. He'd finish three years of varsity play at UCLA with numerous school records. His 1,915 career rushing yards would stand for more than thirty years. KARIN COHEN COLLECTION

The Los Angeles Rams signed Woody Strode in May of 1946. He rarely played and suspected the Rams signed him to be Washington's roommate on the road. (Some teams signed two black players so there would be no question of white players being asked to share hotel rooms with their black teammates.) AP IMAGES

Marion Motley and Bill Willis celebrate in the locker room after the Cleveland Browns beat the New York (football) Yankees 14–9 in the inaugural All-America Football Conference Championship Game in 1946. Cleveland coach Paul Brown signed Willis and Motley several months after the Rams signed Washington and Strode. CLEVELAND PRESS COLLECTION, CLEVELAND STATE UNIVERSITY LIBRARY

The Cleveland Browns offensive starters at Cleveland Municipal Stadium in December of 1947. Fullback Marion Motley is second from left in the backfield. Bill Willis is fifth from left in front. Motley and Willis were crucial members of the Browns teams that dominated the AAFC from 1946 through 1949. BETTMANN/CORBIS/AP IMAGES

Loy Harrison (LEFT), Sheriff J. M. Bond (MIDDLE), and coroner W. T. Brown (RIGHT) stand where a mob lynched two black couples on July 25, 1946, near Monroe, Georgia. The lynchings sparked national protests and led to a federal investigation. AP IMAGES

The Monroe lynching victims were Roger and Dorothy Malcom and George Dorsey and Mae Murray Dorsey. On July 28, 1946, friends and relatives gathered at Mount Perry church to mourn the deaths of George Dorsey and his sister, Dorothy Malcom. Some relatives refused to attend for fear of being targeted next. AP IMAGES

Woody Strode and Ezzrett "Sugarfoot" Anderson sing and play guitar in this undated photo. Strode joined the Calgary Stampeders in 1948 and helped them win their first Grey Cup championship. Anderson joined in 1949. He still lives in Calgary with his family and celebrated the team's 2015 Grey Cup victory. SUGARFOOT ANDERSON COLLECTION

40:—AERIAL VIEW OF EUCLID BEACH PARK, CLEVELAND, OHIO

1405

A main attraction for Clevelanders in the 1940s, Euclid Beach Park barred black patrons from the bathing beach, roller skating rink, and dance pavilion (here inland from pier). In 1946, protesters repeatedly used nonviolent direct-action tactics to protest the exclusion, and park security reacted with violence.

Juanita Morrow and Wally Nelson enjoy a picnic in Cleveland in 1946. Morrow, a CORE leader, helped organize the Euclid Beach protests. She'd previously collaborated with Pauli Murray on civil rights actions near Howard University. She and Nelson married and later moved to Massachusetts where they became war tax resisters. JUANITA MORROW NELSON COLLECTION

The Los Angeles Rams celebrated Kenny Washington's retirement at halftime of his last game on December 12, 1948. He received numerous gifts, including the car he's sitting in here. He was given a trophy that he then gave to his alma mater, Lincoln High. To this day the school presents the trophy to the football team's MVP.

KARIN COHEN COLLECTION

Bill Willis and other Cleveland defenders lunge for a fumble by Brooklyn Dodgers halfback Glenn Dobbs. The Browns beat the Dodgers 26–7 on October 6, 1946. Cleveland won the AAFC title each of the league's four years of existence before being absorbed by the NFL prior to the 1950 season.

C. J. NICHOLS/BETTMANN/CORBIS/AP IMAGES

Marion Motley tries to run against Tank Younger and the Los Angeles Rams defense during the 1950 NFL Championship Game on December 24, 1950. The two teams had the best offenses in the league and had the most black players of any teams in the NFL as well. AP IMAGES

Everyone watches Lou Groza's field goal attempt in the waning moments of the 1950 NFL Championship Game. The Cleveland Browns trailed the Los Angeles Rams 28-27 and Groza's attempt amid blustery winds would decide who won the NFL title. CLEVELAND PRESS COLLECTION, CLEVELAND STATE UNIVERSITY LIBRARY

rusher from the right. In those extra seconds, Graham spotted Dante Lavelli getting ahead of his man. The quarterback spun the ball inches beyond the outstretched arm of a defensive back. Lavelli caught the ball and trotted into the end zone, giving Cleveland its first lead of the game. Groza hit the extra point to put Cleveland ahead, 20–14.

On the ensuing kickoff, Los Angeles back Tommy Kalmanir caught the ball three yards deep in his end zone and weaved his way to the Ram 28-yard line. Waterfield repeatedly found Tom Fears, Elroy Hirsch, and his running backs over the middle to move the Rams down the field. Once inside Cleveland's 10-yard line, Los Angeles looked to smash the ball into the end zone. In this area of the field the Rams got predictable, often relying on Dick Hoerner to slam his way into the end zone.

And that's just what Los Angeles tried to do. At the nine-yard line Waterfield handed off to Hoerner, who ran left and was gang-tackled at the seven. Hoerner ran again, this time inside. The Los Angeles center and left guard buried Willis, and Hoerner went over him for three yards and a first down at the four. Waterfield tried yet another inside handoff to Hoerner. This time Willis stood up, the Rams' left guard and Browns lineman Abe Gibron submarined Hoerner, who went down at the three.

On second down, Waterfield spun the wrong way and Willis tomahawked him as he shoveled an underhand pass to Hoerner sweeping right. Browns defenders dragged down Hoerner at the one-yard line. Third and goal.

At the snap, Willis shot through the gap between center and left guard. The ball had barely reached Waterfield's hands when Willis split the line. The Ram quarterback spun to hand off, his back to Willis. Waterfield extended the ball toward Hoerner as Willis's arms slammed down around him from behind. Waterfield crumbled to the turf, but the pigskin stayed tucked in Hoerner's gut, and the fullback dove forward for a touchdown. Waterfield converted the extra point to nudge Los Angeles back in front, 21–20.

With a little over a quarter left it seemed that whoever had the ball last would win the game. The Los Angeles kickoff pinned the Browns inside their 20-yard line, and Cleveland turned to Motley, the NFL's top rusher, to pound them into better field position. In the AAFC, Motley had played his best in title games.

But the Rams knew the Browns would rely on the fullback and prepared accordingly. Graham handed off to Motley at the 20-yard line, and the back headed left. As he neared the edge of the line, he saw the Rams defense had him hemmed against the sideline. He spun back the opposite way and swung back through the backfield, hoping to get to the opposite side of the field. Rams linemen Jack Zilly and Larry Brink were a step behind him. Motley, one of the few Browns who had stuck with wearing cleats on the icy field, slipped. Zilly and Brink slammed into him. Motley felt the ball squirting away as he fell. He lunged, but the football tumbled out of reach.

By the time Graham and the other Browns realized the ball was loose, Brink had picked it up at the seven-yard line. On the ground Motley saw flashes of the play surge the other way. He heard his opponents' shouts of joy and knew exactly what had happened. Touchdown, Los Angeles.

Motley pushed himself up from the cold turf and walked to the sideline. Coach Paul Brown kept his distance. Motley didn't need to be reminded of his occasional problems with holding on to the ball, or that he had stuck with wearing cleats while most of the team had switched to basketball shoes for better footing. He sat on the bench in the freezing air and stared out at the field.

Like Motley, the Cleveland fans were stunned. Just minutes before they'd held the lead for the first time in the game. Cleveland had to regroup quickly after Motley's fumble. With half of the third quarter gone, the Browns might have only a handful of drives left, and they needed to score twice. (The NFL did not adopt the two-point conversion until 1994.) Cleveland's Ken Carpenter took the kickoff out to the 35-yard line. Graham hit Dante Lavelli for 13 yards and a first down. But on the next play Graham took a sack and the Browns eventually punted.

Despite nursing an eight-point lead and fighting the swirling winds, the Rams went back to the air. Waterfield continued to pick apart the Browns defense with short passes over the middle. Los Angeles drove into Cleveland territory, and Browns fans worried that the Angelenos were about to put the game away.

But on Waterfield's next drop back, the Browns pressured him from both of the ends and through the middle. From nearly 15 yards behind the line of scrimmage, Waterfield chucked the ball. Far downfield, Cleveland defensive halfback Warren Lahr plucked it from the air. He raced upfield to his own 35-yard line. The Browns were in business again.

CHAPTER 13

92 Yards

Los Angeles Memorial Coliseum
Los Angeles, California

1947

WHEN THE LOS ANGELES RAMS ENDED THEIR 1946 season, both Kenny Washington and Woody Strode had reason to be optimistic about the upcoming year. For one, Washington would be a year away from serious knee surgery. He'd have the off-season to more fully recover and prepare his joints for their next round of beatings. For Strode, a change in leadership opened the possibility of more playing time.

Just two days after the Los Angeles Rams closed out their 1946 campaign, head coach Adam Walsh resigned. Little was written about why he left or whether he had been pushed out. Walsh did say he was open to other head-coaching offers, which many took as a sign that owner Dan Reeves had canned him. Backfield coach and T formation expert Bob Snyder was named the new head coach. No one knew whether Snyder would play Strode more, but he could barely play him less than Walsh had.

In the first week of February, the *Los Angeles Times* and the *Pittsburgh Courier* reported that Los Angeles had re-signed Woody Strode for another year. When asked about Washington, Reeves said he hadn't yet met with Kenny but expected to soon. If Washington's legs were better, he was expected to be a key cog in the Rams backfield.

As training camp approached, the press asked Snyder how the Rams under his guidance might differ from previous squads. He said he would still focus on the T formation, but he would also incorporate plays from the single wing, the offense that Kenny Washington, Tom Harmon, and other backs on the team were more familiar with. As several sportswriters noted, quarterback Bob Waterfield was the only Rams player who was particularly suited for the T. Snyder also said he might give Washington more reps at quarterback and officially switched him back to halfback from fullback. Washington officially signed for the 1947 season in early March.

Waterfield, Washington, and Jim Hardy split time at quarterback during the team's first full scrimmage in training camp, and each threw a touchdown pass. The next scrimmage saw Les Horvath also get reps at quarterback. The following week Snyder moved Horvath to halfback and signed another potential backup quarterback. Washington was reported to have an ankle injury that could take several weeks to heal. Snyder also brought in two ends, Jack Zilly and Frank Hubbell—even more competition for Strode.

In a public intrasquad scrimmage at Gilmore Field, the Rams Blues edged the Golds, 35–34. Hardy shone, and Washington made a spectacular catch in the end zone before being knocked out of bounds. "The Kingfish played one of his great games and nobody's going to run him off the squad no matter how much whittling Snyder does to his backs," wrote Braven Dyer in the *Los Angeles Times*, using a common press nickname for Washington that referenced a black hustler character in the popular *Amos 'n' Andy* radio program.

Strode wasn't so lucky. The Rams played their annual charity game against Washington on Friday, September 6. On Saturday, offensive line coach George Trafton asked Strode to meet with him. When they sat down, Trafton broke the news. The Rams were cutting six players and Strode was one of them.

Strode sat quietly, stunned. "They're trying to say you're too old and that they're trying to rebuild," Trafton continued. "Woody, it's not because of your ability that you're getting fired. I tried to tell them that Negroes don't age like white people." Strode was 33, an age by which many pro players had already retired. But he had maintained his carved decathlete physique and was faster than anyone else on the team except Tom Harmon.

Strode said nothing. He thought about how often he had been stuck on the bench. The coaches only threw him into games for a few minutes here or there to blunt the attacks of bigger lines. When he got in the game, he often excelled. "In my generation players never defended their right to play," Strode later explained. "We just tried to prove ourselves in practice, which I did."

Los Angeles had brought in two more ends at the beginning of training camp and had nine on the roster at one point. Head coach Snyder said he had no alternative to cutting Strode. He wanted to get younger at the position and planned to carry only five ends during the season.

Strode talked with Washington. "It's not your ability; it's your lifestyle," Washington told his friend. "Dan Reeves does not approve of your marriage to Luana and your Hawaiian lifestyle." Strode had met his wife, a descendent of Liliuokalani, the last queen of the Kingdom of Hawaii, when the UCLA Bruins had played in the Pineapple Bowl in Hawaii after their 1938 season. Princess Luana pursued Strode, and several years later they married. Unlike many other black stars in Los Angeles, Strode eschewed living near Central Avenue or in South Los Angeles. He and Luana lived among a community of Pacific Islander entertainers who clustered near Hollywood.

Reeves's distaste for Strode's marriage perplexed him at the time and perplexed his son decades later. "I don't know what it was that the owner of the Rams had against his marriage," Kalai Strode said. "If it had been a white-black situation, I can kinda see that [at the time]. But this was a black-brown situation. That is what I don't get."

"Maybe it was more of a punishment for your mom for not following the rules?" Kalai's wife, Pam Larson, said. "She was a rebel. She was a very flamboyant woman. She didn't follow mainland social standards, and there was resentment from men and women."

"Even my dad's mother didn't like it," Kalai Strode said. "He never smoked, drank, or partied before meeting Luana. He probably started that [partying] when he met her, and my grandmother didn't like that. [Luana] was leading him astray down the path to paganism. Others thought that, too, the men more from jealousy and the women more for propriety."

The day after Strode was cut, several friends of Washington's from Lincoln Heights stopped by Strode's house. "We were [out] having dinner last night, and we heard Dan Reeves and Bob Snyder talk about cutting you from the team," one of the visitors told Strode. "They were falling-down drunk and they were talking so bad about you and Luana that we sent our wives home," relayed another. "We don't like what they're doing. Do you want to fight them?"

"This was the mob asking me this," Strode later wrote. "I looked at them and said, 'You know, I've lived here thirty-two years and I've never had a racial incident. I don't want to start one now.'" Strode told them no. "'Anyway, how do you fight someone with a hundred million dollars?'" he said, referring to the Rams' owner.

Through the fall and into winter Strode tried to stay busy with cooking, cleaning, and taking care of his and Luana's eight-month-old son, Kalealoa (Kalai) Strode. "He and Luana were my only joy at that time," Strode said of those months. "After I got cut by the Rams I completely shut down."

In an interview much later, Strode said that, after his experience in the NFL, if he had to integrate heaven, he didn't want to go. Many writers repeated this quote over the years, and in his biography Strode clarified that he simply didn't want to go somewhere where he wasn't wanted.

With Strode having been passed over by the Rams in favor of unproven rookies, other NFL teams showed little interest. The AAFC's New York Yankees sniffed around but did not sign him after he went east for a workout. Strode stopped by Chicago to visit some cousins on his way back from New York. "I got drunk for one week and licked my wounds. I was a warrior, I didn't know anything but football. I didn't know how I was going to support my wife and baby."

When Strode got home, Luana had a message for him. Les Lear, another Ram who'd previously been cut, had called. Lear had gone to Canada to be player-coach of the Calgary Stampeders of the Western Interprovincial Football Union, later part of the Canadian Football League. Lear could hire up to four international players and he wanted Strode. "Bring your shoes and your shoulder pads, I'll get you all the money I can," Lear told his old teammate. Strode jumped at the opportunity. He would be one of several Stampeders with ties to Los Angeles, three of them black, who would spark the team to their greatest seasons and become part of Canadian football lore.

With Strode cut, Kenny Washington entered the 1947 season without his best friend and with an unfamiliar coach. On the positive side, Washington was more experienced with the Rams offense, and the rest seemed to have helped his knees. He certainly looked to have regained some of his explosiveness in the Rams' 2-1 start. Los Angeles opened the season at Pittsburgh. The Steelers had had the best defense in the league the previous year, but the Los Angeles offense steamrolled them, 48–7. Everyone on offense shone, including Washington, who scored from nine yards and four yards out.

The next week the Rams faced the Green Bay Packers at Wisconsin State Fair Park. Both clubs failed to score in the first half. The Packers notched two touchdowns in the third quarter, their drives powered almost exclusively by running plays. Down 17–0, Los Angeles finally woke up in the fourth quarter. The Rams scored off a four-yard run by Pat West, and Washington set up a second Rams touchdown with a 30-yard run where he eluded half a dozen tackles before being brought down on the four-yard line.

Washington played sparingly in the next Rams game, having suffered a gash over his eye at the end of the Packers game. The Rams' other backs did just fine, however, rolling up 296 yards on the ground and beating the Lions 27–13. For their home opener against the Chicago Cardinals, the Rams drew 69,631 fans in 90-degree heat. Los Angeles dispatched the Cardinals 27–7 behind more dominant offensive line play and rushing. Los Angeles running backs netted 260 yards in the game, and Washington dodged three would-be tacklers on a 31-yard dash around end. He only had two more carries in the game, though, totaling 38 yards. The Cardinals had entered the game undefeated, and with the win the Rams tied them for first place in the Western Division with a 3-1 record.

The Rams backs were carrying the team, averaging 221 yards rushing per game. This success on the ground masked an inconsistent passing game. Waterfield and fourth-quarter substitute Jim Hardy had managed only 100 yards passing each of the previous two games, and their numbers were about to get worse.

The Rams traveled to Philadelphia to take on the Eagles. On paper, Philly should have been a prime spot for the Los Angeles passing game to reassert itself. The Eagles had the league's best rush defense but had given up big games to opposing quarterbacks the previous two weeks. The Rams certainly put the ball in the air, throwing 35 times in the game. But three attempts were intercepted and neither Waterfield nor Hardy threw a touchdown. Los Angeles tallied their lone score on the ground in the 14–7 loss.

Next up was a rematch with the Chicago Cardinals. Despite Kenny Washington's touching the ball only a handful of times a game, coaches and scribes were buzzing about his reemergence. Even owner Dan Reeves had commented to Rams staff while traveling with the team that Washington looked more like the scintillating runner that had dominated college ball and the coast semipro scene.

In the first quarter at Chicago, Washington ripped off the best run of his pro career. The Rams were backed up to their own eight-yard line, and the play call was a handoff to Washington. As he had done so often at UCLA and with the Hollywood Bears, Washington started wide and cut inside, slashing through arm tackles at the line and cutting past linebackers. When asked later what he saw in the middle of all those bodies, Washington simply said, "Alleys."

Washington's rushing game benefited from his knock-kneed gait. His feet kicked to the sides as he ran, exaggerating the possibilities of lateral movement. Strode described it from his unique vantage point: "Sometimes I would be forty yards downfield, watching [Washington] fake out guys on his way to me. His legs would go one way and he'd go another." Paul Schissler, Washington's coach with the Hollywood Bears, maintained that Washington was the best open-field runner he'd ever seen.

On his run against the Cardinals, Washington sliced through the line, past the linebackers, and stiff-armed the oncoming safety. Only John Cochran, the defensive halfback on the other side of the field, had a shot to bring him down. Just as Cochran reached him, Washington stutter-stepped, and Cochran's momentum took him off target. Washington straight-armed Cochran to the ground and dashed into the end zone. Washington's teammates had risen from the bench as he got into the secondary and yelled and jumped on each other as he dispatched the last defender. As he came to the bench, the players rushed to hug him and slap him on the back.

The touchdown, as thrilling as it was, couldn't offset the Rams turnovers: four fumbles and three interceptions. Bob Waterfield connected on only five passes all afternoon. Washington was sent in at quarterback near the end of the game in a now-familiar role: Los Angeles trailing late in the game and the opponent expecting long throws. Washington completed one pass for 18 yards and was picked off on another shot. He finished the game with 145 yards rushing on 11 carries in the 17–10 loss. On the strength of his 92-yard run Washington took over the league lead in yards per carry, moving ahead of Eagles star halfback Steve Van Buren.

The following week the Rams lost their third game in a row, and Waterfield threw another handful of picks. Sportswriters speculated that the star quarterback was injured. He and Hardy had totaled zero touchdown passes and 12 interceptions in three games. Why didn't they give Washington a shot at quarterback? Surely he couldn't have struggled more than the incumbents already had.

Even just for the threat of his running, putting Washington behind center might have thrown off defenses and created mismatches the Rams could exploit. Coaches still seemed to doubt Washington's suitability for quarterback in the modern T, though, and ultimately neither Washington nor Rams fans would find out what he could do with a sustained chance to lead the offense. Washington was hurt late in the second Cardinals game, his left knee again, and he would be out for two or three weeks.

Los Angeles dropped three out of their next four, which eliminated them from playoff contention. Waterfield and Hardy continued to split quarterback duties for the rest of the year. Washington scored his last touchdown of the season in the final game, taking a direct snap from center and rushing 23 yards for the tally. The direct snap to a halfback was one of the few times in the year that Coach Bob Snyder called a single-wing play.

For the season, Washington and Tom Harmon led the club in rushes with 60 attempts apiece. Three other halfbacks had at least 40 carries as well. Washington topped the squad in total rushing yards and averaged 7.4 yards per attempt, the 92-yard run certainly padding that number. His average per rush was the highest in the league in 1947. However, given that he'd split carries with so many other backs, he landed just a few carries short of the minimum needed to qualify for the title, keeping him out of the NFL record books. The Rams as a team finished first in the league in rushing yards and rushing average but placed ninth, out of ten teams, in passing yards. Bob Waterfield had his worst year as a pro, tossing only eight touchdowns against 18 interceptions.

Washington's 92-yard run in Chicago was the longest touchdown run in the NFL that year and still stands as the longest touchdown run in Rams franchise history.

THE SUGAR HILL CASE WAS A LANDMARK moment in the covenant fight because it was the first time a state court had decided racially restrictive housing covenants ran afoul of the protections defined in the Fourteenth Amendment. That was all well and good, but Loren Miller knew that the bigger challenge was federal court, specifically the U.S. Supreme Court.

Up through the mid-1940s the picture looked bleak for those hoping the Supreme Court would declare racially restrictive housing covenants unconstitutional. The same Supreme Court decision in 1883 that curbed the protections that the Fourteenth Amendment had provided in the area of public accommodations—that the amendment only protected against discriminatory "state action," not steps taken by businesses, nongovernment agencies, or individuals—held just as true in the area of housing discrimination. Loren Miller was familiar with that case, and not just as a lawyer. His great-uncle Bird Gee was a plaintiff in one of the cases decided collectively as the *Civil Rights Cases of 1883*.

The first time the U.S. Supreme Court ruled specifically on racial housing issues was in *Buchanan v. Warley* in 1917. Buchanan, a white man, had attempted to sell property to Warley, a black man, in Louisville, Kentucky. The house was in an area of town where a city ordinance prohibited black residents from owning property. The Kentucky Supreme Court upheld the local statute, claiming it did not violate the Due Process Clause of the Fourteenth Amendment. The state high court didn't consider it a question of equal protection.

Since feudal times, the Anglo-Saxon legal system had supported the unrestrained use and sale of property. This principle was embodied in U.S. law with "nor shall any State deprive any person of life, liberty, or property, without due process of law," which protected a property holder's right to sell that property to whomever he pleased.

Courts and laws did enforce some limitations on property use and sales for public-policy considerations. Municipal zoning laws, such as ones defining what kinds of industrial businesses could coexist with residential housing, were deemed acceptable since they benefited the common good, even if those laws did reduce the property value of some houses as a result.

In *Buchanan v. Warley* the U.S. Supreme Court disagreed with the Kentucky court and issued a unanimous decision that city ordinances banning property ownership due to race did indeed violate the Due Process Clause. They were also clear examples of state action. Many towns and cities beyond Louisville had municipal laws enforcing racial zoning, and the *Buchanan* ruling made these ordinances illegal. The use of racially restrictive housing covenants had already increased in many cities by the time the Supreme Court decided *Buchanan*. However, the decision in that case likely accelerated their use as a means to achieve the intended discriminatory end, while skirting the most blatant legal roadblocks.

In 1926, the Supreme Court indirectly validated racially restrictive covenants by letting a lower court ruling stand. In *Corrigan v. Buckley* two white men had signed a neighborhood-wide racially restrictive covenant covering their properties in the District of Columbia. Later, Corrigan decided to sell to a black couple, and Buckley sued to stop the sale. A court of appeals panel ruled that the parties to a covenant had the right to dispose of their property as they wished, and an African American's right to property did not compel a sale that violated the covenant.

That the case was in the District of Columbia was an important detail. The district was under no state judicial body, and at the time only matters raising "substantial federal claims" from the District of Columbia were considered within the Supreme Court's jurisdiction. In not hearing this case the justices may have simply deemed it to not have raised substantial federal claims. But many took the court's refusal to hear an appeal as validating the legality of racially restrictive housing covenants.

In the years to follow, state courts in Kentucky, Maryland, Oklahoma, Wisconsin, Missouri, and New York relied on the *Corrigan* outcome to justify covenants. In 1944, the American Law Institute published its summary of then-current housing and property law in its "Restatement of Law" series. The organization, composed of legal scholars, law professors, and practicing attorneys, had been producing such summaries of the status of various parts of law for two decades, and its publications were considered an accurate read on where the law stood. In its "Restatement" regarding property law, it said the validity of the covenants was clear, based on the rulings in six state courts, and then outlined the ways that the covenants benefited race relations.

So while California Superior Court judge Thurmond Clarke had ruled against the covenants' constitutionality, the U.S. Supreme Court had shown no indication of agreeing with him, and many interpreted the Supreme Court as supporting the constitutionality of the covenants. Clarke's decision, and his basing it on the Fourteenth Amendment, did provide a shot in the arm to the lawyers around the country looking to take a covenant case to the Supreme Court, however.

While Loren Miller labored in Los Angeles, numerous other attorneys battled covenants in other states. In 1934 the NAACP hired a young attorney from Baltimore, Thurgood Marshall, and he joined the national staff two years later. In 1940, Marshall became the executive director of the NAACP's legal arm, the Legal Defense and Educational Fund. Under Marshall, the LDF centralized the handling of covenant cases and gave final decision making of which cases to apply for hearing with the Supreme Court to Marshall. Marshall had won two recent cases at the Supreme Court, including the *Smith v. Allwright* decision in which the court struck down all-white primaries.

Marshall sent Loren Miller a congratulatory letter after Miller got the Sugar Hill case thrown out of California Superior Court. The LDF leader knew Miller was the most experienced lawyer in the country in this area of law. Miller, Marshall, and others began meeting regularly to discuss overall strategy and to identify which of the cases moving through state courts they wanted to take to the most powerful court in the land.

and at the beginning of what would become a thirty-year tenure on Cleveland's city council.

Carr was a controversial figure both inside and outside of his ward. He ran on a promise to tolerate Cleveland's numbers racket, an illegal lottery-style gambling operation common in minority communities and working-class neighborhoods of many cities. Carr saw the numbers racket as not that different from a church bingo game. The police and plenty of his constituents disagreed.

Carr had picketed the Euclid Beach Park entrance in early August 1946, after park guards first assaulted protesters. He both supported the protest and recognized the political opportunity it presented. Carr drafted the ordinance and presented it to the council in early September, shortly after Albert Luster was beaten. The proposed law still awaited a public hearing—a prerequisite before it could be considered by the full council—when patrolmen Coleman and Mackey were beaten and Coleman shot. The legislative and safety committees on the council also asked to review the measure before it was brought to a vote.

Meanwhile, local groups met to discuss Carr's ordinance and build support for it. The Equal Rights Committee sponsored a meeting at the Cedars YMCA, at which Carr explained the ordinance. A week later, the Church of All Peoples held a meeting and panel discussion at Euclid Avenue Baptist Church. There the audience heard accounts of the first two incidents at Euclid Beach Park over the summer. A member of American Youth for Democracy narrated the events of July 21. Mrs. Henry Crawford explained what happened on August 23 when CORE members were ejected from the park. Albert Luster described being attacked by Julius Vago.

Following those speakers, Carr read the full ordinance, and a panel composed of himself, the executive secretary of the Cleveland Baptist Association, and State Representative Howard Metzenbaum discussed the ordinance and answered questions. Carr and his allies organized dozens of such meetings in the central neighborhoods and beyond. He also worked behind the scenes to get the ordinance in front of the various council committees who needed to sign off on it.

Nearly five hundred people showed up to a public city council meeting where the measure would be discussed, necessitating the meeting be moved to a larger room. Even then the crowd, mostly supporters of the ordinance, overflowed into the corridor. First to speak was Dr. D. R. Sharpe, the chairman of the Community Relations Board, a task force created the year before to address and relieve racial conflict in Cleveland. Sharpe spoke strongly in favor of the measure and emphasized that it aligned with the board's very purpose.

Charles K. Arter, attorney for the Humphrey Company, argued that race relations at the park had been fine for decades until communist-inspired agitators stepped in. He argued the ordinance was unconstitutional because it specifically targeted Euclid Beach Park over other places of public gathering. Councilman Carr asked the city's assistant law director for his opinion, and he replied that the city's law department had studied the measure carefully when Carr had first submitted it and they were satisfied nothing in it countered any existing law.

Local civil rights attorney Chester Gillespie asked Arter a few questions about which facilities within the park black patrons were and were not allowed to use. To almost all questions Arter responded, "I can't answer that." The public hearing demonstrated broad community support for Carr's ordinance, but more stalling tactics by ordinance opponents delayed a vote.

Meanwhile patrolmen Coleman and Mackey also faced more stonewalling. Mackey's immediate supervisor advised him to drop the charges against his assailants. When Mackey asked the assistant prosecutor for an arrest warrant on Julius Vago, he was told to speak with the chief police prosecutor. He, in turn, told Mackey there wasn't enough evidence to support the warrant. What more, Mackey wondered, was required? A guard had hit him across the face with a club, witnessed by a crowd of people.

The six CORE activists who were thrown out of the park during the confrontation were told the same thing—there wasn't enough evidence to charge the guards. Based on the pattern set in earlier incidents at Euclid Beach Park, the protesters had two choices. They could press for criminal charges of assault and battery against the guards. Or they could sue under the state civil rights statute and seek damages for the discrimination they'd experienced. Protesters kicked out of the park generally had little luck with the first, and some success with the second, though many tried both routes.

The various civil lawsuits against the park for the behavior of guards totaled a possible $100,000 in damages. As the cases mounted, park management went on the offensive, sending a letter to the three major dailies in Cleveland tarring CORE with the communist tag. The civil rights group defended itself. "[CORE] is an interracial organization founded on the Christian principles of the brotherhood of man and the American principles of democracy. Members are committed to the goal of eliminating racial discrimination through methods of direct, non-violent, action."

The white dailies and black weeklies were mixed on how seriously they took the threat of communism. Most black papers thought the charges and fear of communism overblown. White papers tended to sensationalize more. Two features in the *Cleveland Plain Dealer* may have unintentionally underscored the city's lack of support for communism. The reporter visited the state Communist Party headquarters, a one-room office in Cleveland. There were two framed pictures on the walls, one of Abraham Lincoln and the other of V. I. Lenin. The organization had 3,500 members across the state and a few volunteers that organized in cities such as Cincinnati and Akron. Two members were in the office when the reporter visited, and while the members said they supported the protests at Euclid Beach, they seemed perplexed that the reporter asked what their role was in organizing the actions.

Others chimed in that the Humphrey Company's red-baiting was a smoke screen to distract people from the racial discrimination that drove these violent incidents. Near the end of 1946, Albert Luster's assault-and-battery case against Julius Vago finally went to trial. An all-women jury, including two African Americans, heard the case. The prosecutor framed the incident simply: Luster went to the park. He was told to leave. After Luster exchanged words with Vago, the park guard attacked him with a nightstick, fracturing his skull and causing profuse bleeding from the face.

Vago insisted he never struck Luster and only acted in self-defense. His lawyer argued that Luster came to the park looking for trouble, and as proof he pointed to Luster's having left his wife at home that evening. Vago alleged that Luster had called him a Nazi and had come toward Vago, only to grow dizzy and fall suddenly—Vago's feeble attempt to explain Luster's injuries. In less than an hour, the jurors handed in their verdict: Vago was guilty of assault and battery.

While Luster, Morrow, and others pressed their cases in the courtroom, Councilman Carr pushed to get his ordinance before the full council. When the council returned to the matter, the opposition, almost all from white westside wards, had found a new tactic against the measure: They claimed the legislation was unfair because it only focused on amusement parks and not all public spaces.

The dissenters cannily moved to expand the scope of the bill in order to defeat it. Councilman Carr knew he didn't have the votes to pass a broadly defined bill, so he withdrew it, went back to his allies on the board and retooled his approach. Carr's ordinance made it through committee to go before the full council in early 1947. The westsiders again proposed an amendment that would expand the measure to include all public businesses. This time council member Harold T. Gassaway stood and addressed the proposal:

"This is the first time in the history of Cleveland that we have ever had the development of an armed guard for the forces of discrimination. Whenever a super-government sets itself up in our community and brings armed guards and brutal assaults upon our citizens, it is the duty of this council to put a stop to it. Gentlemen, we have just finished fighting a war for democracy, and in a democracy we can't have two kinds of citizenship—there is only one kind for all citizens, and that is first-class citizenship."

The crowd in attendance cheered, then quickly hushed when Mayor Thomas Burke rose to speak. The mayor had quietly, tepidly, supported the ordinance to date, but few knew if he would throw his political weight behind it at this crucial moment. If Burke supported the ordinance and rejected the proposed amendment, many council members were likely to follow suit. All eyes turned to him.

"Gentlemen, I am opposed to the amendment and I am in favor of the Carr Ordinance," Burke said. "I am opposed to this amendment because we do not have discrimination in bowling alleys and theaters and restaurants and other places. My decision in this matter has been most difficult, but the thing that has assisted me most in making up my mind has been the fact that at no time has the management of the amusement park denied that they discriminate ... Gentlemen, we have been left with no choice."

The room burst into cheers once again. The westside councilmen withdrew their amendment and a vote was taken. Twenty-three voted in favor of the Euclid Beach Ordinance and eight were opposed. The room erupted a third time. Gassaway, Carr, and others who had worked for six months on the measure smiled with relief.

"Monday, February 17 will go down in history as a red-letter day for democracy in a liberal city," exclaimed the *Cleveland Call & Post*. "The 40-year reign of a super-government at Euclid Beach has ended with a 23–8 vote in favor of the Carr Ordinance." In May, Euclid Beach opened for the season. The dance pavilion and bathing beach hadn't opened yet, but there were no reports that week of anyone being denied admittance to the roller rink.

CHAPTER 15

Undefeated

Los Angeles Memorial Coliseum
Los Angeles, California

1939

KENNY WASHINGTON, WOODY STRODE, AND THE REST of the UCLA
Bruins recovered from the disappointment of losing to USC in the
penultimate game of the 1937 season. UCLA lost several key seniors
and started 1938 inconsistently. After splitting the first four games, they
went on a three-game conference winning streak, during which they shut
out Idaho, Stanford, and Washington State.

With a 5-2 record, the Bruins stood in third in the conference behind
unbeaten California and USC, who was 6-1. UCLA needed some help in
the last few games to have a chance at the conference title. Then they stumbled on their own. The Bruins lost a close one to #14 Wisconsin, then got
blown out by their crosstown rivals, 42–7.

Their disappointment was assuaged somewhat by the team's making its
first bowl game, the Pineapple Bowl (also referred to as the Poi Bowl),
against the University of Hawai'i in Honolulu. The trip was notable more
for what happened off the field than for the game itself, which UCLA won
handily, 42–7. There, Woody Strode met his future wife, Princess Luana.

After the 1938 season, longtime UCLA head coach Bill Spaulding retired
and assistant Edwin "Babe" Horrell took over. One of the biggest challenges
for Horrell coming into the 1939 season was how to balance the offense
between his unquestioned star at left halfback—Washington—and a heavily
recruited junior college transfer named Jackie Robinson. Robinson had run
circles around the competition at Pasadena Junior College, and Bruins fans

wondered how the new coach would utilize the newcomer's dazzling speed and elusiveness.

Horrell installed Robinson at right halfback and used him as a man-in-motion. Today, *motion* usually describes a back or receiver running parallel to the line of scrimmage and turning upfield at the snap. In the Carlisle wing, the version of the single wing that UCLA ran at the time, the right halfback stood wide right but just behind the line of scrimmage. The ball would most often be snapped back to the left halfback, Washington. Robinson's motion was not upfield but a circle back from the line, a shorter version of a modern-day wide receiver running a reverse.

This set up a number of options for Washington. He could hand the ball to Robinson heading to the left. He could fake a handoff and go right himself. He could fake and hand the ball to the fullback plowing straight ahead. Or he could drop back to pass, sometimes looking for Robinson breaking upfield on the outside. The dual threat of Robinson and Washington rattled defenses and boosted both of their numbers. Washington's rushing average climbed to five yards per carry, and Robinson, who was used as much as a decoy as a ballcarrier, posted an astounding 12.2 yards per carry. The Bruins ripped off five wins and a tie to start the 1939 season. They held on for two more ties and a win to set up a showdown in their final game against rival USC, also undefeated. It was the first time in history that both teams were ranked in the top 10, with UCLA ninth and USC third.

Days before the clash of undefeated Los Angeles football powers, the newswires announced a bushel of various All-America lists from different papers and press syndicates. Heisman Trophy winner Nile Kinnick from Iowa and Michigan's Tom Harmon swept many of the first-team halfback spots. Kenny Washington was named second team on five lists. The Central Press Association's All-America list named Washington's USC counterpart, Grenville Lansdell, to the first team over Washington. This sparked accusations of racism by local and national commentators alike. Lansdell trailed Washington, Harmon, and Kinnick in total yardage. The snub further fueled Bruin enmity for the Trojans.

Not that the game needed additional hype. The winner of the December 9 tilt would go to the Rose Bowl, with a shot at the national title. A local paper described the rivalry as a battle between social classes. "In the case of USC, the collegiate patrician with just a touch of condescension in its attitude of the other, and UCLA, the alleged upstart and social climber, it's the kind of thing well calculated to make the feuds of the Hatfields and the

McCoys pale and insipid, by contrast . . . Everything (and everybody) seems momentarily at the point of violence, real or merely oral."

The rivalry had a racial component as well. UCLA featured three African American stars in Washington, Strode, and Robinson, while a fourth African American, Ray Bartlett, was a key reserve. This made UCLA the "blackest" of mainstream college teams. USC had no black players. The 1939 UCLA team was followed coast-to-coast by African American newspapers from the *Chicago Defender* to the *Baltimore Afro-American*. In November, Sam Lacy, sports editor of the *Washington Tribune*, wrote that he would "give anything . . . to see the Los Angeles lads trim the wicks of the lamps of their Trojan rivals."

The stakes were such that the teams both prepared in secret that week, for fear of tipping off their plans. Each school deployed spies armed with binoculars and notebooks to scope out the opponent's closed practices. Campus guards periodically flushed them from the bushes near each squad's practice field. Several UCLA students caught two USC men in Westwood and took them to fraternity row, where they were painted blue and gold then sent home.

Each school's pep club hosted a bonfire in the days before the game. Students grabbed crates from behind grocery stores, stole wooden outhouses from construction sites, and collected brush in the nearby hills to fuel the flames. UCLA spies reported that USC's pep squad had hung and burned straw figures of the Bruins' three black starters.

The evening before the game, Woody Strode left his parents' home at 34th and Central Avenue and drove his Model T to Lincoln Heights to pick up Washington, as he had done so many times before. Strode pulled up to the Washington house. Inside, the hands that cradled UCLA's Rose Bowl aspirations were grudgingly threading popcorn for the family Christmas tree. Washington smiled when he saw Strode in the doorway. He handed the popcorn string to his grandmother Susie, grabbed his bag, and ran to the car.

They flipped a coin to see who would crank the engine. Strode lost. He challenged Washington to two out of three, to no avail. Strode cranked the car and they headed to Westwood. They drove down Wilshire with the top down, the afternoon dipping into dusk. They laughed as they roared past department stores with mannequins flaunting holiday finery in the windows. "There was no nervousness, no fear, only exhilaration," Strode remembered. "The city of Los Angeles put the spotlight on us, and that was a very prideful feeling."

They met their teammates at Kerckhoff Hall on campus and loaded onto a bus that would take them to the Beverly Hills Hotel, a pink-and-green palace favored by the brightest of Hollywood stars, and the setting for the pregame chat with the press. Strode, Washington, Robinson, Leo Cantor, and Ned Mathews—the whole Bruin backfield plus Strode—sat in the Polo Lounge decked out in silk shirts, gabardine trousers, and leather shoes. They answered reporters' questions about the game while sipping water and snacking on sliced apples.

That core group spent time together outside of team events, making a tradition of going to Strode's favorite deli in Boyle Heights the Friday night before games. For the most part when the UCLA players were together, they had fun. Some of the laughter at practice was at the expense of the team's two biggest stars. Robinson was pigeon-toed and Washington knock-kneed, so when they ran next to each other during warmups or drills, other players who saw them straight on were forced to hide their laughter or risk getting popped extra hard by the two during scrimmages.

Robinson didn't socialize as frequently as some teammates. The football star who arrived at UCLA was not the same man the country would see eight years later in a Brooklyn Dodgers uniform. The Robinson who attended UCLA was described as sometimes sullen and other times fiery and confrontational. Strode and Washington figured it was because Jackie's older brother, Frank, had died in a motorcycle accident shortly before Robinson came to Westwood. Robinson's guardedness was exacerbated by the constant racism his family faced at home in Pasadena.

Before Robinson even stepped onto a field at UCLA, he was involved in an incident. While Robinson was driving in Los Angeles, a group of men pulled up alongside his car and called him names. One version of the story held that Robinson stepped out of his car and struck one of the men. Another version claimed someone else in Robinson's car responded to the racist taunting and Robinson played peacemaker. Whatever happened tarnished Robinson in the view of many Bruin fans.

Regardless of his standing in the eyes of the public, Robinson had a target on his back as far as opponents were concerned. An ex-teammate remembered a game against a Southern team. Robinson was a kick returner, and when the opponent kicked off the players on that team who were supposed to track the ball and tackle whoever caught it instead ignored where the ball went and ran straight for Robinson, burying him under a pile of people. It didn't happen just once, either, but each time they kicked off. The 1940

UCLA yearbook includes a photo of Robinson during a game against Stanford. A defender is tackling Robinson—and also slugging him in the face. As the shutter clicked, the Stanford man's fist smashed into Robinson's cheek, creating a lasting image of the challenges Robinson, and his black teammates, had to confront.

Once Robinson and the rest of the UCLA players in the Polo Lounge had finished answering reporters' questions about the upcoming clash with USC, they retired to their rooms. Washington called his uncle Rocky and then went to bed. Game day dawned cool and overcast. The team boarded the bus again and rode to the Coliseum, arriving just after ten in the morning, four hours before kickoff.

The stadium was quiet, with only the occasional footfalls of concession workers arriving. The players warmed up in the nearly empty concrete bowl, then returned to the locker room to finish their preparations. As they did, the Coliseum began to wake up. Workers opened food stalls, grease sputtered, peanut men plugged snacks into their trays, and ticket takers fanned out to their appointed stations like sentries around a castle.

Underneath the stands Washington and Strode sat next to each other, waiting for the trainer to tape their ankles. Both felt the vibration of people rushing to their seats.

With his eyes looking toward the ceiling, Washington asked Strode, "You nervous?"

"No way," Strode said, shaking out his legs while also glancing upward. "How about you?"

"Nope." Washington shook his head. "I just want to get this thing started."

As Strode dropped his gaze, he saw Washington cross himself.

Once taped, they yanked on their pants and shrugged into their shoulder pads. Next came the jerseys and cleats. Finally, each man unfolded his helmet, put it on, and pulled the strap tight under his chin. Spikes clattered on the concrete as the team clustered under the edge of the stands. One guy playfully pushed another, and soon everyone was pinballing off one another and also the walls of the corridor, anxious to take the field.

They got the signal and raced into the overcast day. The fans roared, 103,303 strong, screaming for one side or the other. This being Los Angeles, celebrities were on hand. Douglas Fairbanks Sr. was there, as were Jane Wyman and other Hollywood stars. But nobody paid them much attention; all eyes focused on the field.

The student sections faced one another across the wide part of the oval. Yell leaders led cheers against the other team and coordinated card stunts where hundreds of students would hold up colored placards on cue to create images almost as tall as the Coliseum itself. The school bands took turns prancing across the turf. Once the gold breastplates and crimson plumage of the Trojan band had left the field, the players grouped together for a last word from their captains.

Then the teams lined up for the opening kickoff, and more excitement crackled through the stadium. The ball rocketed into the sky and the crowd roared. For the players the cheers soon receded, replaced by the thud of bodies colliding and the shouts of teammates. The Trojans got the ball first and drove down the field. Lansdell was the main ballcarrier, tallying 39 rushing yards on the drive—but fumbling the ball on the UCLA 19-yard line. The Bruins recovered. Then Washington promptly gave the ball back two plays later with a fumble of his own.

Several plays later, the Trojans stood just outside the UCLA 10-yard line. Lansdell got the call again. He took a step inside, then shot outside, angling for the end zone. Robinson sliced across the field and launched himself at the Trojan back. When he hit Lansdell, the ball rocketed off Lansdell's chest and into the end zone. It bounced slowly toward the corner, and bodies converged on it. Strode got there first and picked it up. He was hit as he ran the ball out, but broke free at the 10-yard line. Strode saw only green in front of him, but USC's Bob Hoffman tripped him from behind. The return was called back, though, and the play ruled a touchback. The Bruins took over at the 20-yard line.

The teams traded possessions, with Washington quelling a Trojan drive with an interception. Several times UCLA threatened to break off a long play, but none came to fruition. The teams went into halftime scoreless.

Rocky Washington, who attended almost all of Kenny's games, was waiting for Kenny near the locker room. He grabbed his nephew's shoulder and said, "A couple of bad breaks and you start playing scared. You've got to open up, start throwing the ball downfield. You're in a great position to win this game, but you've got to take the fight to them!"

Washington stared ahead and nodded. Some of his teammates had heard Rocky's pep talk and agreed. UCLA came out throwing in the second half, knocking the Trojans back. Washington barely missed on two long passes to Robinson. He then connected with Bob Simpson on a 44-yard pass, but the referee ruled Simpson hadn't gotten his foot down in bounds. The clock ticked down to six minutes left.

The Bruins next got the ball on their own 20-yard line. Robinson ran around right end for 13 yards. Washington followed with a rush to the left for nine yards. Two plays later, Washington hit end Don MacPherson at the Trojan 38-yard line. Then he fired to Robinson at the 26 for another first down.

USC called a time-out to regroup its shaky defense. But the Trojans didn't have any time-outs left and were penalized five yards for the mistake. Several short runs yielded a handful of yards. Washington hit Strode for a completion at the 15-yard line, and then tossed a short pass to Mathews to the 10. Washington plunged into the line for two, and Cantor rumbled for 4. UCLA had a first and goal at the USC four-yard line.

On first down, quarterback Ned Mathews called for a run to the left by Washington, but the Trojan line stopped it for no gain. Next, Mathews sent fullback Leo Cantor to the right. A hole opened and Cantor bulled forward, only to get stoned at the two-yard line by Bob Hoffman. Cantor was injured but staggered to his feet for the next play. Hoping to catch USC off guard, Mathews called the same play again. This time the Trojan line dropped the hobbled Cantor at the four-yard line.

Fourth and goal. Only four minutes left in the game, and the season. A Rose Bowl bid on the line. "The situation didn't even brusquely demand a field goal try," a Los Angeles Examiner columnist wrote. "It fairly shrieked for it, bellowed, trumpeted, clamored, screamed and bleated almost obscenely in a shrill, insensate falsetto."

Guard John Frawley did most of the placekicking for UCLA that season. He hadn't attempted a field goal all year but had converted seven of 12 extra points, an extra point being roughly the same distance as a field goal attempt from where the Bruins sat. Mathews ducked into the huddle and looked around. "What do you want—six points or three?" Five favored a kick and five said go for it. Mathews cast the deciding vote: They would go for the touchdown.

The conventional call would have been an end run by Robinson or an inside run by Washington. Instead Mathews called a trick play. Washington would take the snap, and Mathews, Cantor, and Robinson would all run left. Strode would also run a route to the left. Washington would then freeze and throw the ball the other way to end Don MacPherson, who would hopefully stand unguarded in the right side of the end zone.

The play unfurled. Washington drifted left, as did the decoys. He planted and threw across the field. Only one Trojan defender, Bob Robertson, had noticed MacPherson angling to the right corner, and Robertson bore down on the end as the ball left Washington's hand. To many Bruin fans, the throw seemed to float toward its target. The pass reached MacPherson's fingertips just as Robertson crashed into him, knocking the ball to the ground.

The Trojans took over possession and satisfied themselves with running out the clock. Given USC's higher ranking, the Trojans would go to the Rose Bowl bid if the game ended in a tie.

With 15 seconds left to play, Coach Horrell took Washington out. The senior halfback turned toward the sideline as thunderous applause cascaded down from every row and reverberated around the stadium. His walk off the field resembled a royal visit more than a player leaving the game. Nearly every Trojan on the field, and several from their bench, came over to shake Washington's hand or slap him on the back.

In the stands, several fans, including Jane Wyman, cried. Washington's expression betrayed little emotion, his face stoic and his mouth set. He gamely shook hands with his opponents even as disappointment settled in his chest. At last he crossed the sideline, stopping briefly on the other side of the chalky stripe.

Prior to the contest, a *Los Angeles Times* columnist had written, "With Saturday's game, an era that has brought the Bruins greater glory than any other will come to an end. The era spans the college days of Kenneth S. Washington, who this year has carried the Bruins undefeated to their last game of the season for the first time in history.

"Never before has UCLA battled through a season with fewer than two defeats. Transferring his torch of glory to Jackie Robinson, another star Negro back, Washington will leave behind him a record Bruins backs can look to for inspiration for years to come." Indeed, Washington's career rushing mark of 1,914 yards would stand as a school record for thirty-four years. After the game, the UCLA players trudged down the tunnel to the locker room. There they quietly answered questions from the press as they unlaced their cleats and peeled off their uniforms. They showered, dressed silently, and boarded the bus.

When they got back to campus, rain had begun to fall and the streetlights glittered off the sidewalk. Strode was angry. Not about the game, but because he hadn't put the top up on the car. The seats were wet and cold.

Neither Washington nor Strode said much as they drove back down Wilshire Boulevard.

"I guess we realized one of the most exciting times in our lives had come and gone," Strode later wrote. Rocky Washington was waiting outside the Washingtons' front door when they turned onto Avenue Nineteen. Kenny got out, and Rocky put his arm around his nephew as they walked inside.

On the same day as the USC-UCLA game, the NFL held its annual draft. The Chicago Cardinals picked Tennessee's George Cafego first. The New York Giants selected USC's Grenny Lansdell at the end of the first round, and the Brooklyn Dodgers grabbed Nile Kinnick in the second. Tom Harmon returned to Michigan for his senior year. Nine USC players were drafted. Neither Strode nor Washington was picked. This was the fifth year of the league's draft, and no black players had ever been selected.

Later Strode mused, "Football is so much like life. Every time you get knocked down, you wonder if you want to get up. Sometimes you wonder, 'Is this worth it?' But you pick yourself up, dust yourself off, and keep on going."

CHAPTER 16

Jackie

Ebbets Field
Brooklyn, New York

1947

NOT LONG AFTER KENNY WASHINGTON AND Woody Strode finished the 1946 season with the Los Angeles Rams, speculation swirled around their former college teammate Jackie Robinson. The twenty-seven-year-old infielder had dominated the International League as the star of the Montreal Royals. In his first game, he blasted four hits, including a three-run homer, and stole 2 bases. He continued to hit and to run and led the league with a .349 batting average. The Royals clinched the top spot in the International League with a 100-54 record.

The Royals faced the Louisville Colonels of the American Association in what was called the Little World Series or Junior World Series, the winner being considered the top minor league squad in North America. Game one was in Louisville, the farthest south the Royals would play during the regular or postseason. The Colonel starting pitcher wasted no time in throwing at Jackie, making him dive to the dirt. The fans cheered. Robinson struggled at the plate, but Montreal won the first game, 7–5. Robinson again struggled in game two, going hitless in two at bats. The Colonels tied the series with a 3–0 victory. Louisville slammed the Royals in the next game and won 15–6. Robinson did get his first hit and scored two runs.

The series then moved to Montreal, and the Royals fans were ready. They were incensed by how the Kentucky fans had treated Robinson. During game four in Montreal the 16,000 in attendance booed every Colonel as soon as he stepped out of the dugout. Heading into the bottom of the ninth, the Royal trailed 5–3 to the pitcher who had thrown at Robinson in game one. This time he gave up a bases-loaded walk to tie the game, and Robinson smacked a game-winning hit in the bottom of the 10th inning. The series was tied 2-2.

In game five Robinson notched a single, a double, and a triple in Montreal's win, bringing them to the brink of the Little World Series title. Robinson got another two hits in the title-clinching win. After the game, the nearly 20,000 fans circled the home dugout clamoring for Robinson and singing, "*Il a gagné ses épaulettes*" (He won his bars).

Black newspapers throughout the United States had followed Robinson's every game during the minor league season. Observers buzzed that he had proven himself ready for the major leagues and could well be called up to the Dodgers in the spring. Others staunchly denied he would. Cleveland fireballer Bob Feller pitched against Robinson while on a barnstorming tour that pitted Feller and white stars such as Stan Musial against black stars such as Satchel Paige and Robinson. Feller dismissed Robinson and said he was too muscular to handle major league pitching. During a barn-storming matchup the next year, Jackie smacked two hits off Feller.

In March 1947, Robinson and some of the other Royals opened spring training with the big league club in Daytona Beach. Fans and critics intently dissected his performance in every game, debating the merits of his play and constantly monitoring his chances of breaking camp with the Dodgers.

Dodgers general manager Branch Rickey was already laying plans for Robinson's eventual promotion. Several of the Southern-born players on the Dodgers had circulated a petition to protest Robinson's being named to the club. Rickey threatened to trade anyone unwilling to play with Robinson. Rickey also met with community leaders of Brooklyn's black middle class: teachers, ministers, newspapermen, and a judge. He wanted their help in coaching black fans to behave, for fear that "overzealous" fan reactions might cause controversy or provoke racial confrontations with white fans.

In a paternal and condescending tone typical of the era's race relations, Rickey told the black Brooklynites that the "biggest threat to [Robinson's success] . . . is the Negro people themselves." He urged them to go to their social clubs and congregations and spread the message for black fans not to drink at the games nor boast too loudly about Robinson or cheer opponents' failures. Many signed on to Rickey's campaign, with some taking exception at a request to tell grown people how they should behave in public. Rickey disseminated his message through black newspapers as well and pushed his contacts in black communities to spread the campaign to other National League cities where Robinson might soon play.

With his preparations complete and the team having returned to Brooklyn from spring training, Rickey made the announcement: On April 10, 1947, the Dodgers bought Robinson's contract from the Royals. He'd be coming to New York. In his debut against Boston on April 15, 1947, the rookie reached first on a sacrifice bunt and scored in the bottom of the seventh inning. Three days later the Brooklyn Dodgers played the New York Giants at the Polo Grounds, drawing 37,000 fans who saw Robinson hit his first major league home run. The following day he had three hits in a loss.

The Dodgers returned to Brooklyn for a home stand against the Philadelphia Phillies. Phillies manager Ben Chapman, an Alabaman, ordered his team to lob any and every racist taunt they could think of at Robinson, supposedly "to see if he could take it." One Phillie mocked Robinson's physical attributes, while another described in detail the sores and diseases Robinson's teammates would get if they used the same towel or comb as Robinson. Players in the Philadelphia dugout held their bats like machine guns and made rat-a-tat sounds while pointing them at Robinson. Baseball commissioner Happy Chandler later told the Phillies to stop the verbal abuse, but the damage was done.

Publicly, Robinson downplayed the racism as a non-distraction that didn't bother him, but years later he admitted otherwise. "This day of all the unpleasant days in my life brought me nearer to cracking up than I have ever been," he wrote of the incident with the Phillies. Robinson confessed that he had been sorely tempted to say to hell with Branch Rickey's "noble experiment" and "stride over to that Phillies dugout, grab one of those white sons of bitches and smash his teeth with my despised black fist."

Taunting was only one of the problems Robinson encountered. Several prominent members of the St. Louis Cardinals organized a player boycott of a game against the Dodgers. As the Dodgers headed out on a road trip, Robinson fell into a hitting slump. Those opposed to integration were quick to jump on any struggle of Robinson's to argue he and other black players couldn't compete in the major leagues. But the question of whether

Robinson belonged had already been answered for many men within base-ball. Managers acknowledged that Robinson could play and would likely stick with the Dodgers. He soon broke his slump and went on a hitting streak. By the end of June, Robinson was batting .315, led the league in stolen bases, and ranked second in runs scored.

Kenny Washington and Woody Strode followed Jackie's progress and cheered his success, as did millions of black fans across the country. They also marveled at how their college teammate had changed. "Those of us who knew Jackie Robinson didn't believe he could do it," Strode wrote, referring to Robinson's promise to Branch Rickey that he wouldn't retaliate for any racist abuse. The Jackie they knew from UCLA had a fiery temper and wasn't one to turn the other cheek. But, they figured, Robinson's desire to be the best overcame his desire to defend himself. "Kenny and I discussed that many times," Strode wrote. "They'd have a sign on the locker room saying 'NO N— ALLOWED!' then he'd go out and play baseball. I don't think Kenny and I could have done that."

As the summer progressed, Robinson continued to produce. So his detractors found other aspects of his game to criticize, such as his aggres-sive base running, a style of play common in the Negro leagues but less familiar in the American or National Leagues. Rivals accused Robinson of grandstanding and showing up opponents when he stole bases, their anger likely exacerbated by him being a black man daring to do so, and succeeding.

Opponents, predictably, tested Jackie. He was hit by pitches more than any other player in 1947. Robinson's quick reflexes kept him from getting plunked as much as he might have, although not for a lack of effort by opposing pitchers. A year later, the man who'd bear the brunt of their efforts was the Dodgers' second black star, catcher Roy Campanella. Pitchers who couldn't hit Robinson sometimes took their frustrations out on Campanella, who was not nearly as quick at dodging fastballs.

The Dodgers moved Robinson from his natural defensive position of second base to the less demanding position of first base when the team called him up. This may have been done in an effort to protect Robinson from opponents who might barrel into him at second, ostensibly to break up a double play. Second basemen and shortstops often caught the business end of a base runner's spikes, and not always by accident.

But even shifting Robinson to first could not protect him. Suddenly players were sliding feetfirst into the bag when trying to beat out an infield hit. Robinson ended many a game with bloody gashes halfway up his calves and shins.

Robinson was a lightning rod figure in national news, but he experienced 1947 as profoundly isolating. The Dodgers, unlike the Rams and the Browns, did not sign two black players in their first season of integration. Instead, Branch Rickey had black sportswriter Wendell Smith travel with the team and room with Robinson on the road. In the clubhouse, Robinson was alone. The first few days with the Dodgers were awkward and tense. He didn't want to force his presence on anyone, so he sat alone until teammates asked him to join them. That, by both personality and experience, he was guarded and slow to engage didn't help.

Often on the road Robinson and Smith were forced to stay in separate lodging, and the team could not socialize freely. The one place most players could depend on for camaraderie and support, the field, was even worse. Several Southern teammates on the Dodgers explained to Robinson that during warm-ups and games they couldn't risk standing near the Brooklyn infielder.

Baseball salaries were not enough to ensure permanent financial security in 1947. Many players had off-season jobs and side gigs, and a good number of the Southern players cashed in on their fame by nominally running a gas station, feed store, or restaurant back in their hometown. Southern-born major leaguers actively avoided Robinson anytime a camera might catch them for fear that a picture of them in proximity to Robinson could earn them a reputation as an integrationist and cost them business back home.

Dynamics within the clubhouse were the first to warm. Within six weeks the twenty-eight-year-old rookie was playing cards with and eating with a few of the Dodgers. Rachel Robinson, Jackie's wife, originally sat in the stands alone while watching her husband play. But eventually one of the white wives invited her down to the area where Dodger spouses regularly congregated after a game. The woman introduced Rachel to the others, and soon she was at least partially included in the sorority of baseball wives.

These small efforts didn't make Jackie's situation easy, but they helped make it slightly more tolerable. Robinson's Dodger teammates also eventually rallied around him in the face of opponents vitriol. His presence was also good business for the team, as black and white fans came in droves to see him. Even on the road, Brooklyn spurred a small attendance boom in National League towns whenever the team came to play.

Wendell Smith had been a key cog in convincing Rickey to sign Robinson. Smith talked up the former UCLA Bruin as the ideal player to break the color line: Robinson had played with whites, gone to college, and served in the Army during the war. The Negro leagues had a handful of bigger stars, notably Josh Gibson and Satchel Paige, but few with Robinson's specific experiences. Thus Robinson was chosen as much for his experience living with and working alongside whites as for his considerable baseball talent. Smith's special access to Robinson as his roommate also provided a weekly scoop of mammoth proportions for the journalist and his paper, the *Baltimore Afro-American*.

Smith and many other black writers echoed Rickey's view that it was best for one player to be the focal point of the "noble experiment." This put tremendous pressure on Robinson as the apparent test case for his race's future in big league baseball. Thankfully, Robinson was not alone for long. Eleven weeks after Robinson's major league debut, the Cleveland American League team inked Larry Doby.

The same year Branch Rickey signed Robinson to the Montreal Royals, he also signed Roy Campanella and Don Newcombe to the Class B Nashua Dodgers. The two would join Robinson in Brooklyn in 1948 and 1949, respectively. (Dan Bankhead made four appearances for the Dodgers in 1947 but did not pitch again in the majors until 1950.) Even with the call-up of Doby in the summer of 1947, the narrative of Robinson as the sole trail-blazer stuck. Robinson's success in the major leagues in 1947 only raised the stakes.

A worry that Robinson might fail and thus ruin the chances for other black players weighed heavily on some. Per Rickey's dubious crusade to manage black reactions to Jackie, many voices in the black press and business community called for subdued reactions to Robinson's success or failure on the field. They also advised black fans to dress well when attending a game. At National League parks that year, white fans in short sleeves and caps were seen standing in line at the turnstiles near black families dressed in their Sunday best, including suits, gleaming leather shoes, dresses, and hats. Indeed, some black fans did compare witnessing Robinson play to something akin to a religious experience.

At the end of the 1947 season, Robinson collected Rookie of the Year honors, as voted by the Baseball Writers' Association of America. White players and pundits who had previously said Robinson would never make it had no choice but to admit he had.

CHAPTER 17

Cleveland's Year

Cleveland Municipal Stadium
Cleveland, Ohio

1948

NINETEEN FORTY-EIGHT WOULD BE THE GREATEST year in Cleveland sports history. The city's beloved baseball team reached the World Series, powered by star pitcher Bob Feller and slugger Larry Doby, the man who broke the color barrier in the American League. Doby debuted for Cleveland less than three months after Jackie Robinson's first game as a Dodger. Like Kenny Washington and Woody Strode, Doby was famous in his day, but as time passed, the heroic narrative of Jackie Robinson overshadowed Doby's legacy.

After Branch Rickey promoted Robinson to the Dodgers, fans and press speculated what team would integrate next. Cleveland was at the top of their lists. Like Rickey, Cleveland owner Bill Veeck prepared for months before deciding on Larry Doby. Veeck hired a scout to cover the Negro leagues, tracking not just which players hit well but who didn't smoke, drink, or curse. Few white men in baseball could meet those expectations and none were expected to, but Larry Doby did.

Doby grew up in South Carolina and New Jersey and served in World War II. (He had also trained at Great Lakes Naval Training Station. That a lot of black military men went through Great Lakes was no accident. The Navy chose Great Lakes as the location for their first training classes for African American recruits. At the time, the Navy was segregated, so Camp Robert Smalls was the home of the black trainees on base. By the end of the war, Great Lakes had integrated their classes and training facilities.)

The war had interrupted Doby's playing for Abe and Effa Manley's Newark Eagles in the Negro National League. In 1946, while Jackie Robinson helped the Montreal Royals to a Little World Series title, Doby and teammate Monte Irvin led the Eagles to a Negro World Series show-down with Satchel Paige and the Kansas City Monarchs. Jackie Robinson had played for the Monarchs before Branch Rickey signed him to the Royals. The Monarchs hadn't missed him much, though, as Willard Brown and Buck O'Neil picked up the slack offensively, and Paige had recovered from an injury and returned to all-star pitching form.

The series went the full seven games, and the Eagles won the last game with a two-out double in the bottom of the eighth to eke out a 3–2 victory. The black press noted a smattering of white scouts from major league teams in the stands throughout the series. Doby and other players were heartened by the signing of Robinson, but owners of Negro league fran-chises had more mixed feelings. They wanted to see their players do well, but they feared the potential talent drain on their teams, and for the viability of their leagues, if more black players were signed by previously all-white teams.

Effa Manley, the only female team executive in any sports league, was vocal in her suspicions of Branch Rickey's motives. She said Rickey's signing of Jackie Robinson was driven more by economics—the desire to sell more tickets—than by a commitment to civil rights or racial equality. She also criticized him for signing Robinson without compensating his former club, the Monarchs.

Just a few years earlier, white scouts couldn't be bothered to watch black teams, and many dismissed the players' skills as not worth their time. Now handfuls of them attended numerous Negro league games with the hopes of finding the "next Jackie Robinson." Some of their general managers saw Negro league players as a way to boost attendance while keeping costs low. The Negro leagues didn't have as rigid agreements around player contracts, salaries, and player movement as Major League Baseball had. But it also likely took some owners by surprise when, after years of disinterest in black players, the major league teams were not only scouting but soon poaching black players.

Cleveland's Bill Veeck had a scout following Doby's performance early in the 1947 season. Doby started the year pounding extra-base hits, and through 36 games he led the Negro National League in homers, doubles, and runs batted in. Veeck made his move. Effa Manley demanded compensation, and on July 3, Veeck offered her $10,000 to buy out Doby's Newark contract.

After announcing the signing, Veeck had player-manager Lou Boudreau make the introductions to the team. For the remainder of the season, Doby was used mainly as a pinch hitter late in games, notching five hits in 32 at bats. He had mostly played infield for the Newark Eagles, but during the off-season Cleveland converted him to an outfielder.

In 1948, Cleveland signed Satchel Paige, Doby's ex-rival and legendary forty-two-ish-year-old pitcher. Paige had also been a rival of new teammate Bob Feller's when they had previously barnstormed together in the off-season. Feller had sparked some ire back in 1946 when the *Sporting News* asked whether any of his black opponents were big league material. "Haven't seen one—not one," Feller said. "Maybe Paige when he was young. When you name him, you're done."

Feller's stance changed over the years, though it's unclear if that was due to having Doby on his team or because he simply didn't want the criticism that came from voicing that opinion, or perhaps he had another reason entirely.

Doby split time between center and right field and batted .301 for the season, holding his own among the major league veterans, finishing fifth on the team in most offensive statistical categories. He also saved his best for last. In a tight pennant race against the Boston Red Sox, Doby scorched the ball for a .375 average in the season's final month, which helped Cleveland go 20-6 in September. The two teams wound up tied, and Cleveland won a single-game playoff 8–3 to advance to the World Series, which they hadn't won since 1920.

In the championship round, Cleveland would face Boston's National League club—which like Cleveland bore a Native American mascot name. The first two games were played in Boston. In the first one, Boston's 24-game winner Johnny Sain outdueled Cleveland star Bob Feller, 1–0. Doby notched a leadoff single off Sain in the sixth inning but was stranded on the bases. In the second game, Doby got two hits off Warren Spahn, including an RBI single, and Cleveland won 4–1. The series shifted to Cleveland tied at one game apiece. Clevelanders packed cavernous Municipal Stadium. Nearly a quarter million fans in total attended the three games in Ohio.

In Cleveland's 2–0 win in game three, Doby mustered a hit and a walk. In the fourth contest, the Tribe faced Sain again, a rematch Doby relished.

He knew he could hit the curveballer after getting two hits off him in game one. Lou Boudreau put Cleveland up 1–0 in the first inning with an RBI double. Doby came up with two outs in the top of the third. On a 1-0 count, Sain delivered. "The pitch fooled me," Doby told the *Call & Post*. "It was a slow curve, just a little outside, but I was able to snap my wrists into it. It felt good!" Four hundred and twenty feet of good, sailing over the wall in right center. This upped Cleveland's lead to 2–0, and their starting pitcher, Steve Gromek, held on to the lead. He gave up a homer in the seventh but otherwise stayed out of trouble to clinch the 2–1 win.

The next day's *Cleveland Plain Dealer* ran a photo of Gromek and Doby on the paper's front page. The two were in the locker room after the game. Gromek had thrown his arms around Doby's neck, pulling him close while screaming with joy. Doby had his hand on Gromek's shoulder and was smiling so hard his eyes were nearly closed. Doby would later say that Gromek's hug meant more to him than the home run. Decades later, many black and white fans in Cleveland remembered that photo more than the details of Cleveland's win or even the series-clinching victory in Boston a few days later. The Ohioans were world champions once again, and Doby led the team with a .318 batting average in the series.

LATER THAT FALL, THE CLEVELAND BROWNS MADE it an Ohio baseball-football sweep with their third straight AAFC championship. This time Paul Brown's men posted an undefeated record of 15-0. Motley had his best year yet, leading the AAFC in rushing with 964 yards. He averaged 6.1 yards a carry, second in the league, and was third in kick-return average with 24 yards. Graham led the AAFC in passing with 2,713 yards. To top it off, Cleveland had the league's top-rated defense as well. Paul Brown called it his best Browns team ever.

Beyond Motley, Graham, and the stingy defense, other Browns showed improvement. End Mac Speedie reached several personal bests after perfecting a curl route where he'd cut back toward the quarterback and jump in anticipation of a high pass from Graham. Speedie was six feet three inches tall and a former basketball player. His height and jumping ability, combined with his hands, made this curl play almost impossible to defend. Years later, timing plays like this would become a staple of systems such as Bill Walsh's West Coast offense, which was based in part on schemes Walsh had learned from Paul Brown much later in Brown's coaching career.

Cleveland also aggressively employed the platoon system, which was becoming more popular in pro football. In 1946, many of Cleveland's offensive stars also played defense, including quarterback Otto Graham, who played defensive halfback. Motley played linebacker as well as fullback. But by 1948 the majority of Cleveland's starting defense focused exclusively on that side of the ball. This included newcomers Tommy James and other defensive backs tasked with covering both ends and running backs as the latter emerged as bigger threats in the passing game.

Historically, defensive strategy in football was simply a reaction to what was being done on the offensive side of the ball, especially in the early years of the sport. As most teams moved from the single wing to the modern T formation, and from more rushing to passing, coaches made changes to accommodate that. As passing became more prominent, defenses positioned fewer players on the line of scrimmage and put in more defensive halfbacks or, as they would become known, defensive backs, then later safeties and cornerbacks.

New York Giants coach Steve Owen was the mastermind behind many of the defensive adaptations used to combat the modern T formation. He created a 5-3-3 defense to better cover the ends and men-in-motion used by teams such as the Los Angeles Rams and the Cleveland Browns. The prevalent defensive set in the late 1930s and early 1940s was a 6-2-3 with six linemen, two linebackers, and three defensive backs. Owen replaced a lineman with a linebacker. This allowed a middle linebacker to plug running lanes in the center of the line while one of the outside linebackers covered the halfback-in-motion coming out of the backfield.

Some squads sent both left and right halfbacks out wide as receivers. Owen then set his outside linebackers farther outside and brought two of the defensive backs closer to the line of scrimmage to clog the passing lanes for receivers coming over the middle. This was especially effective in an environment where defenders could knock players off their routes at will. Several decades would pass before defensive players were barred from bumping receivers once they got five yards past the line of scrimmage. Many of the passing routes run today wouldn't have worked back then because a receiver couldn't have gotten so far across the field without getting clocked by a defender.

Late in the 1940s, Eagles coach Earle "Greasy" Neale took the 5-3-3 a step further and created the 5-2-4. He sacrificed the middle linebacker for a fourth defensive back.

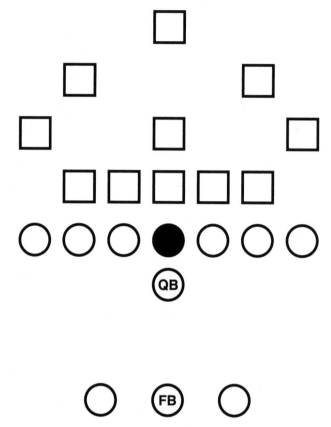

1940s T Formation Offense vs. 5-3-3 Defense
Ends tight to offensive line, backs even in backfield, five defensive linemen, three linebackers, and three defensive backs.

Sometimes two of the defensive backs would come up and serve as semi-
linebackers as well. Having four defensive backs made it possible to cover
the width of the field and mark ends on sideline routes. Neale also set his
two linebackers between the ends and tackles. This enabled the ends to line
up wider, giving offensive ends less room to get off the line and providing
the defensive ends flexibility to stop wide runs or assist on screen passes.

By the third year of the AAFC, Cleveland was clearly the class of the
league, with the New York Yankees and San Francisco 49ers a tier below. The
Browns developed their biggest rivalry with San Francisco, the only team that
could match the Browns in scoring firepower. San Francisco boasted a fright-
ening offense led by T formation wizard Frankie Albert.

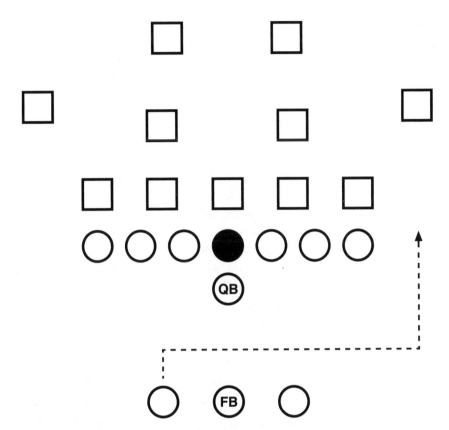

T Formation with Man-in-Motion vs. 5-2-4 "Eagle" Defense
Ends tight to offensive line, halfback goes in motion before snap. Five defensive linemen
with four defensive backs to defend against more receivers.

In 1948, the Browns and 49ers entered their first head-to-head matchup
with each team undefeated, the 49ers at 10-0 and the Browns at 9-0. In the
short history of the league, no two teams had ever met with as many total
wins and no losses between them. (The AAFC played fourteen games a
year; the NFL then played only twelve.) Nearly 83,000 fans crammed into
Municipal Stadium to watch the heavyweight battle. They were in for a
defensive struggle, with Cleveland losing players to injury on nearly every
drive. The Browns ground out a 14–7 win on two rushing touchdowns, one
by Graham and the other by halfback Dub Jones.

A West Coast Browns-49ers rematch just two weeks later featured
the offensive explosion many fans expected. Sixty thousand 49er faithful

cheered on San Francisco at Kezar Stadium on the edge of Golden Gate Park. With a win the 49ers could force a playoff between them and the Browns for the Western Conference crown. If the Browns won, they'd clinch both the conference and home field in the AAFC title game.

Graham's status had been questioned due to a leg injury suffered the previous week, but the Cleveland quarterback was in the lineup. San Francisco fumbled the opening kickoff, and on Cleveland's first offensive play Graham fired a 41-yard touchdown to Dante Lavelli. Shortly after the Browns added a Groza field goal. The 49ers came back, scoring on a two-yard plunge by rookie fullback Joe Perry. Perry and UCLA's Bob Mike were San Francisco's first two black players, signed in 1948. Despite only getting 77 carries in 1948, Perry led the league in rushing touchdowns with 10.

Frankie Albert got on track after San Francisco recovered a Motley fumble. Albert hit end Alyn Beals with a four-yard touchdown pass to give San Francisco a 14–10 lead before halftime. Early in the third quarter the 49er tandem teamed up again for a 29-yard touchdown pass to extend the San Francisco lead.

The Browns clawed back. They chugged down the field on a 73-yard drive, culminating with a six-yard touchdown pass from Graham to Motley. After a 49er punt, Graham drove the Browns down the field again, this time connecting with Lavelli for a 30-yard gain along the sideline and then hitting Dub Jones for a seven-yard touchdown pass to regain the lead, 24–21. An interception of Albert set up Cleveland's last touchdown, a 33-yarder from Graham to Edgar "Special Delivery" Jones (not to be confused with teammate Dub Jones). San Francisco scored one more touchdown on a pass from Albert to Perry, but the Browns won, 31–28. Graham also won the passing battle with Albert. The Browns signal caller tossed four touchdowns and one interception while Albert had three and one.

The AAFC Championship Game proved anticlimactic as the Browns thrashed the Buffalo Bills 49–7. This AAFC Championship Game, like the previous two, was the Marion Motley show. The fullback gashed the Bills defense for 133 yards on 14 carries and scored three touchdowns on runs of 29, 31, and five yards. This tremendous output was merely slightly above his championship game average. In 1946 he ran 98 yards on 13 carries for a 7.5-yard average and one touchdown. In 1947 he ran 109 yards with a long run of 51 yards for an average of 8.4 yards. His 1948 title game average was 9.5 yards a shot, nearly a new first down every time he ran the ball.

Despite the record-setting attendance for the Cleveland–San Francisco matchups, the AAFC's overall financial situation had turned precarious. When the AAFC had launched in 1946, it had benefited from pent-up consumer desire for entertainment in the aftermath of World War II. But competing with the NFL for players quickly raised salaries. Revenue grew steadily for the best teams: Cleveland, San Francisco, and the New York Yankees consistently sold out games. However, the weaker teams, the Chicago Rockets and Brooklyn Dodgers, continued to flounder at the gate in crowded football markets. In 1947, the Dodgers folded, joining the woeful Miami Seahawks on the AAFC's scrap heap.

From the beginning, *Chicago Tribune* sports editor and AAFC founder Arch Ward had hoped to merge the AAFC with the NFL. The league had done well comparatively, outdrawing the NFL game by game, but attendance was down across both leagues from their 1946 highs, and only the top AAFC teams had a shot at turning a profit. The older NFL weathered the revenue challenges of the late 1940s, but AAFC team owners soured quickly from the lack of return on their investment, which led to unsettling ownership shuffles.

To keep the weaker teams afloat, the AAFC reallocated top prospects from the most successful teams to those floundering at the bottom. This is how the Browns lost the rights to future 49er and New York Giant star Y. A. Tittle, whom the Browns had drafted and signed in 1948. Even that leveling effort didn't help much. The younger league would soon enter into talks with the NFL for the senior league to absorb a handful of AAFC teams.

CHAPTER 18

Good-bye

Los Angeles Coliseum
Los Angeles, California

1948

THE LOS ANGELES RAMS HIRED A NEW head coach in 1948, their third in three seasons. This time owner Dan Reeves tapped the creator of the modern T offense, Clark Shaughnessy, who had taught Frankie Albert the T at Stanford. Shaughnessy had advised the Chicago Bears on the T scheme ahead of their legendary 73–0 rout of Washington in the 1940 NFL title game. After the Bears' resounding win, pro teams scrambled to experiment with the new approach. Shaughnessy developed a reputation as a mad scientist who had a Midas touch with pro offenses.

But like many quirky geniuses in a rigid profession, Shaughnessy struggled to fit in. He was prickly and stubborn and tended to wear out his welcome quickly. He was at his most comfortable with a pencil and paper, endlessly drawing out variations of different plays. What he was least comfortable with was the coaching itself. True to form, he wouldn't lead the Rams for long. Black fans hoped that Shaughnessy might bring in more African American players, but the new coach stood pat with Kenny Washington as the sole black player on the Rams in 1948.

In their season opener, Los Angeles crushed the Detroit Lions 44–7. Washington played defense for the first time since his days as a Bruin, and according to observers he seemed to enjoy himself. He scooped up a Detroit fumble to set up the Rams' first touchdown. The veteran also made a number of crunching tackles and generally knocked Lions around the field.

After the game, Detroit's rookie end Bob Mann stopped by the Los Angeles locker room to hunt down Washington. "My pal!?" he chided Washington for a particularly aggressive hit. "I'm sorry," replied Washington, ". . . but I meant to do it," which prompted laughter from both men. Mann was the first African American player Detroit signed. A year later he led the league in receiving yards. The Lions approached Mann after the season to take a 20 percent reduction in salary. He refused, was cut, and later signed with the Green Bay Packers. Mann claimed many clubs blackballed him after he refused the salary reduction.

In their next game, the Rams spotted the Philadelphia Eagles four touchdowns but roared back to salvage a tie. The *Los Angeles Times* framed it as a battle between Kenny Washington, who led the league in rushing average, and Eagles running back Steve Van Buren, who topped the league in rushing yards. In this game, Washington led the Rams on the ground with 49 yards on 8 carries and did that in less than two quarters of work as he injured his left leg and didn't return. Van Buren notched only 28 yards on 17 carries. A bright spot for the Los Angeles offense was the play of rookie end Tom Fears, who would quickly become Bob Waterfield's favorite target in the passing game.

Washington was sidelined for the next game against the Bears and probably came back too soon, as he looked off in his return against the Green Bay Packers, fumbling three times. Coach Shaughnessy signed two extra backs to stand in for Washington and Fred Gehrke, the other starting back, who was also injured. (Gehrke, an aspiring painter, painted Ram horns on the team's helmets prior to the 1948 season. Los Angeles was the first club to sport a design on their helmets. While opponents and others in football—including Paul Brown—initially made fun of them, other teams soon followed suit.)

Washington ran little over the next few games, but in the middle of November, he posted his best day of the year, leading all ground gainers in a 52–37 victory over the New York Giants. He tallied 31 of his 76 yards on a second-quarter touchdown run in which he eluded five would-be tacklers.

Coming off his stellar 1947 season, observers wondered if Washington had anything left in the tank. He clearly did—in 1948 he once again led all Rams runners statistically. But he was thirty years old, an age when many pro football players retired, and his body had taken a beating for fourteen of those years, even if only two-plus of those were in the NFL.

Essentially, Washington's legs gave out. His left hip, knee, and ankle all troubled him in 1948. Even a minuscule falloff in speed and cutting ability could be devastating in the NFL. The defenders who had missed him before were able to trip him up or slow him down. The holes he had sliced through in the past closed as he hit them.

Few would have argued that he could no longer contribute to the Rams' rushing game or couldn't have continued on defense. But just getting his body in decent enough shape to play at all, much less leave the game with only moderate pain, was becoming less possible.

Two days after his big day against the Giants, Washington announced his plans to retire at the end of the season. "Football has been good to me," Washington said. "I have made a good living at it. I've bought a home for my wife and son. I have made wonderful friends in the game, yet I'm tired of football now and I've made up my mind to retire."

After Washington made his announcement, Los Angeles mayor Fletcher Bowron declared December 12, the day of the Rams' last home game, to be Kenny Washington Day.

Los Angeles Times writer Frank Finch noted that Washington hadn't gotten a chance in the NFL in his prime. Former Rams coach Bob Snyder observed, "If Kenny had joined the Chicago Bears [who were rumored to be interested in him in 1940] right after he graduated from UCLA, he would have gone down in league history as the all-time best running back." But instead, Washington had to wait six years and reached the NFL with a lot of miles already on his legs. Years later, when a reporter asked Washington what he thought his best game was, the retired star said the 1939 tie with the USC Trojans. The reporter himself chose Washington's breakout game in 1937 where he hit Hal Hirshon with a 65-yard throw and racked up nearly 150 passing yards in the fourth quarter. Indeed, to the football fans who remembered Washington, those two games stood out more than his pro accomplishments.

Kenny Washington's last game in the NFL was the Rams' home finale against the Pittsburgh Steelers. Los Angeles was out of the playoff race, and the day was dedicated to recognizing Washington. The Los Angeles El Centro Recreation Commission sponsored a regional football league for boys twelve to fourteen years of age. That year's youth-league champion was a squad of African American boys. At the end of their tremendous season they were asked what kind of reward they wanted: Medals? A trophy? Team sweaters? No. They wanted to see Kenny Washington play football. Rams owner Dan Reeves arranged for the young footballers to attend Washington's send-off game.

Coach Shaughnessy honored Washington in his last game by starting all the ex–UCLA Bruins on the Rams' roster. Quarterback Bob Waterfield fed Washington the ball, and he ran for 54 yards on 10 carries. Washington also intercepted a Steeler pass in the first half. But it would be Jim Hardy, now ensconced as Waterfield's backup, who would lead the Rams that day with three touchdown passes.

At halftime the team set a microphone stand on the field, and both squads lined up single file along either side. Inside the line of Rams players stood a small cluster of men in double-breasted suits with pocket squares tucked neatly against their chests. Some were team executives, others former coaches of Washington's. A few were local businessmen.

The ceremony honoring Washington was filmed, although the audio has been lost. Bill Schroeder, former general manager of the Hollywood Bears, walked to the microphone clutching a trophy, a plaque, and a piece of paper. He spoke briefly while several of the fourteen photographers squatting in a semicircle in front of him snapped photos. What Schroeder said is lost to time. Schroeder motioned Washington to the front, shook his hand, handed him the trophy, and showed him something on the plaque. Washington, still in his uniform, nodded, and spoke for a few minutes. He handed the trophy to Dr. Thomas Riley, principal of Lincoln High School, his alma mater. To this day, the Lincoln High School football team presents that very trophy to their most valuable player of the year.

When Washington finished speaking to the crowd, Schroeder posed with the man of the hour while the photographers crabbed closer. Another man said a few words and passed the microphone to Fred Naumetz, Rams team captain. Naumetz shook Kenny's hand and spoke for less than a minute before presenting Washington with a watch on behalf of his teammates.

Eight members of the El Centro youth-league championship team came onto the field and gave Kenny a huge crate of the lettuce that their nearby town was known for. Washington shook hands with each of the young men. From the far end of the field, a Rams employee slowly drove a brand-new 1949 Ford Tudor toward the microphone. He pulled up behind where Washington stood. More men stepped forward to shake Washington's hand.

One of the newspapermen opened the Ford's door and asked Washington to sit there with his plaque. Washington acquiesced and the photographers surged in for close-ups.

Soon Kenny Washington ducked inside his new ride and was chauffeured across the stadium's grass. The line of Rams watched the celebration and clapped heartily as the crowd cheered Washington off the field. Waterfield and Hardy then turned toward the bench to prepare for the second half.

AFTER THE RAMS GAVE UP ON WOODY STRODE in 1947, other teams in the NFL and AAFC showed little interest, and Strode took up former teammate Les Lear's offer to join him on the Calgary Stampeders. Strode had never been to the Canadian Rockies and had no idea what to expect. Calgary was open skies, vast plains, and Black Angus cattle, and culturally about as far from Los Angeles as one could get. But Calgary loved its football team. "The Canadian Indians used to bring wild game to my hotel room," Strode recalled, once they confirmed he also had Native blood. "I'm part Indian but you never walk up to them and announce it. They'll see it in you. They came to all the football games.

"It took [the Canadian Indians] a month to ask me what kind of Indian blood I had. I told them, 'American Blackfoot.' The guy who asked me had an interpreter talking for him; he replied, 'We are Canadian Blackfeet.' Well, that made us like brothers."

Woody Strode had discovered he was part Native American when he was in college, although he'd had an inkling long before. Strode remembered a Native American neighbor named Harry who lived next to Strode's childhood home. During the week Harry dressed in suits and went to work, but on weekends he'd dance and chant in his backyard. Strode understood none of it, but it fascinated him. One night when Strode heard Harry start, Strode opened the back door and crept down to the wooden fence that separated the yards. He crouched down and watched Harry through a space in between the slats. "His face had more wrinkles than a dried up old prune," Strode remembered. "But his eyes were bright, like two headlights on a dark country road.

"The moon lit him up so that he was nothing but a silhouette and his shadow flowed across the ground until it piled up against the fence. As he circled around in my direction he saw me peering through the slats . . . He motioned me over and I crawled through the fence. That was the beginning of our friendship."

Over the years, Harry taught Strode about how the U.S. government sought to destroy indigenous tribes, why the buffalo were so important to the Blackfoot, and where various tribes lived in the United States. When someone at UCLA commented on Strode's high cheekbones and asked what his racial makeup was, he asked his father, who told him that on one side his great-grandmother was Creek, and on the other side, his grandmother was full-blooded Blackfoot.

Finding out about his Native American background was the first of several experiences Strode later saw as opening his eyes about race in America. He admitted that he was naive as a youngster and through much of his time in college.

Strode's first job after college was working for District Attorney Buron Fitts. He served subpoenas to addresses in black neighborhoods. "The DA's office was using me but I was too naive to notice," Strode admitted. He played with Kenny on the Hollywood Bears immediately after college but was drafted into the military after the United States entered World War II.

Larger military training bases had baseball and football teams culled from the soldiers stationed there. The teams played other service teams and top college squads as well. Military brass believed the teams helped keep morale up, and proceeds from the games went to families of service members hurt or killed in action. Many of the country's top players ended up on service teams, and their coaches were drawn from the pro, semipro, and college ranks. George Halas of the Chicago Bears, Paul Brown of Ohio State, and even Paul Schissler of the Hollywood Bears managed military teams. Often they pulled strings to get their favorite players assigned to their base rather than shipped overseas. Schissler did just that with Strode and ex-teammate Leo Cantor.

But when Strode first arrived at March Field in Riverside for Army basic training, he found everything and everyone segregated by race. All African American soldiers lived on a part of the compound called Dusty Acres. They did the service jobs: worked the mess halls, cleaned the latrines, etc. The base had separate buses for white and black soldiers, a separate movie house, and a separate military store. "What a slap in the face that was," Strode said. "I had never been kicked [like that] before." Although the camp was in California, the top decision makers in the military opted to bow to the social norms of the South regardless of where a base was located.

For Strode and many other black service members, the blatant hypocrisy of enduring second-class treatment in the military while ostensibly fighting a racist regime in Europe in order to spread so-called American ideals of freedom and fairness was a rude awakening. Strode languished at Dusty Acres for six months before Schissler convinced the base's commanding officer to let the entire football team live together. Many of the players were Southern white boys and had never played with African Americans. Several were amazed to see that Strode had no scars on his back, given their assumptions that all black men had suffered the kinds of beatings they knew about from home.

The football team's reunion also provided a respite for Strode's college teammate Leo Cantor. He hadn't been shunted to a separate camp as Strode had, but he had encountered rampant anti-Semitism from his peers, most of whom didn't realize he was Jewish. Many service members whom Cantor knew blamed Europe's Jewish population for the war the United States was now in. Cantor felt powerless to confront the scapegoating and felt some relief at being reunited with the other football players and ex-teammates, including Strode.

At March Field, Strode first met Jack Jacobs, who was Creek. They played together on the March Field football team and later crossed paths in the PCFL and the NFL. Jacobs split time between halfback and quarterback for Cleveland, Washington, and Green Bay. In 1950 he went to play for the Winnipeg Blue Bombers. Ezzrett "Sugarfoot" Anderson joined the Calgary Stampeders the year after Strode did, and competed against Jacobs for several years in the early 1950s. Anderson remembered that some of the bars in Calgary refused to serve Jacobs or any First Nations people. "Jack told them he'd put a curse on the upcoming Calgary Stampede," Anderson recalled. The Calgary Stampede was the biggest rodeo and multiday celebration in Alberta. "Sure enough it rained for days," Anderson said, laughing at how Jacobs and he had joked about it at the time. "Any time after that the bars let Jack order whatever he wanted."

When Strode arrived in Calgary in 1948, he had to adjust to playing with nineteen-year-old Canadian kids and the handful of internationals the team was allowed. They practiced on a frozen field with lines etched in the ice. Les Lear brought the Rams playbook with him, one of the more complex systems in the NFL, and more complicated than what many Canadian teams used at the time. Lear had convinced Keith Spaith, a quarterback who had been cut by the Rams, to come north and play for the Stampeders. Since the Canadian leagues played different seasons from the NFL, Kenny Washington visited for a week to train Spaith in the modern T formation.

With Strode's help, the Stampeders rolled to an undefeated season in 1948. They faced the Ottawa Rough Riders for the 1948 Grey Cup in Toronto. Calgary's exuberant mix of fans took the train out east or joined along the route, partying most of the way. One newspaper described it as "quite a piece of mobile vaudeville by the time it hit Bloor St. One prairie schooner even had a little prairie schooner tagging along behind it . . . on them all were people peculiarly dressed in great big hats and great big boots and all of them shouting great big boasts."

The championship game was a tight contest, but late in the game a Rough Rider dropped a lateral pass and then stopped, thinking he had heard the referee blow the whistle. But the play was not dead, and Strode picked up the ball and raced the other way, setting up the deciding touchdown. When the final gun sounded, Strode's teammates hoisted him on their shoulders, handed him a bottle of rye whiskey, and carried him off the field.

The team partied at the Royal York Hotel that evening. Strode met up with one of his Blackfoot friends in front of the hotel. He asked to borrow his companion's white stallion. Strode jumped on, and his friend opened the doors leading to the foyer. The horse's hooves clip-clopped on the black-and-white marble floor as Strode rode him to the ballroom. The tuxedo-clad partyers and guests quieted as Strode cleaved the crowd.

Wearing a white-fringed suit, red lizard boots, and a blue scarf tied around his neck, Strode held the reins along with the bottle of rye whiskey in his left hand. In his right he held his white ten-gallon hat. When he reached the middle of the room, he let out a yell and dug his heels into the horse's flanks. The stallion rose and spun. The crowd erupted in cheers as horse and rider rose again, then thundered back out the front door.

The trains full of Calgary fans and the fun they had as they traveled east have become a part of Grey Cup lore, including the legend of the stallion in the York Hotel. Over the years, many people have claimed to be the man on the white horse that evening. A local politician said he was the rider, as did an Ottawa sports reporter. But neither accounted for where the horse came from or whom they had borrowed it from. No photographic proof seems to have survived, and Strode wrote about the scene in detail in his book, *Goal Dust: The Warm and Candid Memoirs of a Pioneer Black Athlete and Actor*. Also consider: The likelihood of a Blackfoot man lending his stallion to a stranger, and not just any stranger but an Eastern city slicker at that, was exceedingly slim.

CHAPTER 19

Fourth Quarter

Cleveland Municipal Stadium
Cleveland, Ohio

1950

THE RAMS HAD LOOKED TO BE ON THE VERGE of taking control of the 1950 NFL Championship Game when Cleveland defender Warren Lahr intercepted Bob Waterfield's pass and returned the pick to Cleveland's 35-yard line. The Browns had the ball and a little over a quarter to overcome a 28–20 deficit. Otto Graham quickly completed two short passes to Dante Lavelli, which brought the Browns to midfield at the close of the third quarter. Lavelli would total 11 catches on the day for 128 yards. Graham hit the end with staccato regularity at the beginning of the fourth quarter, moving the Browns to the Los Angeles 47-yard line, then to the 43.

On this drive, Graham completed nine passes, five to Lavelli. Graham converted a first down on a quarterback sneak on fourth and one at the 43-yard line. On first down, Graham kept the ball again, following Marion Motley's block for six yards. Then halfback Rex Bumgardner caught a short pass, followed by another Lavelli reception. On the next set of downs the Browns faced fourth and four, and Graham again found Lavelli, this time for a seven-yard gain.

Now Cleveland was within Lou Groza's field goal range. They faced another fourth down and Graham converted with a short scramble. Soon after, Motley tied up right defensive end Jack Zilly, and Graham again ducked inside, this time for an eight-yard romp to the 19-yard line, where the quarterback nearly ran over defensive halfback Woodley Lewis.

Motley's ability to direct defenders past Graham helped the quarterback rack up 99 yards on the ground for the game. Several plays after his eight-yard dash, Graham saw Bumgardner rumbling toward the front corner of the end zone with Rams defensive halfback Fred Naumetz blanketing him. The Browns quarterback saw a sliver of an opening and attempted to drop the ball in front of Bumgardner, where Naumetz would have a harder time defending the pass. The flag marking the end zone snapped back and forth in the wind as the ball started to drop amid the swirl. Bumgardner lunged toward the quickly dying pass and grabbed it before it hit the ground. The big back stepped in the end zone, then stumbled out of bounds, scattering the celebrating grounds crew from their wooden bench next to the field.

Groza nailed the extra point. Cleveland had climbed within 1 point, 28–27. Groza's kickoff floated downfield, and the Rams brought it out to the 25-yard line. On first down, Waterfield turned left to hand off to half-back Glenn Davis. But Bill Willis had pierced the line again, beating both the center and the left guard, and he was only a step from Davis when he got the ball. Davis fought to the sideline and tried to turn upfield, but Willis and several other defenders ran him out of bounds for a two-yard loss.

The Rams managed just four yards on the next two plays and punted. Cleveland failed to sustain a drive and punted right back. Halfway through the final quarter, Los Angeles took over the ball on their own 20-yard line. The Rams gave the ball to Dick Hoerner, who gained three before being tackled by Willis. Then Waterfield went back to pass. He dropped back and back and back as Bill Willis bulled through 6-foot-2-inch center Art Statuto. Waterfield dumped the ball off to Elroy Hirsch, but Los Angeles gained only two yards on the play.

Needing five yards for a first down, Waterfield retreated again, looking for Hirsch or Tom Fears. Len Ford bulldozed the Ram left tackle and headed for Waterfield's blind side. The quarterback zipped the ball off target toward Hirsch. Cleveland safety Ken Gorgal got a hand on the pass and batted the ball into the air. As the ball tumbled end over end, Cleveland linebacker Tommy Thompson lunged and pulled it to his chest as he landed on the ground. Interception, Cleveland ball.

The Browns offense jogged on the field as the jubilant but exhausted defenders trotted off. The offense gathered around Graham. The team had the ball just inside Los Angeles territory with less than five minutes to go. Right away, Graham completed a 22-yard pass to Dub Jones. From the Los Angeles 26-yard line Graham called for a quarterback draw. He dropped back as if to pass, then shot forward.

The Browns signal caller veered right around a surprised lineman and cut back left, the ball in his right arm. One of the Rams defensive backs slammed his shoulder into Graham's right hip and wrapped the quarterback's legs just as linebacker Don Paul clocked Graham from the other side. The ball popped backward as Graham spun around and landed on his back. Rams Mike Lazetich and Tank Younger were the first to the ball, with a few Browns close behind.

When the referee unpiled the bodies at the 24-yard line, Lazetich had the ball. Four feet away, Graham was on his hands and knees. His head slumped toward the ground. "I wanted to die," he said after the game. He swiped at the turf in frustration as he pushed himself up.

The Rams had the ball and the lead with three minutes left in the game. If Los Angeles could get two first downs, the game and the championship were theirs. A few of their heartier fans had made the trek to Ohio and exhorted their squad on. As did a handful of the Cleveland locals who still rooted for their old team. Those in Los Angeles followed closely on radio. (The cable needed to transmit television live coast-to-coast was still being laid. The following year the NFL Championship Game would be televised live coast–to-coast for the first time.)

Was Kenny Washington one of the Rams fans in Los Angeles listening to his old team? He didn't follow many games after he retired, according to his daughter Karin Cohen, but perhaps he would have tuned in for the title game to root for his friends and new players such as Tank Younger? As it was midday Pacific time, on Christmas Eve, Washington might have been sitting at the Santa Anita racetrack with friends, a radio filling them in on the NFL action while they watched the ponies. Or he might have been in Lincoln Heights with his family, visiting his former neighbors, hearing the call of the seesaw battle happening 2,300 miles away.

WHEN LOREN MILLER GOT THE SUGAR HILL covenant case tossed out in Superior Court, he hoped he'd get a similar result when the case was appealed to the California Supreme Court. If it had been heard and appealed again, it could have made it to the U.S. Supreme Court. But the California Supreme Court dragged its feet on hearing the case, so Miller moved forward on nationwide preparations with Thurgood Marshall and other lawyers as other cases percolated through state judicial systems.

Miller explored various arguments they could use against the covenants as he wanted to determine what their strongest strategies could be. In one of Miller's earlier cases, *Fairchild v. Raines*, the California Supreme Court ruled that the original conditions of one set of covenants, signed in 1927, no longer existed. The areas covered by the covenants were noncontiguous. Over time more black residents had moved into the units not covered by the covenants, thus changing the racial makeup of the neighborhood. The broader area was no longer exclusively white so the covenants were not upheld.

In related decisions, some courts refused to uphold covenants if they had been only sporadically enforced, such that the conditions of the neighborhood had already substantively changed since the covenants had been agreed upon. Many white neighborhood associations responded by even more aggressively attacking and suing black families who moved in nearby.

In 1944, a relatively new California Supreme Court justice, Robert Traynor, revived the public-policy angle of property law that the U.S. Supreme Court had used to justify some municipal zoning laws. In the covenant cases, Traynor, who would become better known for his rulings validating interracial marriage twenty years before the U.S. Supreme Court followed suit, noted that areas where black residents lived in Los Angeles were severely overcrowded specifically *because* of the residential segregation of black citizens, which was accomplished "not by ordinances, which would be unconstitutional, but by agreements between private persons which the courts have recognized as valid." He concluded that the covenants "must yield to the public interest in the sound development of the whole community."

Few other judges and courts agreed, however, even though another public-policy angle held that forcing large numbers of people to live in squalid, overcrowded areas constituted a public health risk. Loren Miller had yet another approach: No legal definition of race existed. Who was to say what defined someone as black or white? And what about multiracial individuals? Miller related to this personally, having a black father and white mother.

While a deft combination of these approaches might win an individual case, none addressed the core constitutionality of the covenants themselves. Miller didn't want to nibble around the edges; he wanted to strike at the heart of the matter. To him the most direct attack on the covenants was to argue that using the court system to enforce the racially restrictive covenants was "state action" of the sort prohibited by the Equal Protection Clause of the Fourteenth Amendment.

By 1946, the NAACP's national office had prioritized fighting covenants for several years and had organized meetings that brought together lawyers from all over the country who led major covenant cases. When Loren Miller headlined the Conference on the Elimination of Restrictive Covenants in Chicago in May 1946, he met with Thurgood Marshall and the lawyers leading covenant cases in St. Louis, Detroit, and Washington, D.C. The gathered legal minds debated the various strategies they could employ and which cases seemed the best bets to take to the Supreme Court. The case that would become most widely known originated in St. Louis.

In 1911, thirty of thirty-nine property owners in the Greater Ville neighborhood of St. Louis signed a housing covenant barring the sale of their houses to anyone of "Negro or Mongoloid race" for fifty years. In 1945, African Americans J. D. and Ethel Lee Shelley bought a property on Labadie Avenue, two blocks inside the area covered by the covenant.

Louis D. Kraemer sued the Shelleys under the terms of the 1911 covenant. The St. Louis Circuit Court deemed that the covenant documents had not been properly signed. Kraemer appealed and the Missouri State Supreme Court upheld the covenants—which meant the Shelleys would have to move, pending more appeals.

A similar case in Michigan involved Orsel and Minnie McGhee, who bought a house several blocks outside the invisible line corralling one of the African American neighborhoods in Detroit. Residents on the McGhees' street created an all-white neighborhood association and convinced the McGhees' new neighbors, the Sipeses, to sue them.

The local NAACP represented the McGhees and tried a tactic that Miller ultimately eschewed in his Southern California cases: They recruited sociologists and anthropologists to show that no scientifically agreed upon definition of race existed, and therefore terms such as *Caucasian* and *Negro* had no proper legal definition.

Lower courts ruled against the McGhees, as did the Michigan State Supreme Court. The NAACP planned for Thurgood Marshall to consolidate the cases the Supreme Court was most likely to agree to hear and petition the court. As always, the Supreme Court chose what cases it would hear and often declined to hear appeals, letting lower-court rulings stand, as it had done previously in *Corrigan v. Buckley*.

On April 21, George Vaughn, the attorney for the Shelleys in St. Louis, preempted plans to carefully choose which covenant cases to appeal to the Supreme Court by asking the court to hear the Shelley case. NAACP and

Legal Defense and Educational Fund leaders in New York immediately applied for *McGhee v. Sipes*, as did the lawyers for several covenant cases in the District of Columbia. On the last Monday of its term, June 23, 1947, the Supreme Court agreed to hear the covenant cases. Marshall, Miller, and others launched intense preparations. They worked nonstop to cultivate all angles with which to attack the covenants as broadly as possible while still focusing on the state-action angle.

First, they pushed sociologists they knew to publish about both the dire public-policy outcomes of enforced ghettoization and the biological and social challenges in trying to define someone as Caucasian or black. If articles could be published by October and November, the lawyers would have time to cite them in briefs to be submitted to the court by the end of the year.

Second, the lead attorneys of the individual cases met in person numerous times to hash out tactics. Marshall and the D.C.-area lawyers met regularly at Howard University, where they did trial runs of the actual cases with law school faculty playing the roles of each justice. Law school students made up the audience and peppered the attorneys with questions.

They also solicited amicus curiae, "friend of the court," briefs from prominent legal organizations. In October President Truman's Committee on Civil Rights published its findings in a 178-page report, "To Secure These Rights," which documented the widespread discrimination black Americans faced. The office of the solicitor general of the United States contacted the NAACP offices in New York. He offered to write an amicus brief, essentially putting the weight of the federal government on the side opposing the covenants.

All of this work had to be done soon. The Supreme Court would hear opening arguments on January 15, 1948.

CHAPTER 20

Younger

Los Angeles Memorial Coliseum
Los Angeles, California

1949

I N 1949, THE YEAR AFTER KENNY WASHINGTON retired, the Rams
began investing more heavily in black players. Los Angeles signed Tank
Younger, who was a standout halfback at Grambling State and the first
player from a historically black college or university to be signed by an
NFL team. When Younger suited up for the Rams, he wore #13, the number
Washington had worn. It is unclear if he did so to honor Washington or
if, in an era of much tighter team budgets, the Rams simply gave him
the jersey of the person he replaced. The Rams would add four more
black players in 1950: Dan Towler, Woodley Lewis, Bob Boyd, and Harry
Thompson.

By 1950, a handful of teams now had African Americans on their rosters.
The slightly broader level of acceptance may well have played a role in the
Rams' personnel decisions in 1950. The franchise had also gone through
several head coaches in its four years in California. Adam Walsh gave way
to Bob Snyder, who in turn was supplanted by Clark Shaughnessy.
Shaughnessy left after 1949, and Joe Stydahar took over in 1950.

There is no marked evidence that any of these coaches pushed hard for
more black players, or that owner Dan Reeves felt particularly inclined to
meaningfully integrate the team. More likely, the slow emergence of a black
presence on other teams helped push the Rams forward. Their Coliseum
cotenants, the AAFC's Los Angeles Dons, didn't sign any black players in
1946 when the Rams signed Washington and Strode. But by 1949 they had

six. Indeed, AAFC teams signed more black players per team than their NFL peers.

The signing of Younger wasn't the only notable pro football first that year. Indiana halfback George Taliaferro became the first black player chosen in the NFL draft when the Chicago Bears picked him in the thirteenth round. Previously, black players had been signed *after* the draft. This not only brought less attention to the signing but also gave the teams a great deal of financial leverage in negotiating contracts. Teams were more likely to invest money in players they drafted. If a draftee refused to sign, the team would have wasted a draft pick.

An undrafted player likely had no other franchises interested in his services, or at least not interested enough to spend a draft pick on him. Compared to their white peers, black undrafted free agents had even less leverage. This was ameliorated somewhat by the competition between the AAFC and the NFL for players, which also drove up player salaries, but it remained true that undrafted players had less of a shot at a sustained NFL career.

Taliaferro decided not to sign with the Bears but with the Dons of the AAFC, who had taken him in the fifth round of their league's draft, held the same day as the NFL draft. Throughout their short rivalry, the AAFC and NFL jockeyed to sign players and also jockeyed for draft positioning. The AAFC even went so far as to hold secret drafts over the summers prior to their regular drafts so teams could get a jump start on trying to sign their top choices. The new league sought any advantage it could get, as the NFL had the benefit of being the older, more established outfit in swaying high-profile draftees.

The Los Angeles Dons led the AAFC in drafting black players. In the 1948 draft they picked Len Ford from Michigan and Lin Sexton from Wichita State. When they drafted Taliaferro in 1949, the fact that they already had several black players may have influenced Taliaferro's decision to choose them over the Chicago Bears, who had none.

Most black players in the late 1940s carried the weight of representing more than just themselves but their race. If they failed, that could mean fewer chances for other black players. If coaches or owners weren't racist themselves, they were skittish of the attention signing a black player would bring and they feared backlash from white fans. Individual players had to overcome this preexisting negative, not just for themselves but so the coach or owner would consider signing additional black players in the future.

The Los Angeles Rams entered the 1949 season with lofty expectations. They had Waterfield at quarterback, the best end in football in Tom Fears, and Bob Shaw to complement him. Many pundits predicted the Rams would battle the Chicago Bears for the top spot in the Western Conference, while many picked the defending NFL champion Philadelphia Eagles to repeat in the East.

Los Angeles had stocked up on new halfbacks to replace Kenny Washington, and that included not just Tank Younger but Vitamin Smith and Tommy "Cricket" Kalmanir, joining fullback Dick Hoerner in the backfield. Los Angeles signed two other key additions. The Chicago Rockets of the AAFC had struggled to stay afloat and were renamed the Hornets after the 1948 season. Their exciting but oft-injured halfback, Elroy Hirsch, switched leagues, signing with the Rams prior to the 1949 season.

In that year's draft, the Rams took a chance on a quarterback from Oregon. Norm Van Brocklin finally inked with Los Angeles in July, giving him a bit more than a month to pick up the Rams offense as Waterfield's new backup (Jim Hardy left the Rams for the Chicago Cardinals).

Early on, the Rams delivered on the preseason expectations, shooting out to a 6-0 record. In the home opener against the Detroit Lions, Waterfield and Hirsch sparked the Rams to a 17–14 lead. But then Waterfield threw two interceptions in the second half and those turnovers led to 10 points for the Lions. Van Brocklin came in and threw a 19-yard touchdown to Hirsch that set up Waterfield's game-winning field goal with two minutes left. One of the key plays on the drive was a Van Brocklin toss to Younger in the flat that the rookie back turned into a 33-yard gain.

Three weeks later the Rams faced the Bears in front of 42,000 fans at Wrigley Field (the Bears' home until 1970). Chicago jumped out to a 16–3 lead. But the Rams then dominated the line of scrimmage, and their defense nabbed a shocking seven interceptions from the troika of Bears quarterbacks: veteran Sid Luckman, second-year-man Johnny Lujack, and rookie George Blanda. The Los Angeles running game showed some flash with Hoerner lateraling to Hirsch for a touchdown. Hirsch also scored on a reception.

Clark Shaughnessy was keen on finding a better way to utilize Hirsch's speed than running him from the backfield. The halfback had almost exclusively carried the ball on rushing plays while at Wisconsin and during his time with the AAFC Rockets. While Hirsch excelled as a runner, Shaughnessy hit upon the idea of lining him up outside the end, creating the flanker position. This was done partly out of necessity: Hirsch had been troubled by concussions, and the team hoped that starting him outside would reduce the risk of impacts as compared to rushing the ball into the line of scrimmage. Hirsch played well but was hurt a good chunk of the year, partly due to an instep injury and possibly another concussion.

Tank Younger's best games as a rookie came in the middle of the year. He gained 49 yards on nine carries in a 35–7 shellacking of the Green Bay Packers and notched another 52 yards on nine attempts in the rematch against the Bears. The rematch saw the 5-0 Rams draw 86,080 fans to the Coliseum, an NFL record at the time. For the Bears, Johnny Lujack had supplanted Sid Luckman as the starting quarterback, and rookie George Blanda had taken over kickoff duties, fast becoming known for his booming kicks. Shaughnessy started Hirsch, Younger, and Hoerner in the backfield. The Bears held the Rams rushers in check, but Waterfield had one of his best days of the year, connecting on 24 of 42 passes for 303 yards. Lujack threw five interceptions and the Rams won, 27–24.

Much of what the Rams did well against the Bears, they struggled with against their next opponent, the Philadelphia Eagles. Their line blocked poorly for Waterfield and Van Brocklin, who played the entire fourth quarter. Philadelphia scampered to a 24–7 lead when an Eagle defensive back swiped the ball from Hirsch's hands on a run and took it the other way for a touchdown. The Eagles were known for their powerful rushing game, led by future Hall of Famer Steve Van Buren, and their equally imposing rush defense. Against Los Angeles, the Eagles ran for 264 yards while giving up only 27. The Rams also turned the ball over five times in the 38–14 loss.

Los Angeles next tied the Pittsburgh Steelers, 7–7, in a sea of mud. The most notable thing about that contest was that the Steelers didn't complete a single forward pass the entire game.

The Rams offense was formidable the whole year, scoring the second most points in the league and leading the NFL in average yards per play. However, they turned the ball over consistently; their 45 turnovers averaged nearly four a game. Waterfield was one of the main culprits. He threw 17 touchdowns but also 24 interceptions, the most in the NFL.

With their midseason stumble the Rams slid from 6-0 to 6-1-2. However, they still had a two-game lead in the loss column on the Bears, who stood at 6-3. The Rams returned to the winning side of the ledger with a 42–20 beating of the lowly New York Bulldogs. The Rams pulled away by scoring on each of their first four possessions in the second half. Waterfield threw five touchdowns and no interceptions on the day, and Van Brocklin added a 40-yard scoring pass in the fourth quarter.

End Tom Fears was on the receiving end of three of those touchdown passes. He'd caught eight passes total and was nearing striking distance of one of the most revered, and thought to be untouchable, records in pro football: the most receptions in a season, held by Don Hutson. Hutson had nabbed 74 catches seven years earlier when teams played 11, not 12, games. That was nearly three times what the player with the second most receptions had that season, leaving many to predict Hutson's record would never be broken.

While Hutson was setting the season reception record in the manpower-depleted NFL during the war, Fears was in the military. The Rams drafted him in 1945, but Fears chose to go back to school. He finished his college career at UCLA and earned All-America honors in 1946 and 1947. He joined the Rams in 1948 and immediately formed a connection with quarterback Bob Waterfield.

Fears would become one of the first Mexican American stars of pro football. His father met his mother in Guadalajara, where his father had moved to for his work as a mining engineer. Fears was born in Guadalajara and his family moved to Los Angeles when he was six years old. During his playing career few mentioned Fears was mixed race, which was highlighted much more so well after he retired.

But with the 1949 season coming down to its last weeks the focus was on a potential division title and Hutson's record. The Rams needed only a win or a tie in one of the last two games to clinch a division title. With two games left, Fears had 60 receptions, 14 short of Huston's record.

Los Angeles started strong in their next game against the Chicago Cardinals in front of almost 75,000 fans at home. Bob Waterfield passed to Bob Shaw for a touchdown, ran for another touchdown, and kicked a field goal in the first half, giving the Rams a 17–3 lead. In the third quarter Vitamin Smith scored on a 51-yard punt return, showing why he was considered the best kick returner in the league.

But then the wheels fell off. Chicago scored on a run and an interception off Waterfield, climbing to within 7, 24–17. Waterfield added a field goal to push the Rams lead to 10 points halfway through the fourth quarter. The Cardinals' Jim Hardy left the game after completing only four of 19 pass attempts. His replacement, Paul Christman, tossed a 50-yard touchdown to get his squad within three points. As the clock ticked under a minute, the

Cardinals got the ball back. With just a few seconds left, Christman found Billy Dewell for a 24-yard touchdown to steal a victory. The Rams had not trailed in the game until the very last seconds.

The bright spot was Fears's seven catches, bringing him within seven of Hutson's mark. Los Angeles had one more game to clinch the Western Division crown. The Rams faced Washington, who were a disappointing 4-6-1. The game started for the Rams the same as it had against Chicago, with Los Angeles scoring a flurry of points. Waterfield and Van Brocklin traded off drives from the beginning. Waterfield hit Fears for a touchdown, and Van Brocklin connected twice with Bob Shaw. Smith and Hoerner added rushing scores to give the Rams a 34–7 lead. But with the Rams' tendency to give the ball away and lose big leads, few of the nearly 45,000 at the Coliseum felt comfortable.

But unlike the previous week, the Rams continued the onslaught in the second half with Shaw catching two more touchdowns and Fears adding another. On the day, Fears caught 10 passes for 159 yards and two touchdowns. This moved him past Hutson with a new single-season record of 77 receptions. (Bob Mann of the Lions edged Fears for most receiving yardage by a single yard.) But Fears was by no means the only offensive star for Los Angeles. Bob Shaw caught four touchdown passes and the team's full passing arsenal was on display.

Waterfield completed 11 of 17 passes for 235 yards and two touchdowns. Van Brocklin hit six of 10 passes for 142 yards and four touchdowns, meaning only two of the young quarterback's completions didn't wind up in the end zone. The Rams totaled 584 yards in the 53–27 victory. They'd won the West and would host the 11-1 Philadelphia Eagles in the 1949 NFL title game.

It took the Eagles four days to reach California, as their coach, Greasy Neale, preferred taking the train over flying. But by the time the Philadelphia club reached Los Angeles, they were good and ready for the Rams. The Eagles once again held the top defensive ranking in the league and had only twice allowed more than 17 points in a game, making a repeat of the Rams' offensive explosion against Washington unlikely. So did the weather. The forecast called for showers, and the morning of the game looked like a monsoon. Both team owners and players voted to reschedule the game— the rain was expected to drastically dampen day-of ticket sales, which were what player playoff bonuses were based on. But NFL commissioner Bert Bell refused to postpone the game, citing commitments to ABC, which was broadcasting the game on radio and television.

Under a driving rain on a muddy field, the Eagles league-leading rusher Steve Van Buren ran the ball 31 times for 196 yards. The Eagles defense, especially the stout middle of their line, crushed the Rams running game. Los Angeles managed only 21 yards on 24 carries. Hoerner and Vitamin Smith got the bulk of the carries. Younger had no carries and just a six-yard reception.

Philadelphia quarterback Tommy Thompson only attempted nine passes and threw two interceptions, but he connected with end Pete Pihos on a 31-yard touchdown pass in the second quarter to get the Eagles on the board, 7–0. Waterfield and Van Brocklin both struggled. Each only managed five completions and no big plays. With a 7–0 lead, Philadelphia didn't try any passes in the second half. In the third quarter, Ram center Don Paul snapped the ball high to Waterfield on a punt attempt. Eagle Leo Skladany blocked the kick and ran the ball in for an insurance score.

That was more than enough for the Philadelphia defense. The Eagles won the 1949 NFL championship game. For Los Angeles it was a disappointing end to a mistake-prone but highly successful year. They'd go into the off-season with two starting-caliber quarterbacks and the prospect of getting their talented receivers healthy for another run the next year. For the league champion Eagles, the next challenge would be the 1950 season opener against the NFL's newest team: the Cleveland Browns.

CHAPTER 21

Swan Song

Cleveland Municipal Stadium
Cleveland, Ohio

1949

AFTER THE 1948 SEASON, THE BROOKLYN DODGERS merged with the New York Yankees. In baseball this would have been monumental. In the AAFC, it signaled the beginning of the end. With only seven teams left, the AAFC went from two divisions to one and cut its schedule from fourteen regular-season games to twelve. The Browns opened against the Bills, the team they had smoked in the title game the year before.

The Bills raced ahead, aided by Browns turnovers. On one punt Horace Gillom bobbled the snap from center and got tackled behind the line of scrimmage. Later, Otto Graham went back to pass and had the ball stripped from his grasp at his own two-yard line. By the fourth quarter Buffalo had built a 28–7 lead. Graham rallied Cleveland and hit halfback Edgar Jones twice for touchdowns. With two minutes left, Graham lofted a long pass to Gillom, in at right end for the injured Dante Lavelli, and the punter-slash-receiver snagged the ball over three defenders. A few plays later Mac Speedie caught a low pass in the end zone, salvaging a 28–28 tie.

Cleveland reeled off four wins after that, including a strange 14–3 victory over the New York Yankees, in which the Browns managed only five first downs and 36 yards passing but scored touchdowns off a fumble recovery and an interception.

In early October, Cleveland traveled to San Francisco to take on the 49ers, the AAFC's perennial second banana. Thus far, the rivalry had

189

produced one-sided offensive bonanzas. San Francisco had beaten Cleveland in their first-ever matchup in 1946, but had since lost five straight games. In recent contests between the two, Cleveland's defense had made key stops or forced turnovers that led to Browns wins. Nearly 60,000 fans crammed into Kezar Stadium for the teams' first 1949 tilt.

This time, San Francisco won both the little battles and the larger war. Joe Perry shredded the Browns' top rushing defense for 155 rushing yards and two touchdowns. Frankie Albert threw five touchdowns to five different players. The Browns scratched within one score at 28–21 in the second quarter, having fallen behind 21–0. The 49ers pulled away with two scores in the fourth quarter for a resounding 56–28 victory. The loss broke the Browns' 29-game unbeaten streak and also marked the most points posted against the franchise in its short history.

Coach Paul Brown waxed philosophical after the game. "It had to come sometime," he said in reference to the end of the team's unbeaten streak. "Now the pressure is off and maybe we can start playing football again." But the team knew he'd be on them behind closed doors to atone for the thorough beating they'd taken. The team traveled to Los Angeles next to face the Dons. Cleveland took their frustrations out on Los Angeles with a 61–14 thumping. Graham threw six touchdowns, four to Lavelli.

Up next was their chance for revenge versus the 49ers. The Browns faithful came out 72,000 strong for the contest, making it the fourth time in four years that the Browns home game against the 49ers drew more than 70,000 fans. In the previous contest three weeks prior, the San Francisco defense successfully pressured Graham by looping their defensive linemen around each other, mostly with inside defensive linemen stunting outside. This strategy changed which gap in the line the defenders would hit and scrambled Cleveland's pass-protection plans.

Paul Brown and the coaching staff studied the film and called quarterback sneaks up the middle to stymie the 49ers' defensive stunts. Indeed, the sneaks slowed the defense, and Graham scored a touchdown on a 20-yard rush up the middle in the third quarter to give the Browns a 21–14 lead.

One of the many innovations Paul Brown brought to pro football was to use a messenger guard to relay plays from the sideline to Graham. Many teams had picked up the tactic by 1949, but in this game the 49ers took it a step further. San Francisco head coach Buck Shaw wrote plays down on scraps of paper that a player from the sideline would bring in and hand to quarterback Frankie Albert. Perhaps Shaw worried that the crowd noise would drown out the exchange or didn't want the message bearers having to remember what play he'd told them.

But anyone familiar with the weather at Cleveland's Municipal Stadium could have predicted what happened next. The winds off Lake Erie snatched the notes out of the 49ers' hands and spun them in all directions. More than once Albert had to chase down the slip of paper skipping across the turf to find out what play to call. The 49ers soon abandoned the paper-scraps method, but not before the field was littered with notes.

Cleveland bottled up Joe Perry this time, though that only modestly slowed down the San Francisco rushing attack. The teams traded scores up to and through the fourth quarter. A 38-yard field goal from Lou Groza and 12-yard touchdown reception by Mac Speedie gave the Browns a 30–21 lead. The 49ers scored their last touchdown with fifteen seconds to go, bringing the score to 30–28 for the Browns.

Like the Browns' black players, San Francisco running back Joe Perry faced aggressions large and small from opponents. In a game against the Bills earlier that year, Perry was on the ground when Bills guard Rocco Pirro walked by and nonchalantly kicked Perry in the head. Perry jumped up, and his teammates rushed to keep him and Pirro apart. To give Perry a chance to exact revenge on Buffalo, Frankie Albert called Perry's number eight straight times and the running back pummeled their defensive line.

After the 49ers grudge match, the Browns hosted the Chicago Hornets and thumped them 35–2 with Motley scoring two touchdowns, one on a 49-yard run in the third quarter to give the Browns a 21–0 lead. Motley's rushing average dipped in 1949, going from 6.1 the year before to 5.0. He did score more touchdowns—eight, compared to five the previous year.

After a tie with the Bills, Graham notched 382 passing yards in a 31–0 shutout of the New York Yankees. Left end Mac Speedie caught 11 of Graham's 19 completions for more than 200 yards. It would be Speedie's third straight year as an All-Pro, and he'd lead the league in receiving yards with 1,028 over 12 games.

One of the strengths of the Browns' passing game was the number of exceptional receivers the team had, not just starting ends, but backups such as Gillom and running backs adept at catching balls downfield such as Dub Jones and Marion Motley.

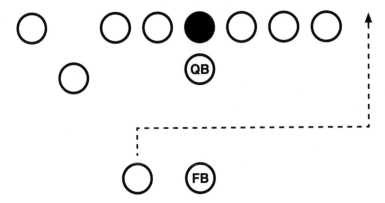

Browns T with Slotback and Man-in-Motion

Multiple receivers going to both sides forces defense to cover more space.

The dire financial straits of some AAFC clubs were apparent on Cleveland's trip to Chicago for a rematch with the Hornets. The players and the sideline staff had to help the Hornets clear snow off the field because the team couldn't afford to hire a groundskeeper. The Browns dispatched the Hornets in a turnover-marred game and proceeded to face the Bills in the first round of the playoffs. The Browns overcame Buffalo with a 31–21 victory in Cleveland. With the AAFC now having only one division, the Browns could finally face their old division rival, San Francisco, for the championship.

Behind the scenes, AAFC leadership, Coach Brown, and others had been negotiating the terms of a merger with the NFL. In the week before the title game, the AAFC announced it would close down after the 1949 season with the Browns, 49ers, and Baltimore Colts entering the NFL the following year. Players from folding AAFC teams would enter a dispersal draft for NFL clubs.

The merger meant fewer roster spots and a glut of talented players which likely worried the league's black athletes the most. Five of the seven AAFC teams had black players, thirteen in total. Meanwhile, the NFL had only seven black players league-wide in 1949. Four of the black AAFC vets didn't make it through the dispersal draft and never played in the NFL.

The announcement of the AAFC's dissolution dampened the enthusiasm for the final game, which was played in front of fewer than 23,000 fans in Cleveland. The offenses couldn't find a way to send the league out with a bang. Graham completed only seven passes and Frankie Albert only nine. Motley didn't have his standard triple-digit rushing-yard game in a championship, but he did gain 75 yards on 8 carries, most of them coming on a 68-yard touchdown run in the third quarter. Graham helped with 62 yards rushing, and it was enough for a 21–7 Cleveland victory.

The Browns won every title in the AAFC's existence. Not long after the merger was finalized, the Browns found out who they would play in the 1950 season opener: the NFL champion Philadelphia Eagles. The Browns—and their doubters—would finally get to see how the AAFC juggernaut stacked up against the best of the NFL.

THE LONGER THE FBI SPENT IN MONROE, GEORGIA, the more proof they uncovered of Loy Harrison's animosity toward his black sharecroppers. They discovered Harrison had beaten members of George Dorsey's extended family several times over the few years prior to the lynchings. The winter before, he'd attacked George's thirty-two-year-old uncle-in-law, Robert Elder. Several men grabbed Elder from the side of the road and blindfolded him. He recognized Harrison's voice saying, "All these damn n—s been to the Army and come back thinking themselves something." Elder was hit in the head and didn't regain consciousness until some other men found him and returned him to his sister's house.

Elder still owed Harrison money but knew he had to escape. He planned to run to Chattanooga as one of his sisters had done. But Harrison found Elder at the bus station and beat him with a lug wrench. After recovering from his injuries, Elder was back in Harrison's field working off his debt.

A week before the lynchings, Harrison had beaten George Dorsey for keeping Harrison's car longer than he had told Dorsey he could use it. Harrison saw Dorsey return and chased him across the yard. He grabbed a stretch of chain from the barn and beat Dorsey before taking the car and driving off. That evening George and Mae walked to the house of some friends down the road who were also tenant farmers. They listened to *Amos 'n' Andy* that evening. "My nerves is all frayed," the Kingfish said. "Even the frayed part is frayed." A week later they would be dead.

The agents uncovered additional inconsistencies in Harrison's story of the evening of the lynchings. He'd claimed that he hadn't seen any cars on the road to Moore's Ford Bridge until he'd rounded the last corner approaching the bridge. And not until he'd looked in the rearview mirror had he seen the cars pull up behind him. But when the agents talked to the young son of the sharecropper who lived nearest the bridge, the boy said he had been in the yard that afternoon and seen Harrison's car sandwiched by two cars in front and two in back well before the last curve in the road.

But as much as the agents suspected Harrison was involved in the lynchings, they still couldn't prove he participated in the killings. And even if they could, they couldn't force local law enforcement to arrest or prosecute him. Perhaps if the agents had focused less on proving who killed the four victims and more on building cases for what the federal government had jurisdiction over, they might have been able to bring charges against those involved. They were still in Monroe trying to marshal evidence against Harrison and several other suspects when they heard the news: A federal grand jury was being convened in nearby Athens to look into the circumstances of the Moore's Ford lynchings.

The federal government had a few ways to become involved in lynching investigations, but the grand jury was one of its best tools. The purpose was to investigate and potentially indict people for federal crimes. Unless waived, a grand jury inquiry was required for a federal indictment. While the feds still needed probable cause to get search warrants, the grand jury didn't need to meet that bar for subpoenas to be issued and for people to be compelled to testify in the investigation of a potential crime. Those subpoenaed could talk with their lawyers outside the grand jury room but counsel was forbidden from joining their clients during their testimony. That didn't mean witnesses were forthcoming, especially white men in lynching cases, but it was one of the best shots the government had.

The two prosecutors brought in to make the case read through the 353-page-plus summary written by the FBI agents who'd been investigating the crimes. The lawyers issued 106 subpoenas with hopes of finally getting to the bottom of what had happened that day on the banks of the Apalachee River. Their primary focus was to find out if anyone in the sheriff's office had aided in the lynchings. If they discovered that someone at the jail had notified the lynchers when Roger Malcom was being released, then that could be probable cause for a federal violation under Section 52. And probable cause would trigger federal search warrants that might then prove who killed the four.

When the grand jury convened, black and white witnesses were kept in separate rooms as they waited to testify. Reporters roamed the halls and around the perimeter of the courthouse, trying to get insight into what was being revealed. The grand jury questioned Loy Harrison for nine hours over two days. They also talked with George Dorsey's mother and his family. Most still lived on Harrison's farm and worked for him.

Some observers thought it was obvious that Harrison had threatened his workers to get their silence or bribed them, or both. Each one repeated stock phrases about believing Harrison's account of the afternoon of the lynchings, and each was tight-lipped upon exiting the jury's chambers.

The grand jury was only a day or two from concluding when the federal lawyers found out a key piece of information that investigators had forgotten to share with them. Major Jones, a black man who was a trustee of the town jail, usually slept in an unlocked room on the first floor of the jail. The first night of Roger Malcom's incarceration, and for two nights after, Deputy Sheriff Lewis Howard changed Jones's sleeping arrangement and had him in a locked cell on the second floor of the jail. He also told Jones it was because he didn't want the mob that was coming for Roger Malcom to grab Jones by mistake.

If the deputy knew a mob was coming for Roger and didn't take steps to protect him, or simply allowed him to be bonded out while a mob waited, he could be in violation of federal law. Other inmates on those nights corroborated Jones's story as they'd also heard the deputy tell Malcom that a mob was agitating against him.

Ignoring or overlooking the value of Jones's information two months prior, when the agents first found out about it, didn't just delay the progress of a federal case. The agents could have taken Jones into custody to protect him, but they didn't. And in the intervening time Deputy Howard had told Jones to lie and say he was moved to the second floor because he was sick. Yes, he was tampering with a federal witness, but to be punished Deputy Howard had to get caught.

The silence of Major Jones effectively ended the grand jury investigation into the Moore's Ford lynchings, and with it the chance the killers would be punished.

CHAPTER 22

Spring Training

New York Giants Spring Training
Phoenix, Arizona

1950

KENNY WASHINGTON STAYED BUSY AFTER RETIRING FROM football. He was a hot ticket for public appearances and in 1949 joined Bob Waterfield in a charity softball triple-header that included the Rockford Peaches of the All-American Girls Professional Baseball League, made famous in the film *A League of Their Own.*

Washington also dabbled in politics. Since he was a former sports star with a high profile in Los Angeles, and particularly within the black community, politicians constantly sought Washington's endorsement. He didn't claim a strong party affiliation at the time and generally backed moderate Republicans of the day, such as Los Angeles mayor Fletcher Bowron and Governor Earl Warren.

In 1950, Washington was listed as an organizer for Independents for Nixon, a group supporting young Republican House representative Richard Nixon in his Senate race against Helen Gahagan Douglas—a former actress who had become the first woman to serve as a Democratic congressional representative from California. Throughout his political career, Nixon was known for currying support among current and former athletes, which some critics ascribed to his thwarted football career at Whittier College.

Washington's daughter, Karin Cohen, suspected her father consciously chose to maintain a middle-of-the-road stance in politics in the years after his retirement. She recalled that her father and her mother both staunchly supported John F. Kennedy over Nixon in the 1960 presidential election, however. That apparent shift in Kenny Washington's political leanings corresponded with a larger charge in black voting patterns across the twentieth century from solidly Republican before the 1930s to evenly split in the late 1940s, then majority Democratic by the late 1960s.

Besides moderate engagement in regional politics, Washington also kept busy with film roles in Hollywood, a favored second career for many sports luminaries in Southern California. In his first major screen role he starred as a barely fictionalized version of himself in the almost-all-black cast of *When Thousands Cheer* in 1940. In the fall of 1949 he costarred in the film *Pinky*, one of the more talked about "race films" of the year.

The title character of *Pinky* was a mixed-race nursing graduate who passed as white in the North and had a romance with a white doctor. She returned South to the black side of her family rather than address her racial background with her boyfriend. There Pinky ends up taking care of an ill white heiress played by Ethel Barrymore.

The heiress bequeaths her estate to Pinky, but the aristocrat's family challenges the will. In spite of long odds, Pinky wins control of the estate. Kenny Washington played Dr. Canady, who advocated for Pinky to turn the estate into a medical training center for black nurses and doctors. Pinky loses the romance with the white doctor, which she deemed hopeless anyway, and opens the clinic. The film was directed by Elia Kazan, later famous for directing *On the Waterfront* and for naming names before the House Un-American Activities Committee, which led to the blackballing of left-leaning artists in Hollywood during the height of the Red Scare. *Pinky* was the subject of some Oscar buzz, but nominations never materialized.

Even as Kenny Washington explored a number of career options, including acting and sales work for a liquor distributorship, he still wanted another shot at pro sports. Some football players thought Washington could still make the grade as a defender, but he chose to pursue baseball instead. On November 17, 1949, the *Los Angeles Times* noted that New York Giants manager Leo Durocher had invited Washington to try out for the Giants the following spring training in Phoenix, Arizona.

In his prime Washington was a more complete baseball player than his father had been. Blue had power and a great arm, like his son, but his size made him less nimble in the field and on the basepaths. Kenny was faster and hit for power and average. In high school he was initially considered too skinny to play football, so he began his prep career on the baseball diamond. In his senior year he led the Lincoln High Tigers to citywide titles in baseball as well as football.

When Washington arrived at UCLA, he played for the Bruin baseball team as well as playing football and running track. He broke the color barrier of UCLA's baseball team in 1937 and led the squad in batting average while splitting time between shortstop and second base. In 1938 he was again near the team leaders in batting average. He blasted a 425-foot home run to dead center off Stanford pitcher Cootie Thompson. It cleared not just the outfield wall but a tall tree behind the diamond. Legend held that Washington was one of only two men to hit a ball over the center field fence at St. Mary's College in northern California. The other was Joe DiMaggio.

Washington had played for several local semipro baseball teams over the years but never for very long. To prepare for his New York Giants tryout, he worked out to drop some bulk from his football playing weight. He thought the year off from competitive sports had helped his body heal, and a local baseball coach described Washington as having good power and a good arm, but acknowledged that the ex–gridiron star had a lot to catch up on to make it in the major leagues.

Giants skipper Durocher thought Washington could work as a backup at third base, which he'd played part-time in college, but thought Washington had a better chance as a reserve right fielder. Washington had never played that position and hadn't spent much time chasing flies since he'd shagged balls for teams at the Downey Avenue Playground in his youth. New York had a number of prospects in right, so Washington would have to beat out several players just to make the roster as a backup.

In the Giants' first game of the exhibition season, Washington manned right field and went hitless. Washington started for New York's "B" team in the next game and hit a screamer that skipped inside first base. Two runners scored, and Washington motored to third base for a triple. In the eighth inning he came up with the bases loaded and launched a grand slam. Washington got another hit in the B team's next game, and then went two for three with two runs batted in in a game against the Seattle Rainiers.

Washington consistently hit, but Leo Durocher wasn't as impressed by his fielding or baserunning. Just before the team packed up to conclude spring training and head back east, Durocher cut Washington.

"Nobody in camp has worked harder than Washington, but lack of experience—if nothing else—will keep him off our club," Durocher said. "Make no mistake, Kenny can really rap the ball, but his speed is only fair and I've been disappointed in his throwing." Durocher quickly agreed that a Triple A team should take a shot on the thirty-one-year-old ex-Bruin and that maybe Washington would earn another look from a major league squad.

Kenny Washington took one last shot at baseball. But this time he wasn't willing to play far from home. He signed with the Los Angeles Angels of the Pacific Coast League, a high-level minor league. He played for the Angels for a handful of weeks, from late March to late April of 1950. He struggled with his hitting, despite having smacked the ball so effectively for the New York Giants just weeks previously.

One day in April, Washington asked one of the Angels coaches a question during batting practice. How could he increase his chances of catching on with a major league club? (Some have attributed this to a conversation Washington had with the Giants manager Leo Durocher.) Despite the success of Jackie Robinson and Larry Doby, most big league squads were still much less willing to sign African Americans than other players, an unpleasant fact the manager would have known.

The man replied, perhaps jokingly or perhaps not, that it would help Washington's chances if Kenny pretended to be Cuban. Washington looked out at the field for a moment, the amber sun sinking in the west across from the foothills that still pointing skyward in the east. "I am American," he said, looking at the coach. Shortly after, he turned and headed to the bench, picked up his bag, and walked toward the field's chain-linked exit.

WASHINGTON, D.C., SHIVERED ON A TWENTY-DEGREE morning as Thurgood Marshall, Loren Miller, and their colleagues walked up the steps of the Supreme Court on January 15, 1948, to argue the consolidated *Shelley* v. *Kraemer* cases. When they entered the chambers for the beginning of oral arguments, they saw six of the nine justices were present. The seats for Stanley Reed, Robert Jackson, and Wiley Rutledge were empty; these three justices had removed themselves from the case. When a justice recused himself, no explanation was required, and none was offered in *Shelley*.

Observers speculated that the recused justices owned property covered by racially restrictive covenants, and this was quite possible. Reed, a Southern Democrat from Kentucky, had written the majority opinion in *Smith v. Allwright*, which struck down the all-white Democratic primary in Texas.

Smith v. Allwright was one of the cases that expanded the understanding of "state action" and was key to Marshall and Miller's argument against the covenants. But despite that decision, Reed was generally conservative on social issues. Years later, during *Brown v. Board of Education*, he was the last justice to join the unanimous decision to overturn the doctrine of "separate but equal."

Justice Jackson's decision to recuse himself may have been influenced by a long-standing feud with Justice Hugo Black, who had, Jackson believed, failed to recuse himself from cases where he should have. Jackson had served as chief U.S. prosecutor at the Nuremberg war crimes trials at the end of World War II, and his decision to avoid the covenant issue irked racial-equality activists. One telegram sent him read, "The perpetrators of the massacre of the Jews in the ghetto of Warsaw . . . have been vindicated by your decisive actions." Another critic compared him to Pontius Pilate washing his hands of responsibility in the crucifixion of Jesus.

With only six justices sitting on *Shelley*, the case could end in a split decision, which would allow the lower-court rulings to stand. Miller, Marshall, and the others needed at least four of the justices to rule in their favor.

On the day the hearings opened, Solicitor General Philip Perlman spoke first. The oral arguments in the titular *Shelley* case came next, followed by oral arguments in the McGhee case—the handling of which the McGhees' attorneys had passed to Miller and Marshall. The oral arguments in the consolidated Washington, D.C., cases would come at the end.

In his remarks, Solicitor General Perlman relied on many of the public-policy points highlighted by the President's Committee on Civil Rights, about how racially restrictive housing covenants hindered the federal government's ability to effectively address issues in housing and public health.

Attorney George Vaughn spoke on behalf of the Shelleys, and he began by focusing on the state-action argument. He used his country-lawyer oratory skills to denounce the role of covenants in modern society. These restrictions were the Achilles' heel of American democracy, he said, adding that as a son of a slave himself, he saw black Americans knocking on the nation's door and pleading, "Let me come in and sit by the fire. I helped build the house."

The lawyer representing the Missouri covenanters rebutted that the question before the court was a legal one, not a public-policy one. He emphasized that many individuals would be affected by whatever ruling came down in the case, and that many of those affected would be white homeowners. He added to like or dislike, pick or choose, was human nature, and thus the covenants were an exercise of natural rights.

Justice Felix Frankfurter took the lead in querying both sides. "Are there any contract clauses your courts have struck down as contrary to public policy?" he asked the attorneys for the covenanters. When they said yes, Frankfurter asked them where the courts got the power to do so.

Thurgood Marshall and Loren Miller argued the McGhee case. They identified the ways that enforcement of the covenants constituted state action and reiterated recent Supreme Court cases where the definition of state action had been broadened by the court's decisions. Marshall emphasized the impact of covenants on public health, that the overcrowding they created increased the risk of unsanitary conditions, and their impact on African American morale.

The Detroit and D.C. covenanters were represented by James Crooks, who argued that the homeowners had a right to choose their associates and that they used the covenants to protect that right. If that right meant anything, then it should be enforced. Frankfurter interjected, "But the citizens couldn't enforce it themselves. They need the full strength of the state's judicial power to enforce something which the state could not itself declare as state policy. Is that a fair statement of the case?"

"Yes, I think so," Crooks replied.

On May 3, the Supreme Court returned its decision. At one P.M. James Crooks rushed a terse telegram to his colleagues: "All covenant cases decided adversely. Was in court when opinions rendered. Letter will follow." The Supreme Court ruled unanimously that the covenants were legal in themselves but courts could not be used to enforce them. Such enforcement would make a branch of government an actor in discrimination. Marshall, Miller, their colleagues, and the black homeowners had won.

Chief Justice Fred Vinson outlined the relevant issues and reasons for the decision: "Among the civil rights intended to be protected from discriminatory state action by the Fourteenth Amendment are the rights to acquire, enjoy, own and dispose of property." Judicial enforcement of covenants was state action, and that state action deprived African Americans of the protections guaranteed under the Fourteenth Amendment.

The next day, J. D. Shelley came home from his construction job to find his wife, Ethel, sitting on the porch reading the newspaper. She looked up, smiled, and held the news out to him. The next day, local papers ran pictures of the Shelleys sitting on their couch, their children around them, enjoying the home that was now theirs to keep.

The impact was not lost on legal experts or close followers of civil rights issues. While the institution of Jim Crow still stood, the *Shelley* decision had set a precedent for dismantling it. As one observer wrote, "The Court appears . . . to have seriously undermined the foundation of an extensive field of state segregation laws previously deemed unassailable."

CHAPTER 23

Goalposts

Cleveland Municipal Stadium
Cleveland, Ohio

1950

THE BROWNS KICKED OFF THEIR INAUGURAL NFL season against the league's very best, the 1949 NFL champion Philadelphia Eagles. Philadelphia coach Greasy Neale had been one of the more vocal NFL voices in dismissing the Browns and repudiating the racial integration personified by Willis, Motley, and others. In the off-season, the Browns had added two more black players, rookie Emerson Cole from Toledo University (now the University of Toledo) and Len Ford, the end who had previously played with the Los Angeles Dons of the AAFC. Ohio fans knew Ford well from his days with the University of Michigan, where he teamed with Bob Mann to form one of the most successful pass reception tandems in the Big Ten. (Ford had played both ways in college, but Paul Brown used Ford mainly on defense.)

Philadelphia's star rusher Steve Van Buren missed the season opener with an injury. But that alone didn't account for the 35–10 beating they took from the Browns. Bill Willis knocked down four passes, and Len Ford repeatedly dropped Eagles runners for losses. Marion Motley anchored an early goal-line stand as a linebacker, making up for a fumble that had set up Philadelphia in Cleveland territory.

The biggest surprise was how thoroughly the Browns demolished the Eagles defense. The Eagles were known for a 5-2-4 defense that had previously thwarted more pass-focused T formation teams. But in replacing a linebacker with a defensive back, Philadelphia had removed a middle linebacker. Paul

Brown had his ends and backs run every which way, dragging the defense wide and softening the middle for punishing runs up the gut with Motley. With no middle linebacker and the ones outside cheating wide to support pass defense, Motley bulldozed up the middle time and time again.

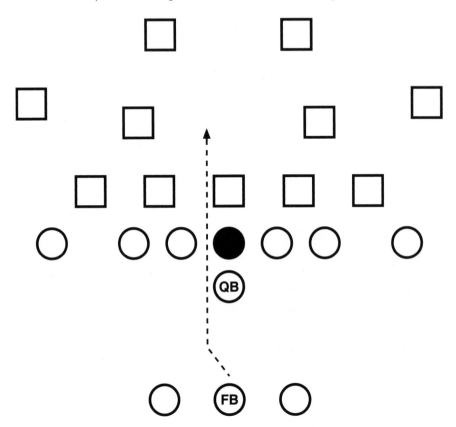

Browns T formation with Ends Split Wide vs. 5-2-4 Eagle Defense
Spreading ends wide forced defenders wider, opening up the middle for Motley.

When the defense drifted back inside to slow Motley, Otto Graham went to the air. He hit Dub Jones for a 59-yard touchdown in the first quarter and Dante Lavelli for a 26-yard score in the second. He tacked on a touchdown throw to Mac Speedie in the third quarter and dove one yard for another score in the fourth. Graham would finish 21 of 38 for 346 yards, with three passing touchdowns to two interceptions.

The Browns demolished most of their competition during the 1950 regular season, except for the New York Giants. In their third game of the season Clevelend lost to New York 6–0. Giants coach Steve Owen had driven to Philadelphia the first week of the season to scout the Browns. He saw Graham throwing to Speedie and Lavelli along the sidelines and to the backs in the flats. Owen realized that the Eagle linebackers were taking the wrong angles on the outside throws.

Owen had previously created a 5-3-3 defense with some success early in the 1940s. Philadelphia's Neale had taken the idea a step further with the 5-2-4. But the Browns had found a flaw in the scheme and exploited it with rushes up the middle. So how could Owen have sufficient pass coverage without sacrificing run defense in the middle of the field? What he came up with was the precursor to the modern 4-3 defense.

The Giants had gotten a wealth of defensive-back talent from the dissolved AAFC New York Yankees franchise: future coaching legend Tom Landry, Harmon Rowe, and Otto Schnellbacher. These three joined Emlen Tunnell to make the best defensive backfield in the sport. Owen decided to use four defensive backs as Neale had, but with Landry and Rowe at the corners and Schnellbacher and Tunnell at safety.

But Owen also kept John Cannady stationed at middle linebacker to thwart Motley in the middle and used six linemen. The trick was, Owen flexed his defensive ends so they sometimes rushed the quarterback and sometimes dropped into coverage as if they were linebackers. To execute the scheme he needed the players to not only understand the system but make quick adjustments on the field. In stepped Tom Landry.

"Steve was a great guy on concepts, but he wasn't a great detail man," Landry said. "He just drew the thing up on the board and handed me the chalk and left me to explain it . . . Emlen played next to me. We sort of worked things out on our own, on the field."

In the first Cleveland–New York matchup, the Giants scored on a short run in the first quarter and shut out the Browns the rest of the way. Cleveland only managed 250 total yards and turned the ball over five times, three of them interceptions of Graham. The Giant defense started the game double-covering both Speedie and Lavelli. "In the second half Brown had Graham rolling out and throwing underneath the retreating defensive ends," Landry noted. "So the ends started blitzing and the cornerbacks rolled up, and it gave them more problems." When New York won 6–0, it was the first time Paul Brown had been shut out as a pro coach.

The upside for the Browns was they only had to wait three weeks for a chance at revenge. But in the rematch, the Browns fared even worse on offense, committing seven turnovers and only netting 130 yards. This time the Giants came out in a 5-1-5 with five defensive backs. No team had ever regularly played with that many defensive backs, though that season would eventually see teams use up to six defensive backs in a desperate attempt to thwart passing juggernauts like the Browns and Rams. The Browns did manage to score in their second battle with the Giants but still lost, 17–13.

The Browns thrashed the Pittsburgh Steelers the following week and continued to handle all non–New York teams. They beat the Eagles a second time. This time Paul Brown stubbornly refused to call a pass play all game after Greasy Neale dismissed the pass-happy Browns as more of a basketball team than a football team after his squad lost to them in the opener. The Browns still beat the Eagles 13–7. Meanwhile, the New York Giants also ran off a string of victories after suffering two losses early in the season. Cleveland and New York were the class of the NFL's American Division and concluded the season with identical 10-2 records. They'd meet in a playoff to determine who would advance to the NFL Championship Game, to face the best of the National Division.

Cleveland hosted the Giants on December 17. The temperature was in the midteens, the ground frozen, and a thin blanket of snow covered the turf. Neither team had excelled offensively in the previous two meetings, but this third battle underscored just how difficult the conditions were and spotlighted the quality of both defenses.

On their first drive the Browns marched deep into Giants territory, but stalled on the five-yard line. Groza kicked a short field goal to give Cleveland an early three–zero lead. Neither team got closer to the end zone until the fourth quarter, when a great play by Willis and a goal-line stand by Cleveland proved pivotal.

New York had moved the ball to the Browns 36-yard line when quarterback Charley Conerly handed off to speedster Eugene "Choo Choo" Roberts. The scatback broke free around the right end with a clear path to the end zone. Willis, manning the middle of the defense, sprinted back, angling to the sideline to cut off Roberts. Willis flung himself at Roberts's back at the seven and dragged him to the ground at the four. "All I could think of," Willis said later, "was that number on Roberts's back represented the championship running away from me."

But the Giants still had first and goal at the Cleveland four. Two running plays netted only a yard. Conerly's pass on third down was snagged by

Giants end Bob McChesney, but one of the Giants was offside, negating the completion. On the next play the Browns seemed to have escaped unscathed when Tommy James intercepted the Conerly pass, but Cleveland was flagged for holding. First and goal again for New York.

The Cleveland defense held for another sequence, and the Giants settled for a field goal to tie the game at 3–3. When the Browns got the ball back, they decided to rely on the running game. But that didn't mean they handed off to Motley, whom the Giants had keyed on. They used the fullback as a decoy and had Graham run the ball, which had the added bonus of eliminating the possibility of a fumble on the handoff, always a risk with a cold and wet ball. Graham ran numerous quarterback draws and bootlegs to push the ball down the field, five, six, seven yards at a time. The team stalled at the Giants 22, with Graham having picked up 45 yards rushing on that drive alone.

Groza lined up to attempt a field goal with 58 seconds left. The snap and hold were good, and the beefy kicker drilled it through. The Browns led 6–3. In the closing seconds Jim Martin sacked Conerly in the end zone for a safety, securing the Browns' place in the NFL title game, which they would host on Christmas Eve.

Like the Browns, the Rams struggled mightily with one opponent in their division. For them it was the Chicago Bears. For all their firepower, Los Angeles stumbled in its first game with the Bears, losing 24–20. The Rams passed for 263 yards, but one of the Chicago scores came on a returned Waterfield interception. The next week Van Brocklin threw four touchdown passes in a 45–28 thwacking of the New York Yanks (the former New York Bulldogs had adopted the name Yanks, almost the exact same name of the defunct New York AAFC team—a strange merry-go-round of team nicknames). Los Angeles then beat the 49ers 35–14 with Deacon Dan Towler scoring a rushing touchdown for the third week in a row. Unlike the Browns, the 49ers struggled in their first year in the NFL and posted a 3-9 record.

The Rams' second loss saw them surrender 56 points to the Philadelphia Eagles. Philadelphia scored five touchdowns before the Rams even got on the board. Bouncing right back, Waterfield and Van Brocklin combined for 353 yards passing in edging the Detroit Lions, then laid 70 points on the Baltimore Colts and 65 on the Lions in a rematch. Los Angeles blitzed through much of the rest of their schedule, running up more than 40 points per game in two separate wins over Green Bay and in their second date with the Yanks.

Los Angeles took their third loss of the season, and their second to the Chicago Bears, on November 26. The Bears victory gave Chicago the division lead with only a few games left. But they dropped their next contest against their crosstown rivals, the Cardinals, to sink back into a tie with the Rams. Los Angeles finished the regular season at 9-3. They didn't just lead the league in passing. Los Angeles's 466 points during the regular season was 100 more than the next most prolific offense. Their quarterbacks combined for almost 1,000 more passing yards than the next-best team. They were also the first team in league history to attempt more passes than rushes in a season.

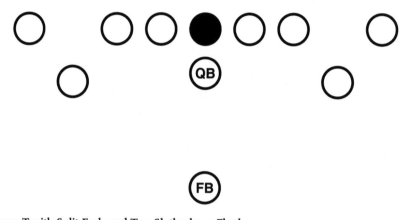

Rams T with Split Ends and Two Slotbacks or Flankers
Everyone wide, running overlapping patterns that stretched the field laterally and vertically.

But because of their middle-of-the-pack defense, they didn't run away with the division. Like the Browns, the Rams would have to beat a team they had lost to twice in the regular season to make the championship game. More than 83,000 fans showed up at the Coliseum to witness the Western battle. The oddsmakers gave the Rams a seven-point edge, even against a team that had beaten them twice. One difference: The weather report called for sun, while the first Rams-Bears game had been contested in rain and the second in snow.

Norm Van Brocklin got the starting nod at quarterback for Los Angeles, partly because Bob Waterfield was suffering from a viral infection and 103-degree fever. But it was Waterfield who gave the Rams the early lead in the first quarter when his 43-yard field goal attempt careened off the right upright and through. Van Brocklin came out wild and missed his first eight passes. The Bears took a 7–3 lead with a rushing touchdown in the second quarter. Waterfield subbed in at quarterback and quickly found his favorite target, Tom Fears. The passing combo lit up the Bears defense. Before the half, Waterfield hit Fears for two long touchdowns, one covering 43 yards and the other 68 yards, to give the Rams a 17–7 lead. On the longer reception Fears turned around defensive back George McAfee so badly that the coverage man tripped and fell down as Fears caught the ball.

In the third quarter Waterfield found Fears for yet another touchdown, this time a modest 27-yarder that put the game out of reach. Fears did all the work on that touchdown, catching the ball in the flat, sidestepping one potential tackler, ducking another, and wriggling out of the grasp of a third before stumbling into the end zone. Waterfield would finish the game 14 of 21 for 280 yards, with three touchdowns and one interception. For once Van Brocklin had a cold hand, connecting on only 2 of 10 pass attempts. Fears caught 11 passes for 198 yards.

The Rams defense held on during several Chicago fourth-down attempts and three Los Angeles defenders intercepted Bears quarterback Johnny Lujack. The Rams defense had never been the key component of their 1950 regular-season success, but this time the unit came up big with six sacks on top of three interceptions and two fumble recoveries. After the game, Bears coach George Halas described the Rams as "the finest passing team I've ever played against."

WHEN OTTO GRAHAM FUMBLED IN THE FOURTH QUARTER of the 1950 NFL title bout, there was only three minutes left in the game and the Browns trailed 28–27. The Rams recovered Graham's fumble and, holding a 1-point lead, decided to play conservatively. They ran the ball twice and quickly faced third and 10. Still they ran, handing off to Glenn Davis, who was tackled four yards short of a first down. Waterfield went back into punt formation and launched a kick that Cleveland returner Cliff Lewis brought back to the 31-yard line. One minute and forty-nine seconds remained.

Cleveland's offense returned to the field for one last chance. On the first play, Graham dropped back to pass. The Ram rush came through and he darted right, stiff-arming a defensive back on his way. He saw a crease down the sideline and scrambled to the Los Angeles 47-yard line. On the next play he saw Rex Bumgardner open and hit him at the Los Angeles 40.

Next came an incompletion and a throw to the opposite sideline to Dub Jones, who snagged the pass and ducked inside to the 23-yard line. Less than a minute left. Bumgardner ran another out to the sideline and Graham threw the pass ahead of him. The fullback stumbled forward, but he plucked the pass with his fingertips before crashing onto the icy ground at the 11. Graham called a quick quarterback sneak to center the ball at the nine-yard line. Thirty seconds to go. The Browns called a time-out and prepared for a field goal attempt.

The gusts off Lake Erie made any field goal attempt at the open end of the field dicey, as the Cleveland players well knew. Some even claimed to have seen a *snap*—not even a kick—sent wide of its mark by the strong winds.

In the huddle center Hal Herring was so confident he asked holder Tommy James where he wanted the laces on the ball to face on the snap. James laughed and Groza smiled. The Browns trudged up to the line with the fate of their first NFL season coming down to this play. Herring nailed the snap, and James grabbed the ball from the frozen air. The holder deftly angled the tip of the ball just as Groza drove his right foot through. The ball knifed through the wind. It sliced to the right but curled inside the upright. The Browns had a 30–28 lead with 28 seconds left. The fans who had survived the brutal weather and the emotional ups and downs of the thrilling game screamed wildly, though their clapping was deadened by gloves and shrieks of joy muffled by the wind.

The game was not over, though. Los Angeles could yet get a good kickoff return and, with a long pass attempt, a game-winning field goal attempt of their own. Although Bob Waterfield's only possible weakness was his lack of arm strength, the Rams had Norm Van Brocklin. He might be able to launch a miracle throw that could give the Rams a shot at victory. Groza kicked off, and Jerry Williams returned the ball from inside the 15 to the Rams 35-yard line. When he got hit, he fumbled and the Browns recovered it. But the referee waved off the play, saying that Groza started forward on the kickoff before the referee had whistled he was clear to go. The kick would be replayed. This time the Rams returned the ball to their own 46-yard line—nearly midfield. Waterfield was a better than average place-kicker, but he'd never connected on 50-yarders as Groza had.

With the goalposts at the front of end zone, the Rams needed roughly 20 yards to try a 40-yard field goal. With the windy conditions and Waterfield's kicking range, they likely wanted to gain 25 yards. And they only had 20 seconds left.

On the first play Van Brocklin backpedaled and looked downfield. He uncorked a long pass down the right sideline, hoping to reach Bobby Boyd. Defensive back Warren Lahr was running right alongside Boyd, and as the ball sailed long it was Lahr who caught it over his shoulder. Cleveland fans leaped to their feet, but Otto Graham and his teammates standing on the sideline swiveled to look at the officials. Lahr had caught the ball inside the 10 and with his momentum carrying him forward, Boyd's tackle pushed him into the end zone. For a second the Browns worried the referee might call a safety, which would tie the game. But the referee blew the whistle and marked the interception good at the seven-yard line.

Fans poured from the stands and swallowed Lahr whole. The Browns bench ran onto the field. Fans jumped on Bill Willis and Len Ford, hugging and congratulating them. Graham made his way across the field to shake Waterfield's hand amid the raucous crowd. Hal Herring's jersey was ripped from his back. Groza barely escaped the press of fans, and teammates had to move quickly to reach the clubhouse in one piece.

The fans who couldn't reach the new champions went after the goalposts, tearing them down in one enormous surge. The uprights soon disappeared, last seen being carted out of the stadium by a gang of souvenir hunters. Demonstrations were equally as riotous in the stands. A bonfire burned in the center field bleachers, although by the time stadium ushers reached it, it had burned out.

Once the Browns had escaped their own delirious fans, they staged a victory celebration of their own in the locker room, shouting, laughing, and hugging one another in delirious exhaustion. Coach Paul Brown went from player to player to offer his congratulations. Usually the epitome of composure, Brown struggled with the emotions evoked by the comeback his team had made. "This is the gamest bunch of guys in the world," he said in barely more than a whisper. "Next to my wife and family, these guys are my life. What a merry Christmas they've made it! This is the greatest football team a coach ever had. Bless 'em all."

CHAPTER 24

Overtime

Lynn Coleman, the black patrolman shot at Euclid Beach, was suspended in March of 1947—for keeping his gun next to his hospital bed while recovering from surgery. His superior officers said he had disrespected them and that he had threatened nurses with the gun. But at a hearing on the gun-related charges, the two nurses admitted under cross-examination from Coleman's lawyer that Coleman had never threatened them in any manner.

Coleman explained later that he kept the gun with him for safety: "Lying wounded in a hospital which was exposed to visits by several entrances, I felt I should keep the gun or have a police detail—which was denied me for protection—particularly after I received threats over the telephone at the hospital and my wife got threatening calls as well."

In the charges of disrespecting superior officers, Coleman's account of events pitted him against a sergeant and a lieutenant who had visited him in his hospital room. Predictably, the word of the senior officers prevailed. The Cleveland Police Department suspended Coleman without pay for ninety days, and he lost all vacation days for a year. Throughout the suspension Coleman maintained that the punishment was not about the gun or his behavior at the hospital, but his actions in supporting the protesters at Euclid Beach the day he was shot.

Coleman continued to fight even after the charges were upheld. He sued Euclid Beach for $50,000. Though he lost, his effort sparked the founding of the Shield Club, an organization of black police officers in Cleveland. He also sued the police department for racial discrimination he'd faced on the force in the 1930s and 1940s. Eventually, the City of Cleveland paid Coleman $21,300. It wasn't justice, but it was more than nothing.

Euclid Beach reopened for the 1947 season in May, with the roller rink under a private membership system and the dance hall and beach still closed. Because Councilman Charles V. Carr's Euclid Beach Ordinance had passed, the Humphrey Company couldn't ban black patrons from these areas without risking financial penalties. They chose to close these attractions until private groups asked to lease those facilities. Whether the Humphrey Company was directly behind the creation of these clubs or simply benefited from them, the result was the same. Private clubs weren't required to follow the Euclid Beach Ordinance regarding their membership practices. They claimed no one would be rejected based on race. However, applicants were required to submit their applications in person, which many observers saw as a means to screen by race.

Activists and the *Call & Post* concluded that these groups amounted to the park's next attempt to enforce segregation on its grounds, a strategy similar to the one state Democratic parties had used in primaries to skirt the Fifteenth Amendment's guarantee of the right to vote. The Supreme Court had struck down the white primaries in *Smith v. Allwright*. But it was unclear if that precedent would also be applied to rights not as starkly guaranteed by the Constitution.

Cleveland municipal leaders, including the mayor, vowed to look into the legality of the private organizations leasing the park's public attractions. No investigation materialized, however, and the roller-skating club received its license to operate at Euclid Beach just before the park opened for the season. A private dance club applied for and received their license to operate the dance pavilion shortly thereafter.

Weeks later, Alberta Crawford received $500 from the Humphrey Company after having sued the company under the state civil rights law for denying her admission to the dance floor. It was the largest fine handed down in Cuyahoga County under the state law, the maximum allowed. Other CORE members settled for undisclosed amounts.

Juanita Morrow's complaint against park guard Alexander Campbell for violating her civil rights was decided with his acquittal. The year earlier she'd met Wally Nelson, another CORE activist, who was one of sixteen men who participated in the first Freedom Ride (called the Journey of Reconciliation), in 1947. Nelson and his fellow riders challenged segregated seating on public transit on buses in the Upper South. Morrow and Nelson married in 1948 and moved to Cincinnati. Morrow resumed her activism at Cincinnati's version of Euclid Beach Park, the Coney Island amusement park.

Morrow would later say in an oral history that it was interesting she spent so much time and effort to get into amusement parks when she had never liked them. But they were popular, and thus a visible site for activism. Over the next several years Morrow and other activists achieved marginally more success at Cincinnati's Coney Island than they had at Euclid Beach.

None of these civil rights protestors could know that urban amusement parks connected to public transportation were on the wane. The next wave of amusement facilities would effectively achieve segregation through location and accessibility, without requiring the outright banning of black visitors. In 1955 Disneyland opened in Anaheim, California. Patrons needed a car to get to the park, which had parking and entrance fees. At Euclid Beach, visitors wandered the grounds for free and only paid when they went on a ride, visited a specific attraction, or bought food.

Disneyland put these costs up front, effectively excluding those on the economic margins. Disneyland's phenomenal success made it the blueprint for future entertainment attractions. The amusement parks that didn't move to the suburbs decayed. In the 1960s activists finally succeeded in pressuring park owners to fully desegregate. More black patrons came to urban parks, but with white flight to the suburbs in full force, far fewer white ones did.

Instead of maintaining urban amusement parks, many owners let the facilities fall into disrepair and then sold the land—which had appreciated over the decades—to developers of office buildings or high-rise apartments. Civil rights activists eventually won the battle for equal access only to see the parks razed and replaced by buildings that were nearly as exclusionary as the most segregated amusement parks had been.

Throughout the 1940s and beyond, Juanita Morrow Nelson maintained a correspondence with her mentor from the Howard University sit-ins, Pauli Murray. While at Howard, Murray had dreamed of joining Thurgood Marshall at the NAACP's Legal Defense Fund. But she tired of the blatant sexism she encountered in both legal work and among her black male would-be colleagues. She coined the phrase Jane Crow to describe the overwhelming barriers black women faced from both whites along racial lines and black men along gender lines.

During her college years and after, Murray grappled with her sexuality. In her private writings she didn't sound ashamed about her attractions to women or desperate to hide her romantic relationships. The term homosexual didn't fit her, though, and she didn't feel that she related to women romantically as a woman, but more as a man. Whether Murray would have identified with any of the more modern terms (queer, butch, stud, trans, etc.) is impossible to know. But mainstream society clearly frowned on her sexuality, her gender presentation (she frequently wore pants at a time when women rarely did in their professional lives), and her unwillingness to completely hide those aspects of herself.

In 1938 Murray challenged the University of North Carolina's ban on black students in seeking admission to its law school. When rejected by the school, she sent information about her case to Thurgood Marshall, thinking hers would make an excellent test case related to a recent Supreme Court decision. "I then got the shock of my life," Murray remembered. "I learned that the NAACP very carefully picks its cases . . . They had to win every case and go carefully into the background of the person who is going to be the bearer of the case . . . The way that I read this was, 'We have to be very careful of the people that we select. They have to be simon-pure and you are not quite simon-pure enough.' I was too maverick."

After her time in California, she returned to the East Coast and worked in private practice in the late 1940s. In 1951 she published *States' Laws on Race and Color*, which Thurgood Marshall called the "bible of the civil rights movement," a bittersweet honor given her exclusion from the opportunities, and acclaim that a top legal position with one of the best-known civil rights organizations might have provided. Marshall incorporated Murray's arguments in *States Laws' on Race and Color* in his successful argument of *Brown v. Board of Education*.

As with contemporary Bayard Rustin, reactions to Murray's sexuality likely curtailed her chances of having a prominent public role within the civil rights movement of the 1950s and '60s. But this exclusion did not stop Murray from continuing her battles against racism and sexism.

In 1965 she was the first African American to receive a J.S.D. from Yale Law School. In 1966 she cofounded the National Organization for Women, which would struggle to address racism as much as the NAACP and other typically male-led organizations did with sexism. Morrow taught at the Ghana School of Law and Brandeis University before becoming the first black woman ordained as an Episcopal priest in 1977.

In 1971 the Supreme Court's ruling in *Reed v. Reed* extended the Fourteenth Amendment's Equal Protection Clause to women for the first time. Future Supreme Court justice Ruth Bader Ginsburg won the Reed case and she listed Pauli Murray as coauthor of her brief in honor of Murray's groundbreaking legal work and advocacy.

THE SUPREME COURT'S RULING IN *SHELLEY V. KRAEMER* resolved the legality of racially restrictive housing covenants—technically legal but unenforceable by the judicial system—but it didn't stop covenanters from trying to segregate housing. After the *Shelley* decision, the Los Angeles Realty Board and the California Real Estate Association proposed a state constitutional amendment to restore convenants.

If covenanters couldn't sue to remove black homeowners or renters from their homes, perhaps they could sue the white people who broke the covenants? In one Los Angeles neighborhood, a group of white residents had agreed to a covenant that required the terms of the pact—including a ban on non-Caucasian tenants—to be carried through all transfers of land ownership. One signee subsequently sold his property to a black family, in breach of the covenant. The covenanters reasoned that if they took no action against the black residents but sued the white seller for damages, they could skirt the issue of discriminatory state action.

Loren Miller took the lead in defending the white seller who broke the covenant. California state courts held that the ruling in *Shelley v. Kraemer* also negated this new tactic to enforce housing segregation. The covenanters petitioned to the U.S. Supreme Court, which agreed to hear the case in 1953. This time, Miller was the lead counsel and Thurgood Marshall was listed as cocounsel on the brief.

The Supreme Court upheld the state rulings by a tally of 6–1. The justices substantively agreed that while the legal action being taken was now against a different party in the dynamic, the outcome was the same. Using state courts to execute lawsuits against covenant breakers was deemed discriminatory state action. But the effort to preserve covenants didn't immediately stop with these decisions. Developers and neighborhood associations still wrote covenants into housing agreements. And residents still had to defend themselves in court. That slowly waned through the 1950s and 1960s.

In 1964 Loren Miller was appointed to the Superior Court of California, where he sat for three years until his death. During that time he wrote *The Petitioners: The Story of the Supreme Court of the United States and the Negro,* outlining the fraught position of black Americans in relationship to the

Supreme Court. Miller decried the need for, and reliance on, judicial efforts to achieve civil rights goals.

Court action might be the best option when neither the legislative nor executive branches were capable of or willing to create change. But this also put all the pressure and burden of asserting equality on black Americans—the petitioners—to come up with the money, time, and specialized resources to take on the legal system in court.

Miller's family continued his legacy after his death and put them in a unique position in California state history. Miller's son, Loren Jr., also became a judge in the California Superior Court system. In 2003, Robin Miller Sloan, Loren's granddaughter, was appointed to the Superior Court of Los Angeles County, making the Millers the first family in California to have three successive linear generations serve as judges in the state. Now Loren Miller Elementary School sits a few blocks from the corner of West Florence and South Vermont, in the narrow part of South Los Angeles between Inglewood and South Gate, an area covered by racially restrictive housing covenants before the school's namesake began his work.

THURGOOD MARSHALL REFUSED TO HIDE HIS FRUSTRATION at how the Monroe lynching case had gone. In a memo to NAACP executive secretary Walter White, Marshall wrote, "I have no faith in [FBI director J. Edgar] Hoover or his investigators and there is no use in my saying I do. With them on the spot the next day and having been down there with that many men, that they can't find one member of the mob . . . to me it is unbelievable."

Lamar Howard, a young black man who worked at the ice plant in Monroe, was one of the townsfolk subpoenaed by the grand jury at the end of the case. Under oath, he had said that the day before the lynchings one of the suspects, James Verneer, had stopped by the ice plant with two guns and cleaned them. Verneer's guns matched the make and type of two of the weapons used in the murders. Howard also testified that several hours before the lynchings, he saw Verneer speaking with Loy Harrison, the man who had brought the victims to the bridge under the pretense of bailing out Roger Malcom.

A month after the grand jury disbanded, several men stopped by the ice plant and took Lamar Howard out back and pistol-whipped him. When Howard got home, his family took him to the hospital. They reported the assault to the county sheriff. The sheriff told them that because the assault happened in town, it fell outside his jurisdiction.

Fearing he might be the next lynching victim, Howard and several family members left Monroe. Howard reported the attack to FBI agents at the bureau's Atlanta office. Shortly after the report, an anonymous call to the FBI claimed any federal investigators attempting to arrest Verneer would be driven out of town. This threat was relayed to J. Edgar Hoover, who ordered agents to arrest Verneer and his brother. The two men were arraigned on charges of intimidating a federal witness. Because the pistol-whipping was in retaliation for Howard's testimony in the lynching grand jury, a conviction had the potential to reopen the Moore's Ford case.

Several months later, James Verneer was tried. Numerous people at or near the ice plant testified that they heard or saw the beating, or that Verneer had admitted to the assault to them later that day. Verneer's own brother volunteered that after the beating he saw blood on his brother's knuckles. Howard repeated what he had told FBI agents after the beating. A guilty verdict seemed like a formality.

The case was in a federal court, but was still tried with a jury pool of Southern white men, who were more interested in preserving white supremacy than pursuing justice. The jury deadlocked and the judge declared a mistrial.

Lamar Howard returned to his new life in Atlanta, where he worked at the Butler Street YMCA and lived in Sweet Auburn. He likely did not know he lived and worked a few blocks from the spot where a horde of white men had threatened to kill future NAACP executive secretary Walter White's family four decades prior. Howard changed his last name so co-workers and others in Atlanta would not suspect his connection to the infamous lynchings in his hometown. But they found out anyway and gave him the nickname Monroe.

The Moore's Ford Bridge lynchings have never been solved. Several times over the decades the case has come under new scrutiny, when someone has come forward claiming to know who did it or that a now-dead relative had been involved in the murders. None of these leads have yielded definite answers, leaving the entire town under the shadow of both the lynchings themselves and the subsequent cover-up.

The history and meaning of the Monroe killings lives on in the present. Black activists in Atlanta reenact the lynchings annually to keep the memory of the victims alive, and to protest the continued violence against black Americans in the South and elsewhere.

THE PACIFIC COAST LEAGUE'S LOS ANGELES ANGELS cut Kenny Washington at the end of April 1950, and his baseball career ended. Shortly after that, he took a regional sales position for the local Cutty Sark distributor. He and his wife, son, and daughter lived a comfortable life in Los Angeles, where he remained well known and well loved.

Washington supported many community-building efforts behind the scenes, whether it was raising money for the YMCA or a new wing at the local hospital, or smaller efforts. "He gave money to everyone," his daughter, Karin, recalled. His former daughter-in-law agreed. "He took care of everybody," Marvel Washington said. "He'd go down to Mr. Potato [a produce store], in downtown L.A. and stock the truck full of fruits and vegetables. He'd drive through the neighborhoods and pass them out. And he always started out in Lincoln Heights."

As he got older, Kenny Washington's weeks mostly consisted of his work in sales, occasional trips to Santa Anita racetrack with friends, and dinners with his family. His son, Kenny, was fourteen and a half a years older than his daughter, Karin, and had a family of his own. Washington spent time at home with Karin and his wife, June, and visited his son's family as well. In the early 1960s the Washingtons became the first black family to buy a house in the Los Angeles neighborhood of Baldwin Hills. After retiring from sports Kenny would relax in the yard, wearing slacks and a polo while practicing golf, well, putting, or joking over cigars with his buddies while enjoying the view over much of South Los Angeles. If he thought about his NFL career or what might have been, he didn't show it. "I think he always continued to look forward," grandson Kirk Washington said. "From what Dad mention he didn't seem bitter."

Kenny and June divorced several years later. June and the kids kept the Baldwin Hills house, and Washington moved a mile away, on the other side of his daughter's school. When health problems arose later in his life, Washington moved back into the house with June and Karin, and they took care of him.

Karin remembered the days before his death he called family members to his hospital room. "He used to have people come by the hospital, and he would send his bets to the racetrack every day," Karin Cohen said. "His friends would place the bets and bring the money back. So he called us all there and he handed out money: fifty dollars to Kenny Jr., forty dollars to Marvel, thirty dollars to me, twenty dollars for [grandson] Kirk and ten dollars for [grandson] Kraig. These were the last winnings that he had from that day. He died either the next day or the day after."

Kenny Washington died from polyarteritis on June 24, 1971, sixteen months to the day before Jackie Robinson passed away. Washington was fifty-two years old when he died; Robinson was fifty-three. After Robinson's early death, many speculated that the emotional toll of breaking the color line as well as the physical stress of pro sports had cut short his life. It's possible the same could be said of Kenny Washington. After Washington's death, both Bob Waterfield and Jackie Robinson said he was the best football player they had ever played with.

Lincoln Heights has continued to recognize and celebrate Washington. Since 2011 the Kenny Washington Stadium Foundation, an organization of locals who seek to upgrade Lincoln High's field and dedicate it to Washington, have hosted a Kenny Washington Memorial Game every fall, complete with throwback jerseys and ceremonies honoring Washington's family, many of whom still live in Southern California.

THE YEAR AFTER WOODY STRODE JOINED THE Calgary Stampeders, he brought Sugarfoot Anderson north to join him. The Stampeders made it to the Grey Cup again in 1949, but failed to repeat as champions. Tales of their fans traveling across the country to the game drew almost as much interest as the contest itself. Anderson remained with the Stampeders for five more years, and he and his family settled in Calgary.

After retiring from football he worked as a car mechanic, and patrons often marveled at his ability to palm a car battery in each hand. Anderson later got an engineering degree and helped build the berm at the curve of the Bow River that cradles downtown Calgary. Still a legend in the city, Anderson is a beloved tie to the Stampeders' earliest glory days. He and the rest of the city celebrated another Grey Cup championship in 2014.

Strode injured his shoulder in 1949 and realized he wouldn't likely play again. He returned to Los Angeles not long after hanging up his cleats and transitioned to a career in film. His big break was in *Spartacus*, in which he played Draba, a gladiator who defeats the title character in combat, but then spares his life. The role was initially set to go to decathlete Rafer Johnson, but Johnson learned taking paid acting work might jeopardize his amateur standing and make him ineligible to compete in the 1960 Olympics. So Strode got the job instead. Early on, he won roles via his physique and athleticism. But as he continued in the industry, his acting steadily improved.

By the 1960s movie directors tapped Strode for a broad array of roles. He played an Ethiopian king in the *Ten Commandments*, and John Wayne's African American manservant in John Ford's *The Man Who Shot Liberty Valance*. He played Native American and Asian warriors and also took the lead in Ford's *Sergeant Rutledge*, a film about a black cavalryman accused, and then exonerated, of rape. Other notable performances came in *The Professionals* and *Once Upon a Time in the West*. Strode's last film credit was *The Quick and the Dead*, which was dedicated to him.

BILL WILLIS AND MARION MOTLEY HELPED LEAD the Browns to several more championships after their 1950 title. Willis retired after the 1953 season. In 1977 he was inducted into the Pro Football Hall of Fame. After hanging up his cleats Willis served as chairman of the Ohio Youth Commission. Willis spent thirty years with the commission. But his decades of work with youth stood as a greater achievement than his considerable gridiron prowess. He and his wife, Odessa, were members of the NAACP and the Urban League. They stayed in Ohio, living for a time in Cleveland and later in Columbus. Music and movies were two of his passions after he retired. He loved listening to jazz: Lionel Hampton, Lester Young, Miles Davis. He liked horror films and always caught the latest Woody Strode western.

"I remember in one of his last interviews," Clem Willis said, "it was kind of touching because he compared himself to a grain of sand. [The interviewer] asked if he felt like a pioneer. He said he felt like he was a grain of sand and doing what he was doing and doing his best at it. He realized that if it were not for other people, certain things wouldn't happen. He was fortunate enough for others to make opportunities for him, and later on he tried to make as many opportunities for others."

Like Woody Strode in Los Angeles, Marion Motley initially felt like an afterthought when he was signed, there more as a roommate for Willis than on his own merits. But when he retired, he had set an NFL record for rushing average at 6.7 yards per carry and that record still stands. Whether or not Paul Brown initially considered Motley secondary to Willis, the big fullback proved himself one of the greatest rushers and all-around players in NFL history. In 1968 Motley became the third Brown enshrined in the Hall of Fame, after Paul Brown and Otto Graham.

Like Willis, Motley spent his later career working with kids in Ohio. He regularly stated that the example of Willis, Washington, Strode, and himself breaking the color line in pro football encouraged Branch Rickey to promote Jackie Robinson to the major leagues in 1947.

"Branch Rickey was also in 1946 a part owner of the football Brooklyn Dodgers who played against the Cleveland Browns in the All-America Football Conference," said Joe Horrigan, executive vice president of the Pro Football Hall of Fame in the *Forgotten Four* documentary. "Branch Rickey once told Marion Motley, 'Had I not had the experience of seeing you and Bill Willis play in a contact sport without incident, I might not have had the courage to bring Jackie Robinson up into the majors.'"

OF ALL THE INDIVIDUALS IN THIS BOOK, Halley Harding is the one whose later life is least known. After the Rams arrived in L.A., he jumped from the *Los Angeles Tribune* to the *Los Angeles Sentinel* and wrote sports columns for a time. His byline disappeared from the paper, but he may have continued writing under the pseudonym Joe Raceman. He later moved to the Chicago area and wrote for several Chicago weeklies, including the *New Crusader*. Little is known about his life outside of work. But his reputation as a crusader remained.

"Halley used to tell the ofays that he got up every morning and proceeded to put his boxing gloves on as soon as he shaved and showered, to get ready to battle them and their prejudices!" Herman Hill, the West Coast correspondent for the *Pittsburgh Courier*, told *Ebony* magazine in 1970. Harding continued the fight when he moved to Chicago, where he was one of the sportswriters who exhorted the Cubs to sign their first black player, Ernie Banks. Harding worked at the *New Crusader* for fifteen years, until his death by stroke in 1967.

In the long-accepted history of the NFL's integration, Harding plays no role. For many years, the story went like this: In 1946, Leonard Roach, president of the Los Angeles Coliseum Commission, refused to give the Rams a lease to the stadium until they tried out black players. And, yes, Roach stated his opposition to racial discrimination and had signed a document binding the Rams to audition black players at the January 15, 1946, meeting. But Roach did not refuse a lease. The commission gave the Rams a lease well before the team signed Kenny Washington.

That same summer Halley Harding also pushed the AAFC's Los Angeles Dons to integrate their squad. But they too signed a lease without making any moves toward hiring black players. When Harding went to the commission to demand they uphold the agreement Roach had signed, Harding was told no such agreement existed. He and Herman Hill continued to attend Coliseum Commission meetings well after January 15, 1946, to pressure the commission and the Dons on integration. In one meeting's notes, the commission acknowledged that the newspapermen had attended, but the commissioners agreed, perhaps after Harding and Hill left, that the commission had no standing to tell teams who they could and could not hire. Leonard Roach did not attend the meeting, and signed the notes without comment.

CHAPTER 25

On History

THE INACCURATE STORY OF LEONARD ROACH'S LEADING the charge to integrate the Rams was taken up as gospel by local and national writers, white and black. The repetition of the story likely gave it more weight, as people assumed someone must have confirmed the story's truth. Moreover, most writers and readers may have assumed that because Jackie Robinson had a powerful white advocate in Branch Rickey, Kenny Washington and Woody Strode must have had someone similar.

Roach certainly did play a role. His verbal support of Washington's hiring might have provided Rams management the cover they needed from white fans who would oppose the signing of a black player. But the role of black sportswriters, and the larger black communities of Los Angeles, has been overlooked as the driving factor in the integration of pro football. "Kenny Washington had the support of the community and he had the support of the black press, which at that time was a lot more powerful than you might imagine it to be today," said Jarrett Bell, NFL columnist for USA Today.

Los Angeles in 1946 was a perfect time and place for their efforts. Washington and Strode had performed well on the field as collegians and semipros and were well liked off it, which gave Harding and his colleagues ideal candidates to argue for. The black press was at the height of its influ-ence in the 1940s. Despite the small size of the black community in Los Angeles compared to the numbers in Chicago, New York, or Detroit, the city supported three major black weeklies. The community also focused on achieving political power. "[The push to integrate the Rams] came off of World War II, the Double V campaign, the "Don't Buy Where You Can't Work" campaign. All of these are local campaigns where African Americans have been able to leverage significant political support despite being a very tiny percentage of the overall minority population," said Christopher

Jimenez y West, Assistant Professor of History at Pasadena City College, in explaining why pro football integration first happened in Los Angeles. "This (in the 1940s) is still largely an African American multi-generation of elites who have a relationship with—not one of patron and servant, and co-equal would be too far—but a constellation of elites that while they don't rotate in the same axis as white elites there is an acknowledgement that there is an axis over here that [white elites] have to at some level grapple with."

Kenny's friends from his old neighborhood, Lincoln Heights, might have provided an assist as well. After the Rams cut Strode in 1947 several of Washington's friends stopped by Strode's house and asked if he wanted retaliation on Rams owner Dan Reeves. Strode knew the guys were members of the mob. Might some "friends of Kenny's" have also "put in a good word" with the Rams management in 1946? "I could see that," said Karin Cohen. "That wouldn't surprise me at all."

The valorization of Roach in the story of pro football's integration brings up a larger question about how history is told. There can be no single telling or universal perspective on history. But it might surprise us to know the extent to which we tell our history, consciously or subconsciously, to reinforce what we want to believe about America as a country and about ourselves as Americans. "American historians, like their counterparts elsewhere, have often sought to construct an intellectually plausible lineage for the nation, while, until recently, excluding those . . . who seemed little more than obstacles to the expansion of Anglo-Saxon liberty and national greatness," noted historian Eric Foner in *Who Owns History?: Rethinking the Past in a Changing World.*

Jackie Robinson's story can be fit into a national narrative of immense individual accomplishments leading toward ever-greater freedom and equality. We believe that Robinson's great talent, will, and perseverance enabled him to overcome great odds and racial barriers. His story is told not just as the American Dream in action but a story of exceptional individualism—the Great Man Theory—played out on a baseball diamond.

"In America, there's been a long tradition of seeing the singular, exceptional black person as a stand-in, not for the story of black heroism, courage and triumph, but the story of American exceptionalism," explained Khalil Gibran Muhammad, director of the Schomburg Center for Research in Black Culture when he was interviewed for the *Forgotten Four.* Later in life, Robinson himself also resisted this simplified version.

The idealizing of Jackie Robinson's individual traits in overcoming the racial barriers in baseball didn't just render invisible many others who contributed to that moment. The association of success with virtue leads to a backlash against those who don't succeed in the same way. As Jennifer Hochschild wrote in *Facing Up to the American Dream: Race, Class, and the Soul of a Nation*, "Devaluing losers allows people to maintain their belief that the world is fundamentally just, even when it patently is not."

Kenny Washington's and Woody Strode's stories cannot be framed in the same way as Robinson's. Robinson's UCLA teammates did not fail, but in the American imagination their lack of undeniable success in the NFL weakens their significant accomplishments. Racism delayed their chance in the pros, which meant they were past their prime in the NFL. They could not play their best on the biggest stage the way Bob Waterfield or Otto Graham did. In some sense, their stories don't just complicate, but repudiate, the American narrative of inexorable progress toward greater equality.

"The emotional potency of the American dream has made people who were able to identify with it the norm for everyone else," Hochschild wrote. "Thus the irony is doubled: not only has the idea of universal participation been denied to most Americans, but also the very fact of its denial has itself been denied in our national self-image."

Our notions of history perpetuate and reinforce our worldview. To value what Washington, Strode, Willis, and Motley did is to also wonder, "Whom else have we ignored?" That answer would have to include the many activists of the 1940s whose courage and accomplishments are overshadowed in our national memory by one-dimensional stories of Rosa Parks and Martin Luther King Jr.

Another element of Jackie Robinson's story bears review: his assumed acceptance by white fans. While Robinson is revered today, many fans and observers did not accept his presence: not at first, not after he won Rookie of the Year, and not after he led the Dodgers to a World Series victory. Many white fans loathed Robinson. The black star's success did not push them to reevaluate their racial views of white superiority. Instead, Robinson's detractors reframed his success to diminish it and paradoxically reinforce white supremacy. They shrugged and claimed that of course he played well on the field. Were sports not a form of entertainment? And weren't African Americans generally excellent at entertaining white audiences?

The same twist happened with boxing at the turn of the twentieth century. The conventional wisdom was that whites were stronger, faster, and more skillful than black boxers, and that this natural superiority would be reflected in the ring. But when black fighters beat white ones, that achievement was not used by racists to question their underlying belief. Instead, they reframed the black achievement to reinforce their existing worldview.

In the view of many white spectators Jack Johnson and other black boxers won not because they were as good as or better than their white opponents, but because black boxers benefited from the jungle savagery of their ancestors and supposed unfair physical benefits—such as thicker muscles or, in the case of sprinters in track and field, elongated heel bones.

When racial bias has taken the form of pseudologic, the response has often been to disprove the statement at hand. Since white athletes beating black ones on the field of play was used to claim white superiority, it made sense that black athletes outplaying whites would call into question that core assumption.

Often those who were defending concepts of white supremacy would declare that more would be needed to prove racial equality. This "moving the goalposts" is a logical fallacy that plays out constantly in American discussion of race. It's no accident that sports metaphors are frequently used to discuss broader equality issues, from moving goalposts to the desire for a "level playing field." Sports are sometimes referred to as a microcosm of society, but this description is too simple. Sports function not just as a reflection of society in miniature but also as an idealized version of it, where gray dissolves into black and white.

In sports, what is in bounds and out of bounds is clearly marked. Chalk lines note obvious progress or loss. The scoreboard makes clear at all times who's winning, and the clock ticks down to a mutually agreed-upon end. Sports is order and structure, and the promise that perhaps within its structure will be a fair battle.

In the far messier arena of society, the fight for equality is much more fraught. Not only do the goalposts move, but the "opponent" is more diffuse and all-encompassing. "Our understanding of racism is shaped by the most extreme expressions of individual bigotry, not by the way in which it functions naturally, almost invisibly (and sometimes with genuinely benign intent), when it is embedded in the structure of a social system," wrote Michelle Alexander in *The New Jim Crow: Mass Incarceration in the Age of Colorblindness*.

It doesn't require a mustache-twirling or devil-horned villain for racism and other forms of discrimination to continue. To thrive, discrimination requires only that the majority of people do not act against the systems that reinforce it. Neutrality is as much an enemy of freedom and equality as bigotry is.

Kenny Washington's experience in the NFL was not unlike the travails of the unnamed protagonist in Ralph Ellison's novel *Invisible Man*. The mainstream public certainly oohed and aahed over Washington's long throws. The *Los Angeles Times* gawked at his majestic passes from high school through his semipro days. His throw to Hal Hirshon against USC as a sophomore carried the promise that "no longer would he be underestimated again." Then he'd constantly be underestimated in terms of the range of skills he brought to the game and often was reduced to a cannon arm and little else. In the pros, he wasn't given a true shot as a passer. The Rams only trotted him out at quarterback at the end of games when they needed to score and the opposing team knew Washington had no choice but to pass. It was no surprise, then, that it rarely worked.

None of this diminishes Washington's achievements or those of these other three men who integrated pro football in 1946. And Washington, Motley, Strode, and Willis understood the value of their accomplishments better than most. Woody Strode's son, Kalai, explained, using a bricklaying metaphor. "You lay the bricks one by one to build a wall. A wall doesn't just appear. My dad built his life brick by brick. You also had to pull the plumb line to make sure [the bricks lined up] straight. That plumb line was my grandfather, it was Paul Robeson, it was everyone who came before my dad. The plumb line was every idealist who came before."

"I think he would also feel proud, even though under Sodium Pentothal he wouldn't tell you, that he had some small part in leading to this success. He and the lions of 1946," Willis said of the long history from pro sports integration to legal victories to the first black American being elected president of the United States. "But we're not at the finish line," he warned. "The race is just getting started."

In not a single one of these little campaigns was I victorious. In
other words, in each case, I personally failed, but I have lived to see
the thesis upon which I was operating vindicated, and what I very
often say is that I've lived to see my lost causes found.
—PAULI MURRAY

Acknowledgments

First, I want to thank the family and the friends of the people I write about here. Without your cooperation, time, and energy, this book wouldn't exist. It can't be easy to have random strangers sifting through your family histories and then interpreting the stories of your loved ones. How could you not wonder with some trepidation whether the result would be an honest or fair telling? To all those who talked with me, I appreciate the trust you showed in my intentions, and I hope my work is a realistic and accurate telling of who your loved ones were.

I also want to thank the people who made this book a reality. Many thanks to my book editor, Pete Beatty, who spent more time with me on this book than anyone else. I appreciate your support and your editorial guidance more than you know. To Mollie Glick, who originally signed me to Foundry Media, thank you for believing in me and in this work when it was, frankly, a big mess. Thanks to Bloomsbury USA for bringing the book into the world. I greatly appreciate the expertise publisher George Gibson provided, but also the entire staff who edited the copy, did the page layout, etc. All of these are crucial roles in getting a work of words into physical form.

Many thanks to the freelance editors who contributed to making this book better than it ever would ever have been without their contributions: Laurie Pendergast, Dana Crumb, Elizabeth Stark, and Peter Fornatale. I'm also indebted to Brian Tyler for the football diagrams and photo optimizations. Thanks to Dana Crumb and Lisa Gold for their help fact-checking this book.

In "Selected Sources" I mention the libraries, archives, and other sources that I used most heavily in researching this book. They were and are incredible resources, and all of the staff members I interacted with were amazingly helpful and patient. A special thanks to the local public libraries, though, who provide such a crucial service for their communities, whether as a place to find good books to read, to write a paper or a book, or simply to gather with friends. Most especially I'd like to recognize the A. C. Bilbrew Los Angeles County Library and its Black Resource Center. Many periodicals are accessible online now, but I started my research when this wasn't the case. I spent many hours at their microfilm machine, and when I needed something or had questions, the staff was always helpful. Many of the archives of black newspapers and magazines are still not online. If you can, contribute to making these critical resources broadly available to the public.

The Los Angeles Central Library, the Cleveland Public Library and its Sports Research Center, the San Francisco Public Library (my "home" library), and the Atlanta Central Library helped jump-start my research and I am beholden to them for their help. I also owe many of my colleagues at Pac-12 Network a big thank you for their ongoing support of and excitement about this project.

There is no one I appreciate more than my friends Ammi, Cameron, Kristine, Stefanie, Maureen—and many, many more!—for your emotional support and feedback on my writing. I'm blessed with many friends who are themselves writers and who provided great advice and resources along the way. My friend Lazaro Cuevas deserves a gold medal for the many times he graciously let me crash at his place when I came to Los Angeles to meet with people or to do research. We enjoyed the visits, too, but he didn't have to be as accommodating as he was, and I'll always appreciate that.

Last, but never least, thank you to my family—my sister, Amy Atwood; my mom, Karen Atwood; my dad, Douglas Atwood; and my aunt, Janet Ell—for not just supporting my work on this book, but supporting my love of reading, writing, sports, and history throughout my life.

And thanks to my late grandfather Robert Ell who took me to watch my first NFL practice when I was seven years old. He lived outside St. Louis, and this was when the Arizona Cardinals were the St. Louis Cardinals. The Cardinals held their training camp in St. Charles at Lindenwood College (my mom's alma mater) in those days. My grandfather took me to their practices, and I remember getting players' autographs and later pointing out the players on the screen when my grandfather and I watched games on television. We sometimes bet Oreo cookies or M&M's on the outcomes of games if we didn't have a personal rooting interest.

It didn't occur to me at the time that it was unusual for a man of his generation to support his granddaughter's keen love of football, but I am so thankful he did. A year before he died, the St. Louis Rams won the 2000 Super Bowl. "I must be real old," he said with an impish chuckle. "I lived long enough to see a St. Louis football team win the Super Bowl!"

Notes

Prologue

1   "Kenny Washington watched": Woody Strode and Sam Young, *Goal Dust: The Warm and Candid Memoirs of a Pioneer Black Athlete and Actor* (Lanham, MD: Madison Books, 1990), 56.

1: First Quarter

3   "Prevailing opinion held": Paul Brown and Jack Clary, *PB: The Paul Brown Story* (New York: Atheneum, 1979), 196.

4   "the Rams and the Browns were the first": Paul Zimmerman, *The New Thinking Man's Guide to Pro Football* (New York: Simon and Schuster, 1984), 98.

4   "In 1949, the Rams had": Ibid., 223.

5   "For all the images": Robert W. Peterson, *Pigskin: The Early Years of Pro Football* (Oxford: University of Oxford Press, 1997), chaps. 2–5.

5   "Nonfans likened it": Michael Oriard, *King Football: Sport and Spectacle in the Golden Age of Radio and Newsreels, Movies and Magazines, the Weekly and the Daily Press* (Chapel Hill: University of North Carolina Press, 2001), 103.

6   "Playing professional football at that time": Ibid., 5.

6   "The driving force behind": Charles K. Ross, *Outside the Lines: African Americans and the Integration of the National Football League* (New York: New York University Press, 1999), 46.

6   "In the fall of 1945": Jules Tygiel, *Baseball's Great Experiment: Jackie Robinson and His Legacy* (Oxford: Oxford University Press, 1997), 35, 56.

7   "was asked to take a 20 percent reduction in pay": Ross, *Outside the Lines*, 123.

7   "Early in 1950": John R. Williams, "Bob Mike Released After Argument," *Chicago Defender*, September 9, 1950.

7   "he had his equipment manager": Edward Prell, "Browns Win Title in Final 20 Seconds," *Chicago Daily Tribune*, December 25, 1950.

8   "He wanted Los Angeles to": Andy Piascik, *The Best Show in Football: The 1946–1955 Cleveland Browns, Pro Football's Greatest Dynasty* (Lanham, MD: Taylor Trade Publishing, 2006), 178.

9   "Paul Brown scrapped": Ibid.

10   "'My dad always felt'": Frank Litsky, "Marion Motley, Bruising Back for Storied Browns, Dies at 79," *New York Times*, June 28, 1999.

10   "Motley had also mastered": Piascik, *Best Show in Football*, 19.

10   "Graham's gain was partly": *1950 NFL Championship: Cleveland Browns 30 / LA Rams 28*, NFL Films, DVD.

11   "On the next play": Ibid.

11   "The Rams had come up with": Brown and Clary, *PB*, 210.

2: THE LAST WORD

13   "Few people realized": Davis J. Walsh, "Cleveland Rams Transfer Pro Grid Franchise to Los Angeles," *Los Angeles Examiner*, January 14, 1946.

14   "It didn't want to cede the entire region": Hal Wood, "Pros Set for West Coast Grid War," *Los Angeles Daily News*, December 28, 1945.

14   "The football teams of the": "Pros Open Fight for Coliseum," *Los Angeles Daily News*, January 14, 1946.

15   "He frequently called out racism": A. S. "Doc" Young, "The Black Sportswriter," *Ebony*, October 1970.

15   "One story swapped over chuckles": Gary Ashwill, "Halley Harding," *Agate Type*, http://agatetype.typepad.com/agate_type/2013/02/halley-harding.html.

15   "'he was a loudmouth'": Ross Greenburg (producer), Johnson McKelvy (director), *Forgotten Four: The Integration of Pro Football* (EPIX/Ross Greenburg Productions, 2014)

15   "Standing before the dais": Ross, *Outside the Lines*, 78.

16   "commission president Leonard Roach": Michael MacCambridge, *America's Game: The Epic Story of How Pro Football Captured a Nation* (New York: Anchor Books, 2004), 19.

16   "Chile Walsh stood and replied": Al Santoro, "Rams Seek Use of Coliseum," *Los Angeles Examiner*, January 16, 1946.

16   "Harding asked Roach": Halley Harding, "So What?," *Los Angeles Tribune*, June 1, 1946.

16   "[The resolution] stipulated": Ibid.

17   "The nightclubs closed": RJ Smith, *The Great Black Way: L.A. in the 1940s and the Lost African-American Renaissance* (New York: PublicAffairs, 2006), 5–9.

17   "That evening, Halley Harding": Untitled photo caption, *Los Angeles Sentinel*, January 31, 1946; and "Rams Mentor Entertains Negro Press," *California Eagle*, January 31, 1946.

17   "A who's who of black newspapermen": Untitled photo caption, *Los Angeles Sentinel*, January 31, 1946.

18   "'What if I could'": "Rams Mentor Entertains Negro Press"; and untitled photo caption. And Strode and Young, *Goal Dust*, 141. "Los Angeles 11 interested in Young and Kenny Washington," J. Cullen Fentress, Pittsburgh Courier, Feb. 2, 1946.

19   "He convinced Washington to try with his left leg": "Washington Having Best Grid Season," *Los Angeles Daily News*, December 28, 1945.

20   "'Kenny's running around'": Ezzrett "Sugarfoot" Anderson, interviewed by author, Calgary, Alberta, Canada, April 4, 2014.

21   "The *Los Angeles Tribune* ran a photo": "Kenny in Hospital; Gets Knees Fixed," *Los Angeles Tribune*, April 13, 1946.

21   "Dick Hyland of the *Los Angeles Times* questioned": Dick Hyland, "The Hyland Fling," *Los Angeles Times*, March 22, 1946.

21   "Halley Harding shot back": Halley Harding column, *Los Angeles Tribune*, March 30, 1946.

3: CITY OF ANGELS

23   "Abie Robinson of the *Los Angeles Sentinel*": "Woody Strode Signed by Rams," *Los Angeles Sentinel*, April 25, 1946; and "Los Angeles Rams Admit They Signed Strode," *Los Angeles Sentinel*, May 16, 1946.

23 "In the mid-1800s": H. D. Barrows, "Memorial Sketch of Dr. John S. Griffin," *Annual Publication of the Historical Society of Southern California and Pioneer Register, Los Angeles* 4, no. 2 (University of California Press, Historical Society of Southern California): 183–85, doi:10.2307/41167720. Also http://lincolnheightsnc.org/about-us2/.

24 "Like so many of their neighbors": Strode and Young, *Goal Dust*, 51.

24 "It was said": Ibid., 52.

24 "Blue was a precocious athlete": Mark V. Perkins, "Edgar 'Blue' Washington," Society for American Baseball Research, http://sabr.org/bioproj/person/b347deac.

24 "Some family members said": Karin Cohen, interviewed by author, California City, CA, February 27, 2010.

24 "When he wasn't barnstorming": Strode and Young, *Goal Dust*, 53.

24 "Marian tired of Blue's frequent absences": Cohen interview.

25 "who raised him": Strode and Young, *Goal Dust*, 52.

25 "Washington was often at church": Ibid., 50.

25 "As a senior he": *Los Angeles Times*, September 1935 to December 1935.

25 "Washington's large hands": Jack Singer, "All-City 'Dream Team' Selected by Coaches," *Los Angeles Times*, December 1, 1935.

25 "'Washington is what'": Ibid.

25 "The *Times* speculated": *Los Angeles Times*, September 1935 to December 1935.

25 "Washington favored Notre Dame": Marvel Washington, interviewed by author, Whittier, CA, February 28, 2010.

25 "The USC coach later admitted": Leonard Knight, "A Talk with Bert Ritchey," *Journal of San Diego History*, 42, no. 2 (Spring 1996), http://www.sandiegohistory.org/journal/96spring/ritchey.htm.

26 "Woody Strode later joked": Strode and Young, *Goal Dust*, 30.

26 "Shortly thereafter": Ibid., 7.

26 "Black home ownership": Douglas Flamming, *Bound for Freedom: Black Los Angeles in Jim Crow America* (Berkeley: University of California Press, 2005), 51.

26 "When slavery yielded only slightly": Douglas A. Blackmon, *Slavery by Another Name: The Re-enslavement of Black Americans from the Civil War to World War II* (New York: Doubleday, 2008).

26 "While black migrants": RJ Smith, *The Great Black Way: L.A. in the 1940s and the Lost African-American Renaissance* (New York: PublicAffairs, 2006), 23.

26 "'My daddy would buy'": Strode and Young, *Goal Dust*, 8.

27 "Many of the newcomers": Barry M. Pritzker, *A Native American Encyclopedia: History, Culture, and Peoples* (Oxford: Oxford University Press, 2000).

27 "Many of the new settlements": Alysa Landry, "Native History: California Gold Rush Begins, Devastates Native Population," Indian Country Today Media Network, January 1, 2014, http://indiancountrytodaymedianetwork.com/2014/01/24/native-history-california-gold-rush-begins-devastates-native-population-153230.

27 "When the Great Depression hit": Strode and Young, *Goal Dust*, 20.

28 "Like many of the other": David M. P. Freund, *Colored Property: State Policy and White Racial Politics in Suburban America* (Chicago: University of Chicago Press, 2007), 5.

28 "Woody's father had helped erect": Strode and Young, *Goal Dust*, 2.

28 "'I looked like a broomstick'": Ibid., 24.

28 "changed his name to Edelson": Kalai Strode, interviewed by author, Honolulu, HI, March 21, 2010.

28 "'He was probably discriminated'": Ibid.

28   "Edelson taught Strode": Strode and Young, *Goal Dust*, 24.

28   "At one track meet": Ibid., 38.

28   "He had to take most": Ibid., 33.

29   "This was true of many": Dave Gaston, interviewed by author, Pasadena, CA, March 2, 2010.

29   "'I remember sitting in algebra'": Strode and Young, *Goal Dust*, 37.

29   "Strode was asked": Ibid., 39.

29   "The painter, Hubert Stowitts": "About," Stowitts Museum and Library, http://www.stowitts. org/index.html.

29   "shut down the exhibit": Ibid.

29   "later sent a message": Strode and Young, *Goal Dust*, 40.

29   "Strode was initially taken aback": Ibid., 50.

30   "Washington took advantage": Ibid., 51.

30   "Slats, was the main agitator": Gaston interview.

30   "'I can't play next to a'": Strode and Young, *Goal Dust*, 64.

30   "The university commissioned a report": Gaston interview.

30   "'When we would scrimmage'": Ibid.

31   "that a Stanford football coach": Gregory John Kaliss, "Everyone's All-Americans: Race, Men's College Athletics, and the Ideal of Equal Opportunity," dissertation (Chapel Hill, University of North Carolina, 2008), 42.

31   "'We'd listen to Al Jarvis'": Strode and Young, *Goal Dust*, 51.

31   "It started in the early": Rolf Pendal, Arthur C. Nelson, Casey J. Dawkins, and Gerrit J. Knaap, "Connecting Smart Growth, Housing Affordability, and Racial Equity," in *The Geography of Opportunity: Race and Housing Choice in Metropolitan America*, ed. Xavier de Souza Briggs (Washington, DC: Brookings Institution Press, 2005), 220.

31   "Restrictive covenants worked in": Amina Hassan, *Loren Miller: Civil Rights Attorney and Journalist* (Norman: University of Oklahoma Press, 2015), 158–62.

32   "The latter was more common": Josh Sides, *L.A. City Limits: African American Los Angeles from the Great Depression to the Present* (Berkeley: University of California Press, 2003), chap. 4, "Race and Housing in Postwar Los Angeles."

32   "Powerful real estate associations": H. Roy Kaplan, *The Myth of Post-Racial America: Searching for Equality in the Age of Materialism* (Lanham, MD: Rowman and Littlefield Education, 2011), 178; and Sides, *L.A. City Limits*, chap. 4, "Race and Housing in Postwar Los Angeles."

32   "South Pasadena's city manager": "So. Pasadena for 'Whites Only' Says City Mgr. Telling of Racial Bias," *California Eagle*, September 12, 1946.

32   "The FHA often *required* building developments": Clement E. Vose, *Caucasians Only: The Supreme Court, the NAACP, and the Restrictive Covenant Cases* (Berkeley: University of California Press, 1968), 225–28; and Joseph Watras, *Politics, Race, and Schools: Racial Integration, 1954–1994* (New York: Garland Publishing, 1997), 82.

32   "'inharmonious racial groups'": Kaplan, *Myth*, 178.

32   "The FHA also used a color-coded system": David R. Goldfield, ed., *Encyclopedia of American Urban History* (Thousand Oaks, CA: Sage Publications, 2007), 265.

33   "In 1920, racially restrictive housing covenants": Loren Miller, "Covenants in the Bear Flag State," *Crisis*, May 1946; and Hassan, *Loren Miller*, 157.

33   "Between 1942 and 1946": Mark Brilliant, *The Color of America Has Changed: How Racial Diversity Shaped Civil Rights Reforms in California, 1941–1978* (Oxford: Oxford University Press, 2010), 92.

34   "Well-off African Americans": Hassan, *Loren Miller*, 155.

34   "When black actress Hattie McDaniel": "Sugar Hill Residents Battle to Keep Their Homes," *California Eagle*, March 24, 1943; and Hassan, *Loren Miller*, 154.

34   "their older neighbors": Hassan, *Loren Miller,* 164–65.

34   "Numerous peers": "Actress Fights Home Covenants": *Baltimore Afro-American,* September 14, 1946.

4: MOORE'S FORD BRIDGE

35   "'We will use Kenny'": "Kenny Washington Signs Up with the L.A. Rams," *Los Angeles Tribune,* March 23, 1946.

35   "'In other words'": Strode and Young, *Goal Dust,* 148.

35   "'I am going to try Washington'": "Kenny Washington Signs Up."

35   "and followed Washington's exploits": Strode and Young, *Goal Dust,* 147.

36   "became friends on and off the field": Ibid.; and Karin Cohen, interviewed by author, California City, CA, February 27, 2010.

37   "Strode suspected the Rams": Strode and Young, *Goal Dust,* 142–47.

37   "Writers such as Vincent": Vincent X. Flaherty, *Los Angeles Examiner,* January 21, 1946

37   "'We can't lose'": "Ken, Strode to Help New Grid League," *Pittsburgh Courier,* June 1, 1946.

37   "Dr. Charles Wesley Hill": "Fans Give Kenny Pro League Sendoff," *Los Angeles Tribune,* July 20, 1946.

37   "Days later, on July 25": "Lynching Arouses Nation! Citizens March on White House; FBI Agents Enter Lynch Probe," *Cleveland Call & Post,* August 3, 1946.

38   "They slowed and more cars": James Edmund Boyack, "Georgia 'Mass Murders': Monroe Massacre Shocks Nation; Protests Pour In," *Pittsburgh Courier,* August 3, 1946.

38   "one of the women in the car": "Lynching Arouses Nation!"; and Boyack, "Georgia 'Mass Murders.'"

38   "'One . . . Two . . .'": Laura Wexler, *Fire in a Canebrake: The Last Mass Lynching in America* (New York: Scribner, 2003), 63.

38   "a cursory inquest was held": Ibid., 64–66.

38   "A young white couple": Ibid., 72–74.

39   "The coroner recorded sixty bullet wounds": Boyack, "Georgia 'Mass Murders.'"

39   "He recalled the sounds": Wexler, *Fire in a Canebreak,* 74.

39   "On July 30, a black man": "Mania Grips Dixie; Three New Deaths Revealed," *Chicago Defender* (national edition), August 10, 1946; and "Lynch Mobs Roam 2 States: NAACP Rescues Survivor of Bestial Louisiana Mobsters," *Cleveland Call & Post,* August 24, 1946.

39   "Barely a week into August": "Mania Grips Dixie"; and Wexler, *Fire in a Canebreak,* 130.

39   "The man who survived": "Lynch Mobs Roam 2 States."

41   "'What's wrong?'": Strode and Young, *Goal Dust,* 151.

41   "At midnight Bob Waterfield": Ibid., 152.

41   "*Times* columnist Braven Dyer thought": Braven Dyer, "Washington May Start at Quarter," *Los Angeles Times,* August 29, 1946.

5: OFFSIDE

43   "Rams owner Dan Reeves": Davis J. Walsh, "Cleveland Rams Transfer Pro Grid Franchise to Los Angeles," *Los Angeles Examiner,* January 14, 1946.

44   "Brown immediately contemplated": Paul Brown and Jack Clary, *PB: The Paul Brown Story* (New York: Atheneum, 1979), 129.

44   "When weighing signing Willis": Ibid.

44 "Willis's sons say": William Willis Jr., Clem Willis, and Claude Willis, interviewed by author, Columbus, OH, January 16–17, 2010.

44 "According to him": Ibid.

45 "'I'll stake my reputation'": Brown and Clary, *PB*, 130.

45 "Willis dug his cleats": Ibid.

45 "'He had a crouch almost like a frog'": Willis, Willis, and Willis interview.

45 "'He's going early'": Piascik, *Best Show in Football*, 37.

45 "'Run the play again'": Ibid.

46 "For years afterward": Ibid., 38.

46 "Willis explained": Brown and Clary, *PB*, 130.

46 "Motley so intimidated other players": Piascik, *Best Show in Football*, 41.

46 "When Motley heard": Ibid., 39.

47 "'Our backfield coach'": Duey Graham, *OttoMatic: Otto Graham* (Wayne, MI: Immortal Investments Publishing, 2004), 74.

47 "Brown realigned Graham's stance": Brown and Clary, *PB*, 131.

47 "Several teammates remembered": Piascik, *Best Show in Football*, 39.

47 "'I'm sure when'": Willis, Willis, and Willis interview.

47 "'Once they got to a point'": Ibid.

48 "'He and Motley . . . they'": Ibid.

48 "'We had this cleavage'": Ross Greenburg (producer), Johnson McKelvy (director), *Forgotten Four: The Integration of Pro Football* (EPIX/Ross Greenburg Productions, 2014)

48 "'On the field'": Ibid.

48 "Their favorite game was Dirty Hearts": Willis, Willis, and Willis interview.

49 "'Motley would always let'": Ibid.

49 "On July 21 several black couples": Charles H. Loeb, "Eject Mixed Party from Euclid Beach: Park Management Admits Negro Patrons Barred from Swimming, Dancing, Skating": *Cleveland Call & Post*, July 27, 1946.

50 "When reached by the *Call & Post*": Ibid.

50 "Civil rights demonstrations continued": Sidney R. Williams, "On the Whole . . . ," *Cleveland Call & Post*, August 17, 1946.

50 "One hundred protesters marched": "Assail Euclid Beach Jim-Crow: Pickets Attack Fascist Policy of Management," *Cleveland Call & Post*, August 10, 1946.

51 "'No such thing happened'": Williams "On the Whole . . ."

6: ASSAULT

53 "It was a crucible": Victoria W. Wolcott, *Race, Riots, and Roller Coasters: The Struggle Over Segregated Recreation in America* (Philadelphia: University of Pennsylvania Press, 2012), 2–5.

54 "The legislators who penned the Reconstruction amendments": Loren Miller, *The Petitioners: The Story of the Supreme Court of the United States and the Negro* (New York: Pantheon Books, 1966), 14; and Eric Foner, *Who Owns History?: Rethinking the Past in a Changing World* (New York: Hill and Wang, 2002), 181.

54 "The U.S. Supreme Court's": IIT Chicago-Kent College of Law, "The Civil Rights Cases," Oyez, https://www.oyez.org/cases/1850-1900/109us3.

54 "Citizens' Committee": Charles A. Lofgren. *The Plessy Case: A Legal-Historical Interpretation* (Oxford: Oxford University Press, 1987), 29–32.

54 "the Southern coastal version": Mark S. Foster, "In the Face of 'Jim Crow': Prosperous Blacks and Vacations, Travel and Outdoor Leisure, 1890–1945," *Journal of Negro History* 84, no. 2 (Spring 1999): 130–49; and Wolcott, *Race, Riots, and Roller Coasters*, 24.

54 "They drafted Homer Plessy": Lofgren, *Plessy Case*, 31–35.

55 "the 1893 Chicago World's Fair": Wolcott, *Race, Riots, and Roller Coasters*, 24.

55 "The fear of interracial flirting": Ibid., 16.

55 "To Humphrey this meant": Ibid., 29.

55 "Cleveland School Board": "Board Bans School Picnics at Euclid Beach," *Cleveland Call & Post*, July 21, 1934.

56 "CORE was less concerned": Paul Finkelman, *Encyclopedia of African American History, 1896 to the Present: From the Age of Segregation to the Twenty-First Century* (Oxford: Oxford University Press, 2009), 480–83.

56 "White City Roller Rink": August Meier and Elliott M. Rudwick, *CORE, a Study in the Civil Rights Movement, 1942–1968* (Champaign: University of Illinois Press, 1975), 27.

57 "On August 23, 1946": "Clevelander Beaten, Evicted, by Private Police at Euclid Beach," *Cleveland Call & Post*, August 31, 1946.

57 "He later reported that": Ibid.

57 "The officers who arrived": Ibid.

58 "'It didn't happen in Monroe'": "Euclid Beach Authorities Openly Flout Civil Rights Laws; Members of Core to Sue After Manhandling," *Cleveland Call & Post*, August 31, 1946.

58 "A week after the beating": "Reveal Man Suffers Skull Fracture in Attack by Euclid Beach Police," *Cleveland Call & Post*, September 7, 1946.

58 "The same issue": "No Record of $600 Bond in Ga. Lynching," *Cleveland Call & Post*, August 31, 1946.

59 "Miami's owner and head coach": Piascik, *Best Show in Football*, 48.

59 "People did have a glimpse": Jules Tygiel, *Baseball's Great Experiment: Jackie Robinson and His Legacy* (Oxford: Oxford University Press, 1997), 101–19.

59 "Branch Rickey's lobbying": Ibid., 106–10.

59 "except for one altercation": Piascik, *Best Show in Football*, 50–51.

60 "'Professional grid foes'": Cleveland Jackson, "Headline Action," *Cleveland Call & Post*, September 7, 1946.

60 "'How do you expect'": Piascik, *Best Show in Football*, 48; and Paul Brown and Jack Clary, *PB: The Paul Brown Story* (New York: Atheneum, 1979), 177.

60 "'We knew Bill Willis'": Brown and Clary, *PB*, 177.

60 "unusual kicking ritual": Duey Graham, *OttoMatic: Otto Graham* (Wayne, MI: Immortal Investments Publishing, 2004), 177.

61 "The *Call & Post* boasted": Cleveland Jackson, "Bill Willis, Marion Motley to Encounter Dixie Bred Stars as Cleveland Browns, Miami Seahawks Open All-American Conference Play," *Cleveland Call & Post*, September 7, 1946.

62 "The first time the Rockets": Piascik, *Best Show in Football*, 50; and Cleveland Jackson, "'Beat the Browns' Is Cry as Buffalo Bisons Set Up Road Block for Locals," *Cleveland Call & Post*, September 21, 1946.

62 "the *Cleveland Plain Dealer* praised": Harold Sauerbrei, "Browns Triumph, 20 to 6: Motley's Rushes Defeat Rockets," *Cleveland Plain Dealer*, September 14, 1946.

7: Second Quarter

63 "Paul Brown sent the halfbacks out wide": Paul Brown and Jack Clary, *PB: The Paul Brown Story* (New York: Atheneum, 1979), 210.

64 "Many teams had a code word" American Football Coaches Association, *Complete Guide to Special Teams: Techniques, Drills, Training* (Champaign, IL: Human Kinetics Publishing, 2005), 208.

64 "James fired a pass": *1950 NFL Championship: Cleveland Browns 30 / LA Rams 28*, NFL Films, DVD.

64 "Above the field": Ibid.

65 "He was known for his hang time": Duey Graham, *OttoMatic: Otto Graham* (Wayne, MI: Immortal Investments Publishing, 2004), 94–96, 109.

000 "15-yard drop": Piascik, *Best Show in Football*, 72.

66 "'Everyone kept asking him'": William Willis Jr., Clem Willis, and Claude Willis, interviewed by author, Columbus, OH, January 16–17, 2010.

66 "Paul Brown would eventually tailor": Piascik, *Best Show in Football*, 156.

66 "The Rams handed off": *1950 NFL Championship*.

66 "Davis dove desperately": Ibid.

66 "Waterfield spun to feed": Ibid.

67 "'The Cards began to taunt us'": Harold Sauerbrei, "Bell Rescinds Slugging Fine When Notified Ford Undergoes Facial Surgery: Browns' Star End Out Indefinitely," *Cleveland Plain Dealer*, October 17, 1950.

67 "On the next play Harder": Brown and Clary, *PB*, 205–6; and Piascik, *Best Show in Football*, 168.

68 "Ford's face was already": "Len Ford Injured by Blow in Final Minute," *Cleveland Plain Dealer*, October 16, 1950.

68 "Several days later": Harold Sauerbrei, "Movies Show Harder, Not Ford, Was at Fault," *Cleveland Plain Dealer*, October 18, 1950.

68 "'The pictures clearly showed'": Brown and Clary, *PB*, 205–6.

68 "NFL commissioner Bert Bell": Sauerbrei, "Bell Rescinds Slugging Fine."

68 "BROWNS, CARDS IN NEAR RACE RIOT": "Browns Players Deny 'Riot' Story," *Cleveland Call & Post*, October 28, 1950.

69 "The players termed the *Courier*": Ibid.

69 "In Atlanta in 1906": Gregory Mixon and Clifford Kuhn, "Atlanta Race Riot of 1906," *New Georgia Encyclopedia*, http://www.georgiaencyclopedia.org/articles/history-archaeology/atlanta-race-riot-1906.

69 "For several weeks prior": Rebecca Burns, *Rage in the Gate City: The Story of the 1906 Atlanta Race Riot* (Athens: University of Georgia Press, 2009).

69 "W. E. B. Du Bois": Ibid.

70 "A clerk at a store": Alfred L. Brophy, *Reconstructing the Dreamland: The Tulsa Riot of 1921: Race, Reparations, and Reconciliation* (Oxford: Oxford University Press, 2002); and Scott Ellsworth, *Death in a Promised Land: The Tulsa Race Riot of 1921* (Baton Rouge: Louisiana State University Press, 1982).

70 "But the newspapers got": Brophy, *Reconstructing the Dreamland*, 24.

71 "[Motley] pointed out that": "Browns Players Deny 'Riot' Story."

71 "John Fuster visited": John E. Fuster, "Ford Won't Pose and We Do Not Blame Him," *Cleveland Call & Post*, October 28, 1950.

71 "I don't remember anybody": Ibid.

8: BLACK LIGHTNING

73 "'there is no sane reason'": Braven Dyer, "Trojans Slight Favorites Over Bruins Today," *Los Angeles Times*, December 4, 1937.

73 "'If we weren't playing USC'": Strode and Young, *Goal Dust*, 67.

74 "Lansdell slammed into": "Lansdell Leads Trojan Eleven to Victory," *Los Angeles Times*, December 5, 1937.

74   "UCLA started the second quarter": "Play-by-Play Story of Trojan Victory Over Bruins," *Los Angeles Times*, December 5, 1937.

75   "USC started using more": "Lansdell Leads Trojan Eleven to Victory."

75   "A few plays later": Bill Henry, "Washington's Pass Measures 62 Yards," *Los Angeles Times*, December 6, 1937.

76   "'I was calling signals'": Frank Finch, "Inside Story of Record Toss Revealed," *Los Angeles Times*, December 6, 1937.

76   "'I was pretty tired'": Ibid.

76   "'Only a goof'": Braven Dyer, "Trojans Beat Bruins, 19–13," *Los Angeles Times*, December 5, 1937.

76   "The previous record": Bill Henry, "It's a New Record! Kenny Passes 72 Yards," *Los Angeles Times*, December 5, 1937.

76   "Fox Movietone": Henry, "Washington's Pass Measures 62 Yards."

77   "'It came at me like a bullet'": Strode and Young, *Goal Dust*, 70.

77   "The most popular postgame topic": Henry, "It's a New Record!"

77   "Washington said after the game": Henry, "Washington's Pass Measures 62 Yards."

77   "The next day local papers": "George Washington Threw Silver Dollar Across Potomac—Kenny Threw Record Pass," *Los Angeles Times*, December 7, 1937.

77   "'The well-groomed colored boy'": Ibid.

78   "saying after the game": Halley Harding, "So What?," *Los Angeles Tribune*, October 5, 1946.

78   "'You can't take the'": Ibid.

78   "According to Harding's contacts": Ibid.

78   "'The scam to advertise names'": Strode and Young, *Goal Dust*, 153.

78   "The opposing left end": Ibid., 152.

79   "'It's hell being a Negro, Jim'": Ibid., 153.

79   "'I think the Rams' brass'": Ibid.

79   "'Woody, what the hell'": Ibid.

80   "Strode streaked past him": Ibid., 154.

80   "'Kenny gave the'": "Christman Leads Cards to Victory Over Rams," *Los Angeles Times*, October 28, 1946.

81   "He had suspected": Strode and Young, *Goal Dust*, chap. 14, "Just a Roommate."

9: Backlash

83   "He called the NAACP": Wexler, *Fire in a Canebreak*, 78.

83   "He and his father saw the crowd run down": Walter White, *A Man Called White* (1948; repr., New York: Arno Press, 1969), 5–12.

84   "'That's where that'": Ibid.

84   "'This thing's got to be done'": Tarleton Collier, "'Gene Told Us' Says Farmer in Walton County, Georgia," *Louisville (KY) Courier-Journal*, July 27, 1946.

85   "'They hadn't ought'": Ibid.

85   "The catch was that men": Alan Greenblatt, "The Racial History of the 'Grandfather Clause,'" *Code Switch*, NPR, October 22, 2013, http://www.npr.org/sections/codeswitch/2013/10/21/239081586/the-racial-history-of-the-grandfather-clause.

85   "White bosses threatened": Wexler, *Fire in a Canebreak*, 50.

86   "By July 1946, the number": Donald L. Grant, *The Way It Was in the South: The Black Experience in Georgia* (Athens: University of Georgia Press, 2001), 364.

86   "He paid African Americans to sit": Wexler, *Fire in a Canebreak*, 37.

87   "Talmadge volunteers were given": Ibid., 49.

87   "many local black residents saw the murders": Mark Auslander, "Holding On to Those Who Can't Be Held: Reenacting a Lynching at Moore's Ford, Georgia," *Southern Spaces*, November 8,2010, http://southernspaces.org/2010/holding-those-who-cant-be-held-reenacting-lynching-moores-ford-georgia.

88   "Real estate firms": Evan McKenzie, *Privatopia: Homeowner Associations and the Rise of Residential Private Government* (New Haven, CT: Yale University Press, 1994), 73.

88   "This led to surreal neighborhood meetings": David Grant, "Covenanters Routed in Ocean Park; Jews, Vets Blast Anti-Negro Move," *California Eagle*, September 12, 1946.

88   "Signers were told": Ibid.

88   "'The whole world is too small a place'": Ibid.

88   "This was true for Pauli Murray": Kenneth W. Mack, *Representing the Race: The Creation of the Civil Rights Lawyer* (Cambridge, MA: Cambridge University Press, 2012), chap. 9, "The Trials of Pauli Murray."

89   "Murray wrote in a first-person account": Pauli Murray, "Pauli Murray Will Not Move," *Baltimore Afro-American*, August 29, 1944.

89   "After arriving in Los Angeles": Pauli Murray, *Pauli Murray: The Autobiography of a Black Activist, Feminist, Lawyer, Priest, and Poet* (Knoxville, TN: University of Tennessee Press, 1987), 254–55.

89   "one of her early cases she handled": Oral history interview with Pauli Murray, February 13, 1976, interview G-0044, Southern Oral History Program Collection (#4007), Southern Historical Collection, Wilson Library, University of North Carolina at Chapel Hill.

90   "O'Day Short, had bought": Cyril Briggs, "3 Dead in Fontana Fire After Vigilante Threats," *California Eagle*, December 20, 1945.

90   "the Shorts had gone into Los Angeles": Oral history interview with Murray.

90   "'They were building'": Ibid.

90   "An arson investigator": Cyril Briggs, "Jury's Refusal to Dub Fontana Fire 'Accident' Puts Probe on Agenda," *California Eagle*, January 3, 1946; and Cyril Briggs, "Grand Jury Hears Report on Fontana Fire Tragedy," *California Eagle*, January 10, 1946.

90   "'I recall writing up the case'": Oral history interview with Murray.

90   "She'd remember her work": Ibid.

90   "During most of the 1930s": Amina Hassan, *Loren Miller: Civil Rights Attorney and Journalist* (Norman: University of Oklahoma Press, 2015), 56–60.

91   "far-left African American activists": Ibid., 59–63.

91   "Local black elites accepted": Ibid., 120–29.

91   "He opposed the forced": Mack, *Representing the Race*, 203.

92   "Miller partnered with A. L. Wirin": Ibid.

92   "California had a more complicated process": Ibid., 201–2.

92   "Miller claimed that": Hassan, *Loren Miller*, 167.

93   "He wrote in his": "Victory on Sugar Hill," *Time*, December 17, 1945.

10: CHAMPIONS

96   "After the game Dons coach": Duey Graham, *OttoMatic: Otto Graham* (Wayne, MI: Immortal Investments Publishing, 2004), 81.

96   "Motley's occasional": Paul Brown and Jack Clary, *PB: The Paul Brown Story* (New York: Atheneum, 1979), 132.

97   "According to Otto Graham": Graham, *OttoMatic*, 87–88.

97 "The *Call & Post* favored": Cleveland Jackson, "Headline Action," *Cleveland Call & Post*, November 23, 1946.

97 "Later Brown informed the": Brown and Clary, *PB*, 132.

98 "'Not every situation'": Ibid.

98 "Otto Graham and his wife": Graham, *OttoMatic*, 87–88.

98 "A Spree Grows": Ibid., 89.

99 "Morrow's account": Juanita Morrow, "Shooting Closes Euclid Beach: Eyewitness Story of Beach Bigotry," *Cleveland Call & Post*, September 28, 1946.

11: SHOTS FIRED

103 "Several other Howard University": "Juanita Nelson: Full Interview," *First Person: Twentieth-Century History as Told by People Who Lived It and Made It*, Memorial Hall Museum Online, Pocumtuck Valley Memorial Association, 2014, http://www.memorialhall.mass.edu/centapp /oh/interview.do?shortName=nelson_interview.

103 "'We actually opened'": Ibid.

104 "'This is one reason why'": "Empty Heads and Loaded Pistols," *Cleveland Call & Post*, September 28, 1946.

104 "Department of Public Safety": Bob Williams, "Guards Assault, Shoot Policeman," *Cleveland Call & Post*, September 28, 1946.

104 "The head of the police race relations": Ibid.

104 "Smythe and Ungvary": Ibid.

104 "Coleman, his wife, and Mackey": "Patrolman Mackey's Story of Assault at Euclid Beach," *Cleveland Call & Post*, September 28, 1946.

105 "'Only two hoodlums said'": Ibid.

105 "'Park police No. 33'": Ibid.

105 "Ungvary told Mackey": Ibid.

106 "'Under ordinary circumstances'": Ibid.

106 "He kept his gun next": "A Frame Up?," *Cleveland Call & Post*, October 5, 1946.

106 "Brown claimed he": Piascik, *Best Show in Football*, 72.

107 "the big rusher often": Ibid., 41.

107 "'He wasn't going to run'": Ross Greenburg (producer), Johnson McKelvy (director), *Forgotten Four: The Integration of Pro Football* (EPIX/Ross Greenburg Productions, 2014).

108 "But as Graham later said": Duey Graham, *OttoMatic: Otto Graham* (Wayne, MI: Immortal Investments Publishing, 2004), 95–96.

108 "'Seeing Motley crouched'": Ibid., 96.

110 "'My binoculars caught Motley'": Zimmerman, *New Thinking Man's Guide*, 394.

12: THIRD QUARTER

111 "In the press box": Tim Brulia, "A Chronology of Pro Football on Television: Part 1," *Coffin Corner* 26, no. 3 (2004): 20.

111 "his struggles in": Red Grange and Ira Morton, *The Red Grange Story: An Autobiography* (Urbana: University of Illinois Press, 1993), 50–51.

112 "Why not move more": Jeffrey J. Miller, *Pop Warner: A Life on the Gridiron* (Jefferson, NC: McFarland, 2015), 71–75; and Sally Jenkins, *The Real All-Americans: The Team That Changed a Game, a People, a Nation* (New York: Doubleday, 2007), 223.

112 "whose opponents often outweighed them": Jenkins, *Real All-Americans*.

113 "The change had little impact": Robert W. Peterson, *Pigskin: The Early Years of Pro Football* (Oxford: Oxford University Press: 1997), 46.

113 "with passers holding": "First Real Football Tests the New Rules: Spectators Divided as to the Success of Experimental Changes," *New York Times*, September 27, 1906.

113 "On September 5": "This Week in College Football History," *Phanatic Magazine*, August 31, 2007.

113 "He worked with": Peterson, *Pigskin*, 52.

113 "St. Louis's success did not": Knute K. Rockne, "Beginning at End," *Collier's*, October 25, 1930.

114 "Notre Dame ran a version": Jeremy Stoltz, "Chalk Talk: The Notre Dame Box," *Bear Report*, Scouts.com, June 28, 2007, http://www.scout.com/nfl/bears/story/655115-chalk-talk-the-notre-dame-box.

114 "That summer he": Richard O. Davies, *Sports in American Life: A History* (Malden, MA: Wiley-Blackwell, 2012).

114 "'The Westerners flashed'": Harry Cross, "Inventing the Forward Pass," *New York Times*, November 1, 1913.

114 "'The press and the football'": Fred Eisenhammer and Eric B. Sondheimer, *College Football's Most Memorable Games* (Jefferson, NC: McFarland, 2010), 11.

114 "world champion strongman": Murray Greenberg, *Passing Game: Benny Friedman and the Transformation of Football* (New York: PublicAffairs, 2008), 9–11.

116 "on this play Gillom": *1950 NFL Championship: Cleveland Browns 30 / LA Rams 28*, NFL Films, DVD.

117 "Waterfield spun the wrong way": Ibid.

117 "As he neared the edge of the line": Ibid.

118 "Waterfield chucked the ball": Ibid.

13: 92 Yards

119 "In the first week of February": Paul Zimmerman, "Baldwin Signs Contract to Play with L.A. Dons," *Los Angeles Times*, February 6, 1947.

120 "In the team's first": Braven Dyer, "Rams Look Sharp in Initial Scrimmage," *Los Angeles Times*, August 11, 1947.

120 "Washington was reported": Ibid.

120 "'The Kingfish played one'": Braven Dyer, "Head-Cutting Task Gives Ram Coach Headache," *Los Angeles Times*, August 29, 1947.

120 "On Saturday, offensive line coach": Strode and Young, *Goal Dust*, 154.

120 "'They're trying to say'": Ibid.

120 "'In my generation'": Ibid.

121 "'It's not your ability; it's'": Ibid., 155.

121 "'I don't know what'": Kalai Strode, interviewed by author, Honolulu, HI, March 21, 2010.

121 "'Maybe it was more of a'": Pam Strode Larson, interviewed by author, Honolulu, HI, March 21, 2010.

121 "'Even my dad's mother'": Kalai Strode interview.

121 "'We were [out] having dinner'": Strode and Young, *Goal Dust*, 155.

121 "'This was the mob asking'": Ibid.

122 "'He and Luana'": Ibid., 157.

122 "Strode clarified": Ibid., 155.

122 "'I got drunk for one week'": Ibid., 158.

122 "Luana had a message for him": Ibid.

122 "'Bring your shoes'": Ibid.

123 "coaches and scribes were buzzing about": Braven Dyer, "The Sports Parade," *Los Angeles Times*, October 21, 1947.

123 "Washington started wide": "Rams Lose to Cards; 49'ers Whip Dons: Christmas Passes to 17–10 Win," *Los Angeles Times*, November 3, 1947.

123 "Washington simply said, 'Alleys'": Strode and Young, *Goal Dust*, 156.

124 "'Sometimes I would be forty'": Ibid.

124 "Paul Schissler": Alexander Wolff, "The NFL's Jackie Robinson," *Sports Illustrated*, October 12, 2009.

125 "Loren Miller was familiar": Miller, *Petitioners*, 3–5.

126 "Since feudal times": Vose, *Caucasians Only*, 2.

126 "*Buchanan v. Warley*": Jeffrey D. Gonda, *Unjust Deeds: The Restrictive Covenant Cases and the Making of the Civil Rights Movement* (Chapel Hill: University of North Carolina Press, 2015), 16–18.

126 "*Corrigan v. Buckley*": Ibid., 16–20; Vose, *Caucasians Only*, 17–19; and Miller, *Petitioners*, 253–54.

126 "'substantial federal claims'": Miller, *Petitioners*, 323.

127 American Law Institute: Vose, *Caucasians Only*, 4–5.

127 "it said the validity": Ibid.

127 "While Miller labored": Amina Hassan, *Loren Miller: Civil Rights Attorney and Journalist* (Norman: University of Oklahoma Press, 2015), 168–69.

127 "Under Marshall": Ibid., 173–74.

127 "congratulatory letter": Ibid., 168.

14: FROZEN OUT

129 "they determined the lynchings": "Hint Georgia Lynchings Rehearsed," *Pittsburgh Courier*, August 3, 1946; and "The Best People Won't Talk," *Time*, August 5, 1946.

129 "what types of guns": Wexler, *Fire in a Canebrake*, 98.

129 "'I told them not'": Ibid., 69.

130 "A young black girl": Ibid., 119.

130 "When the agents dug": Ibid., 120.

130 "Atlanta-area radio stations": Ibid.

130 "Since 1880": James Harmon Chadbourn, *Lynching and the Law* (Clark, NJ: Lawbook Exchange, 2008), 13–14. There are few records of any court-ordered punishment for lynchings or attempted lynchings in the United States. Much of the data that is cited comes from research at Tuskegee University, http://192.203.127.197/archive/handle/123456789/507. More recently, the Equal Justice Initiative (*Lynching in America: Confronting the Legacy of Racial Terror*, 2015, http://www.eji.org/lynchinginamerica) has reported roughly seven hundred more deaths than records had accounted for. This could lower the 0.8–1 percent conviction rate of lynchers even further.

130 "leaving only two": Wexler, *Fire in a Canebrake*, 107–110; and James Edmund Boyack, "Tom Clark Informs *Courier*," *Pittsburgh Courier*, November 2, 1946.

131 "Truman created": "Executive Order No. 9808 Establishing the President's Committee on Civil Rights," *Federal Registry* 11 FR 14153, December 7, 1946; and Louis Lautier, "President's Civil Rights Committee Launches Study of Discrimination," NNPA News Service, January 25, 1947.

132　"Lincoln Bedroom": David McCullough, *Truman* (New York: Simon and Schuster, 1992), 471.

132　"stream of letters": "Letters Flood Justice Department in Lynch Protest," *Chicago Defender* (national edition), October 19, 1946.

132　"Charles V. Carr drafted": "Council Weighs Ordinance to Curb Park Discrimination; Hearings Soon: Law Provides License Loss for Offenders," *Cleveland Call & Post*, September 28, 1946.

133　"He ran on a promise": Mansfield B. Frazier, "Carr Talk," *Cleveland Magazine*, November 2009, http://www.clevelandmagazine.com/ME2/dirmod.asp?sid=E73ABD6180B44874871A 91F6BA5C249C&nm=&type=Publishing&mod=Publications::Article&mid=1578600D8080 4596A222593669321019&tier=4&id=0FBEBCF6DC37432EA313F4698DB39613.

133　"Carr had picketed": "Interracial Picket Line Protests Discrimination at Euclid Beach," *Cleveland Call & Post*, September 7, 1946.

133　"Following those speakers": "Beach Ordinance Public Hearings, Oct 16," *Cleveland Call & Post*, October 12, 1946.

133　"Nearly five hundred people": Bob Williams, "Civic Leaders Support Park Licensing Ordinance: Committee Hears Supporters, Foes," *Cleveland Call & Post*, November 23, 1946.

134　"argued that race relations": Ibid.

134　"'I can't answer that'": Ibid.; and Bob Williams, "Pressure Will Pass Park Ordinance for Council Sees Will of the People," *Cleveland Call & Post*, November 30, 1946.

134　"Mackey's immediate supervisor": "Attorney Relays Coleman's Story from Hospital Bed," *Cleveland Call & Post*, September 28, 1946.

134　"The six CORE activists": "Euclid Beach Park Assault Victim Asks $50,000 Damages," *Cleveland Call & Post*, October 5, 1946.

135　"'[CORE] is an interracial organization'": "CORE Challenges Euclid Beach 'Communist' Smear," *Cleveland Call & Post*, October 12, 1946.

135　"Two features in the": Chads O. Skinner "State's 3,500 Communists Analyze News Just Like Joe," *Cleveland Plain Dealer*, August 10, 1946; and Chads O. Skinner, "Few Hands, but Deft, Hold Hammer of Reds," *Cleveland Plain Dealer*, August 11, 1946.

135　"An all-woman jury": "Find Park Guard Guilty in Assault," *Cleveland Call & Post*, November 16, 1946.

135　"Vago insisted he never": Ibid.

136　"The dissenters cannily": "Committee Members Ask More Time to Study Anti–Jim Crow Measure," *Cleveland Call & Post*, December 14, 1946.

136　"'This is the first time in the history'": Bob Williams, "Mayor's Plea Routs Foes of Law to End Beach Jim-Crow," *Cleveland Call & Post*, February 22, 1947.

136　"'Gentlemen, I am opposed'": Ibid.

137　"'Monday, February 17'": Ibid.

15: UNDEFEATED

140　"Horrell installed Robinson at right halfback": "Understanding UCLA Single Wing Football—the Positions," *Classic UCLA Bruins, Rediscovered*, April 11, 2014, https://lvironpigs.wordpress .com/2014/04/11/understanding-ucla-single-wing-football-the-positions/.

140　"who was used as much as a decoy": "Understanding UCLA Single Wing Football—Man-in-Motion Offensive Scheme," *Classic UCLA Bruins, Rediscovered*, May 9, 2014, https://lvironpigs .wordpress.com/2014/05/09/understanding-ucla-single-wing-football-man-in-motion -offensive-scheme/.

140 "This sparked accusations of": Thomas G. Smith, "Outside the Pale: The Exclusion of Blacks from the National Football League, 1934–46," *Journal of Sport History* 15, no. 3 (Winter 1988): 255–81.

140 "'In the case of'": Davis J. Walsh, "I Speak My Mind," *Los Angeles Examiner*, December 9, 1939.

141 "'give anything'": Gregory John Kaliss, "Everyone's All-Americans: Race, Men's College Athletics, and the Ideal of Equal Opportunity," dissertation (Chapel Hill: University of North Carolina, 2008), 86.

141 "both prepared in secret": Strode and Young, *Goal Dust*, 97.

141 "UCLA spies reported": Ibid., 98.

141 "threading popcorn": Ibid.

141 "'no nervousness'": Ibid.

142 "Strode's favorite deli in Boyle": Ibid., 92.

142 "Strode and Washington figured": Gary Libman, "Jackie Robinson: Recalling a Legend," *Los Angeles Times*, April 6, 1987.

142 "An ex-teammate remembered": Dave Gaston, interviewed by author, Pasadena, CA, March 2, 2010.

143 "the 1940 UCLA yearbook": 1940 UCLA yearbook (covers 1939 season), 258.

143 "Washington called his uncle Rocky": Strode and Young, *Goal Dust*, 99.

143 "'You nervous?'": Ibid., 99–100.

144 "Strode saw only green": Strode and Young, *Goal Dust*, 102.

144 "'A couple of bad breaks'": Strode and Young, *Goal Dust*, 102.

145 "But the Trojans didn't have any": Strode and Young, *Goal Dust*, 102.

145 "On first down": Dick Hyland, "Trojans and Bruins in 0–0 Tie Before 103,300," *Los Angeles Times*, December 10, 1939.

145 "'The situation didn't even'": Strode and Young, *Goal Dust*, 103.

145 "'What do you want'": Hyland, "Trojans and Bruins in 0–0 Tie."

146 "'With Saturday's game'": Strode and Young, *Goal Dust*, 96.

146 "Strode was angry": Ibid., 105.

147 "'I guess we realized'": Ibid.

147 "'Football is so much like life'": Ibid., 104.

16: JACKIE

149 "The Colonel starting pitcher": "Remembering Jackie Robinson: 1945–2006, the 60th Anniversary of His Only Minor League Season," *Minor League Baseball*, http://www.milb.com/milb/features/jackie_robinson.jsp?mc=timeline.

149 "They were incensed": Jules Tygiel, *Baseball's Great Experiment: Jackie Robinson and His Legacy* (Oxford: Oxford University Press, 1997), 142.

150 "'Il a gagné ses épaulettes'": Ibid., 143.

150 "Feller dismissed Robinson": A. S. "Doc" Young, "A Black Man in the Wigwam," *Ebony*, February 1969.

150 "Rickey threatened": Tygiel, *Baseball's Great Experiment*, 170–71.

150 "'biggest threat to [Robinson's] success'": Ibid., 163.

151 "some taking exception": Ibid., 162–63.

151 "Ben Chapman, an Alabaman": Joseph Dorinson and Joram Warmund, eds., *Jackie Robinson: Race, Sports, and the American Dream* (New York: Routledge, 2015) 18–19.

151 "'This day of all the unpleasant'": Tygiel, *Baseball's Great Experiment*, 184.

151 "Several prominent members": Dorinson and Warmund, *Jackie Robinson*, 138.

152 "'Those of us who knew'": Strode and Young, *Goal Dust*, 88.

152 "'Kenny and I'": Ibid., 88–89.

152 "his detractors found": Dorinson and Warmund, *Jackie Robinson*, 95.

153 "bloody gashes": Tygiel, *Baseball's Great Experiment*, 202–3.

153 "they couldn't risk standing": Ibid., 193.

153 "Within six weeks": Tygiel, *Baseball's Great Experiment*, 194–95.

153 "Rachel Robinson": Ibid., 201.

154 "many voices": Ibid., 163–65.

17: CLEVELAND'S YEAR

157 "but who didn't": "Doby, Laurence 'Larry' E.," *The Encyclopedia of Cleveland History*, http://ech
     .case.edu/cgi/article.pl?id=DLLE.

158 "She also criticized": Bob Luke, *The Most Famous Woman in Baseball: Effa Manley and the Negro
     Leagues* (Washington, DC: Potomac Books, 2011), 149; and Jules Tygiel, *Baseball's Great
     Experiment: Jackie Robinson and His Legacy* (Oxford: Oxford University Press, 1997), 213.

159 "'Haven't seen one'": Larry Tye, *Satchel: The Life and Times of an American Legend* (New York:
     Random House, 2009), 174.

160 "'The pitch fooled me'": "Doby Predicts, 'I'll Hit Sain,'" *Cleveland Call & Post*, October 16, 1948.

160 "The next day's": *Cleveland Plain Dealer*, October 10, 1948.

160 "fans in Cleveland remembered": Dave Anderson, "Sports of The Times: Has Baseball
     Forgotten Larry Doby?," *New York Times*, March 29, 1987.

161 "He created a 5-3-3": Zimmerman, *New Thinking Man's Guide*, 127.

161 "The prevalent defensive": Ibid., 120.

161 "the 5-3-3 a step": Ibid., 127.

165 "AAFC's overall financial situation": Piascik, *Best Show in Football*, 124–28.

165 "To keep the weaker teams": Paul Brown and John Clary, *PB: The Paul Brown Story* (New York:
     Atheneum, 1979), 191.

18: GOOD-BYE

167 "Washington played defense": Frank Finch, "Rejuvenated Rams Ruin Detroit Lions by 44–7,"
     Los Angeles Times, September 23, 1948.

168 "'My pal!?'": TK.

168 "Mann claimed": Ross, *Outside the Lines*, 124–25.

168 "The *Los Angeles Times* framed": Frank Finch, "Washington, Van Buren Set for 'Battle of
     Halfbacks,'" *Los Angeles Times*, October 3, 1948.

169 "'Football has been good to me'": Frank Finch, "Kenny Retiring," *Los Angeles Times*, November
     16, 1948.

169 "*Los Angeles Times* writer": Ibid.

169 "'If Kenny had joined'": Ibid.

169 "They wanted to see": TK.

170 "At halftime": Karin Cohen home movie.

170 "Bill Schroeder": Ibid.

170 "He handed the trophy": Ibid.

170 "From the far end": Ibid.

171 "'The Canadian Indians used'": Strode and Young, *Goal Dust*, 159.

171 "During the week": Ibid., 12.

171   "'His face had more'": Ibid., 13.

172   "'The DA's office was using'": Ibid., 110–11.

172   "Dusty Acres": Ibid., 125.

172   "'What a slap in the face'": Ibid.

173   "scars on his back": Ibid., 126.

173   "He hadn't been shunted": Ibid., 125.

173   "'Jack told them'": Ezzrett "Sugarfoot" Anderson, interviewed by author, Calgary, Alberta, Canada, April 4, 2014.

173   "Les Lear": Strode and Young, *Goal Dust*, 160.

174   "Kenny Washington visited": Anderson interview.

174   "'quite a piece of mobile'": Strode and Young, *Goal Dust*, 161.

174   "bottle of rye whiskey": Ibid., 162.

174   "Strode jumped on": Ibid.

19: FOURTH QUARTER

178   "The flag marking the end": *1950 NFL Championship: Cleveland Browns 30 / LA Rams 28*, NFL Films, DVD.

178   "Davis fought to the sideline": Ibid.

179   "'I wanted to die'": Duey Graham, *OttoMatic: Otto Graham* (Wayne, MI: Immortal Investments Publishing, 2004), 118.

179   "He didn't follow many games": Karin Cohen, interviewed by author, California City, CA, February 27, 2010.

179   "Or he might have been in": Ibid.

180   *"Fairchild v. Raines,"*: Vose, *Caucasians Only*, 26, 153.

180   "Robert Traynor, revived": Gonda, *Unjust Deeds*, 99.

180   "'not by ordinances, which'": Vose, *Caucasians Only*, 24–25.

181   "J. D. and Ethel Lee Shelley": IIT Chicago-Kent College of Law, "Shelley v. Kraemer," Oyez, https://www.oyez.org/cases/1940-1955/334us1.

181   "Orsel and Minnie McGhee": Lynne Heffley, "They Built a Home in Which All Could Live," *Los Angeles Times*, February 10, 1999.

181   "preempted plans to": Gonda, *Unjust Deeds*, 135; and George B. Stafford, "St. Louis Scene," *Pittsburgh Courier*, May 10, 1947.

182   "they pushed sociologists": Amina Hassan, *Loren Miller: Civil Rights Attorney and Journalist* (Norman: University of Oklahoma Press, 2015), 189–91.

182   "met in person": Vose, *Caucasians Only*, 199–200.

182   "offered to write": Gonda, *Unjust Deeds*, 170–79.

20: YOUNGER

185   "Shaughnessy hit upon": Michael MacCambridge, *America's Game: The Epic Story of How Pro Football Captured a Nation* (New York: Anchor Books, 2004), 64.

187   "most revered": Christopher L. Gasper, "Don Hutson Was the NFL's First Superstar Receiver," *Boston Globe*, September 6, 2013.

187   "one of the first Mexican American": Earl Gustkey, "Ex-Ram Great Dies," *Los Angeles Times*, January 6, 2000; and Adam Rank, "Muñoz Tops List of Greatest Mexican-Americans in NFL History," NFL.com, May 5, 2011, http://www.nfl.com/news/story/09000d5d81fb1d79/printable/muoz-tops-list-of-greatest-mexicanamericans-in-nfl-history.

21: SWAN SONG

192 "It had to come sometime": Harold Sauerbrei, "49ers Shatter Browns 29-Game Streak, 56–28, Take Conference Lead," *Cleveland Plain Dealer*, October 10, 1949.

192 "looping their defensive linemen": Harry Jones, "Graham Clicks as Ball Carrier in Move to Combat 49ers' Looping Defense," *Cleveland Plain Dealer*, October 31, 1949.

192 "scraps of paper": Ibid.

193 "Bills guard Rocco Pirro": Zimmerman, *New Thinking Man's Guide*, 86.

194 "negotiating the terms": R. D. Griffith, *To the NFL: You Sure Started Somethin': A Historical Guide to All 32 NFL Teams and the Cities They've Played In* (Pittsburgh: Dorrance Publishing, 2012), 95.

195 "'All these damn n——s'": Wexler, *Fire in a Canebreak*, 142.

195 "'My nerves is all frayed'": Ibid., 144.

195 "agents uncovered": Ibid., 146.

196 "A federal grand jury": "Ga. Jury Probing Lynching," *Pittsburgh Courier*, December 7, 1946.

196 "Their primary focus": James Edmund Boyack, "Tom Clark Informs *Courier*," *Pittsburgh Courier*, November 2, 1946.

197 "Many observers thought": Wexler, *Fire in a Canebreak*, 161.

197 "also told Jones": Ibid., 186.

197 "Major Jones to testify": Wexler, *Fire in a Canebreak*, 186–90.

22: SPRING TRAINING

199 "Rockford Peaches": "Kingfish Cavorts on Diamond: Ken Washington Plays in Charity Ball Tilt," *Los Angeles Times*, February 16, 1949.

199 "Independents for Nixon": Printout from RMN Library.

199 "her father consciously chose": Karin Cohen, interviewed by author, California City, CA, February 27, 2010.

200 "In his first major": *While Thousands Cheer*, IMDb.com, http://www.imdb.com/title /tt0033255/?ref_=nm_ov_bio_lk3.

200 *"Pinky"*: Bosley Crowther, "*Pinky* (1949)," *New York Times*, September 30, 1949.

200 "the *Los Angeles Times*": "Washington to Try Out with Giants," *Los Angeles Times*, November 17, 1949.

201 "color barrier of": "Black Pioneers of College Baseball: Kenny Washington (UCLA)," *Black College Nines*, February 16, 2010, http://blackcollegenines.com/?p=790.

201 "Washington was one": Strode and Young, *Goal Dust*, 57.

202 "'Nobody in camp has worked'": Frank Finch, "Leo Says Washington too Green to Make Grade in Major Leagues," *Los Angeles Times*, March 24, 1950.

202 "only six of the nine": Gonda, *Unjust Deeds*, 187.

203 "Justice Jackson's decision": Kermit L. Hall, *The Justices, Judging, and Judicial Reputation* (New York: Garland Publishing, 2000), 27–30, 466–67.

203 "'The perpetrators of'": Gonda, *Unjust Deeds*, 186–95.

203 "'Let me come in'": Amina Hassan, *Loren Miller: Civil Rights Attorney and Journalist* (Norman: University of Oklahoma Press, 2015), 199.

204 "'Are there any contract'": Gonda, *Unjust Deeds*, 186–95.

204 "Marshall reiterated": Ibid.

204 "'But the citizens couldn't'": Ibid.

204 "On May 3, the Supreme Court": *Shelley v. Kraemer* (1948), U.S. Supreme Court, FindLaw, http://caselaw.findlaw.com/us-supreme-court/334/1.html.

204 "'All covenant cases'": Gonda, *Unjust Deeds*, 186–95.

204 "'Among the civil rights intended'": Ibid.

205 "'The Court appears'": *New York University Law Quarterly Review* 24 (January 1949), as quoted in Vose, *Caucasians Only*, 213.

23: GOALPOSTS

207 "biggest surprise was how": Louis Efrat, "Cleveland Browns Halt Eagles, 35–10," *New York Times*, September 17, 1950; and Paul Brown and John Clary, *PB: The Paul Brown Story* (New York: Atheneum, 1979), 201–4.

207 "Eagles were known": Michael MacCambridge, *America's Game: The Epic Story of How Pro Football Captured a Nation* (New York: Anchor Books, 2004), 65–67.

209 "Owen had driven": Zimmerman, *New Thinking Man's Guide*, 127.

209 "Owen had previously": Ibid.

209 "But Owen also kept John Cannady": Ibid.

209 "'Steve was a great guy'": Ibid., 127–28.

210 "came out in a 5-1-5": Ibid.

210 "Brown stubbornly": Brown and Clary, *PB*, 204.

210 "when a great play by": Duey Graham, *OttoMatic: Otto Graham* (Wayne, MI: Immortal Investments Publishing, 2004), 117.

210 "'All I could'": Piascik, *Best Show in Football*, 174.

212 "They were also": Zimmerman, *New Thinking Man's Guide*, 98.

213 "'the finest passing team'": Cal Whorton, "'Rams Have Best Air Eleven' Says Halas," *Los Angeles Times*, December 18, 1950.

213 "stiff-arming a defensive": *1950 NFL Championship: Cleveland Browns 30 / LA Rams 28*, NFL Films, DVD.

214 "In the huddle center Hal": Brown and Clary, *PB*, 212.

214 "But the referee waved off": Piascik, *Best Show in Football*, 181.

215 "Otto Graham and his": Graham, *OttoMatic*, 119; and Piascik, *Best Show in Football*, 182.

215 "Fans poured from": *1950 NFL Championship: Cleveland Browns 30 / LA Rams 28*, NFL Films, DVD.

215 "The uprights soon disappeared": Harold Sauerbrei, "Browns Win World Title, 30–28," *Cleveland Plain Dealer*, December 25, 1950.

215 "'This is the gamest bunch'": Andrew Clayman, "The Cleveland Rams: Remembering the Original L.A. Move and a Rivalry Reborn," *Waiting for Next Year*, January 13, 2016, http://www.waitingfornextyear.com/2016/01/cleveland-rams-browns-nfl-history/.

24: OVERTIME

217 "was suspended in": Bob Williams, "Coleman Case Continued: Nurses Clear Patrolman of Any Misconduct," *Cleveland Call & Post*, March 29, 1947; and Bob Williams, "Patrolman Lynn Coleman Draws Suspension, Loses Vacation Days," *Cleveland Call & Post*, April 5, 1947.

217 "'Lying wounded in'": Williams, "Coleman Case Continued."

217 "suspended Coleman": Williams, "Patrolman Lynn Coleman Draws Suspension."

217 "He sued Euclid Beach": "Officer Coleman, Shot, Sues Euclid Beach for $50,000," *Cleveland Call & Post*, September 25, 1948.

217 "Shield Club": Jacqueline Marino, "Black and Back: The Once Relevant Black Shield Attempts to Rise Again from the Ruins," *Cleveland Scene*, November 2, 2000, http://www.clevescene.com/cleveland/black-and-back/Content?oid=1475561.

217 "paid Coleman $21,800": "Lynn Coleman Wins 41 Year Fight Against Police Bias," *Cleveland Call & Post*, June 24, 1978.

218 "until private groups": Wolcott, *Race, Riots, and Roller Coasters*, 56, 105.

218 "submit their applications": Bob Williams, "License Approved at Euclid Beach, 'None Denied Skating Applications,'" *Cleveland Call & Post*, May 3, 1947.

218 "private dance club": Wolcott, *Race, Riots, and Roller Coasters*, 56, 105.

218 "Crawford received $500": "Pioneers in Euclid Beach Fight Win Cash Judgment," *Cleveland Call & Post*, March 13, 1948.

218 "Morrow's complaint": "Jury Acquits Beach Policeman in Attack on Interracial Party," *Cleveland Call & Post*, March 22, 1947.

219 "next wave of amusement": Wolcott, *Race, Riots, and Roller Coasters*, chap. 6, "'Riotland': Race and the Decline of Urban Amusements."

219 "But she tired": Kenneth W. Mack, *Representing the Race: The Creation of the Civil Rights Lawyer* (Cambridge, MA: Cambridge University Press, 2012), 132.

219 "Jane Crow": Ibid., 207–9.

220 "with her sexuality": Barbara Lau, "Pauli Murray: Imp, Crusader, Dude, Priest" exhibit, Pauli Murray Project, a community-based initiative of the Duke Human Rights Center at the Franklin Humanities Institute, Durham, NC.

220 "'I then got the'": Oral history interview with Pauli Murray, February 13, 1976, interview G-0044, Southern Oral History Program Collection (#4007), Southern Historical Collection, Wilson Library, University of North Carolina at Chapel Hill.

221 "She listed Pauli": Mack, *Representing the Race*, 207.

221 "the Los Angeles Realty Board": Mark Brilliant, *The Color of America Has Changed: How Racial Diversity Shaped Civil Rights Reforms in California, 1941–1978* (Oxford: Oxford University Press, 2010), 105.

221 "Supreme Court upheld": Vose, *Caucasians Only*, 232–34.

222 "Miller decried the": Miller, *Petitioners*, 7–15.

222 "'I have no faith'": Wexler, *Fire in a Canebreak*, 191.

222 "Under oath": Wexler, *Fire in a Canebreak*, TK.

222 "pistol-whipped him": James Edmund Boyack, "Sensational Development May Break Monroe Mob Case," *Pittsburgh Courier*, January 11, 1947.

223 "James Verneer was tried": Wexler, *Fire in a Canebreak*, 199–202.

223 "the nickname Monroe": Ibid., 201.

224 "'He gave money to everyone'": Karin Cohen, interviewed by author, California City, CA, February 27, 2010.

224 "He'd go down": Marvel Washington, interviewed by author, Whittier, CA, February 28, 2010.

224 "Baldwin Hills": Cohen interview.

224 "Karin remembered the": Ibid.

226 "his decades of work": William Willis Jr., Clem Willis, and Claude Willis, interviewed by author, Columbus, OH, January 16–17, 2010.

226 "'I remember in one'": Ibid.

227 "Branch Rickey was also": Ross Greenburg (producer), Johnson McKelvy (director), *Forgotten Four: The Integration of Pro Football* (EPIX/Ross Greenburg Productions, 2014).

227 "The commission gave the Rams a lease": Paul Zimmerman, "Rams Get Three-Year Coliseum Contract," *Los Angeles Times*, January 30, 1946.

228 "Harding was told no": "Petition May Keep Dons from Using Coliseum," *Los Angeles Tribune*, August 10, 1946.

228 "In one meeting's notes": Meeting notes, Los Angeles Coliseum Commission, August 12, 1946.

25: ON HISTORY

229 "'Kenny Washington had the support of the community'": Ross Greenburg (producer), Johnson McKelvy (director), *Forgotten Four: The Integration of Pro Football* (EPIX/Ross Greenburg Productions, 2014).

230 "'I could see that'": Karin Cohen, interviewed by author, California City, CA, February 27, 2010.

230 "'American historians'": Eric Foner, *Who Owns History?: Rethinking the Past in a Changing World* (New York: Hill and Wang, 2002), xv.

230 "'In America, there's been a long'": *Forgotten Four: The Integration of Pro Football*.

230 "'Devaluing losers allows'": Jennifer Hochschild, *Facing Up to the American Dream: Race, Class, and the Soul of a Nation* (Princeton, NJ: Princeton University Press, 1995), 31.

231 "'The emotional potency'": Ibid., 26.

233 "'That's exactly how'": Kalai Strode, interviewed by author, Honolulu, HI, March 21, 2010.

233 "I think he would": William Willis Jr., Clem Willis, and Claude Willis, interviewed by author, Columbus, OH, January 16–17, 2010.

233 "In not a single one": Oral history interview with Pauli Murray, February 13, 1976, interview G-0044, Southern Oral History Program Collection (#4007), Southern Historical Collection, Wilson Library, University of North Carolina at Chapel Hill.

Selected Sources

I'd like to recognize sources that were crucial to the writing of this book. This is not a complete list of all sources; please check the end notes for more details.

BOOKS

Gonda, Jeffrey D. *Unjust Deeds: The Restrictive Covenant Cases and the Making of the Civil Rights Movement*. Chapel Hill: University of North Carolina Press, 2015.

Miller, Loren. *The Petitioners: The Story of the Supreme Court of the United States and the Negro*. New York: Pantheon, 1966.

Piascik, Andy. *The Best Show in Football: The 1946–1955 Cleveland Browns: Pro Football's Greatest Dynasty*. Lanham, MD: Taylor Trade Publishing, 2006.

Ross, Charles K. *Outside the Lines: African Americans and the Integration of the National Football League*. New York: New York University Press, 1999.

Sides, Josh. *L.A. City Limits: African American Los Angeles from the Great Depression to the Present*. Berkeley: University of California Press, 2003.

Strode, Woody, and Sam Young. *Goal Dust: The Warm and Candid Memoirs of a Pioneer Black Athlete and Actor*. Lanham, MD: Madison Books, 1990.

Vose, Clement E. *Caucasians Only: The Supreme Court, the NAACP, and the Restrictive Covenant Cases*. Berkeley: University of California Press, 1968.

Wexler, Laura. *Fire in a Canebrake: The Last Mass Lynching in America*. New York: Scribner, 2003.

Wolcott, Victoria W. *Race, Riots, and Roller Coasters: The Struggle Over Segregated Recreation in America*. Philadelphia: University of Pennsylvania Press, 2012.

Zimmerman, Paul. *The New Thinking Man's Guide to Pro Football*. New York: Simon and Schuster, 1984.

NEWSPAPERS

Atlanta Daily World
Baltimore Afro-American

California Eagle
Chicago Defender
Cleveland Call & Post
Cleveland Plain Dealer
Cleveland Press
Los Angeles Sentinel
Los Angeles Times
Los Angeles Tribune
Pittsburgh Courier

Libraries, Centers, and Archives

Black Resource Center, A. C. Bilbrew Library, County of Los Angeles Public Library
Charles E. Young Research Library, University of California, Los Angeles
Cleveland Public Library
Cleveland State University Michael Schwartz Library
Kirwan Institute for the Study of Race and Ethnicity, Ohio State University
Library of Congress
Los Angeles Public Library
San Francisco Public Library
Southern California Library of Social Studies and Research

Oral Histories

Miller, Loren. "Loren Miller Papers," Huntington Library, San Marino, CA.
Murray, Pauli. Oral history interview, February 13, 1976. Interview G-0044, Southern Oral History Program Collection (#4007), Southern Historical Collection, Wilson Library, University of North Carolina at Chapel Hill.
Nelson, Juanita Morrow. "Juanita Nelson: Full Interview," *First Person: Twentieth-Century History as Told by People Who Lived It and Made It*, Memorial Hall Museum Online, Pocumtuck Valley Memorial Association, 2014, http://www .memorialhall.mass.edu/centapp/oh/interview.do?shortName=nelson_interview.

DVDs

1950 NFL Championship: Cleveland Browns 30 / LA Rams 28, NFL Films.
Black Star Rising, NFL Films.
Forgotten Four: The Integration of Pro Football. Ross Greenburg (producer), Johnson McKelvy (director) (EPIX/Ross Greenburg Productions, 2014).

Index

A Note on the Author

Gretchen Atwood is a writer whose articles on professional football have appeared in *LA Weekly* and is a member of the Professional Football Researchers Association. This is her first trade book. She lives in San Francisco.